8000 Years of Wisdom

8000

Years of Wisdom

Compiled by Michelle Abadie and Mike Cast

ACCENT PRESS LTD

Published by Accent Press Ltd – 2010

ISBN 9781907016530

Printed and bound in Malta

Cover Design by Michelle Abadie

Names
by Wendy Cope

She was Eliza for a few weeks
When she was a baby –
Eliza Lily. Soon it changed to Lil.

Later she was Miss Steward in the baker's shop
And then 'my love', 'my darling', Mother.

Widowed at thirty, she went back to work
As Mrs Hand. Her daughter grew up,
Married and gave birth.

Now she was Nanna. 'Everybody
Calls me nanna,' she would say to visitors.
And so they did – friends, tradesmen, the doctor.

In the geriatric ward
They used the patients' Christian names.
'Lil,' we said, 'or Nanna,'
But it wasn't in her file
And for those last bewildered weeks
She was Eliza once again.

*From TWO CURES FOR LOVE Selected Poems 1979-2006
published by Faber at £12.99*

To Dad

9 February 1919 – 19 February 2008

Mike Cast

Preface

This book is dedicated to Mike's dad who sadly passed away before it was published. The book is based on an idea that came to Mike many years ago when he was having dinner with his family and enjoying his dad's favourite meal (steak and chips followed by hot apple pie and vanilla ice-cream) Mike asked his dad what advice would he give his teenage grandson and granddaughter, having spent over 80 years on this planet. As quick as a flash his dad replied that he would take more risks. Mike asked his mum, also an octogenarian, the same question. Her reply came as quickly, to travel and experience the world for as long as possible. She added that there is plenty of time to grow up. With Michelle's involvement the idea grew into collating anecdotes, memories, opinions, stories and experiences from octogenarians, and a few nonagenarians, from all over the world, some of which conclude with their advice for teenagers or what they have learnt from life.

Introduction

8000 years of wisdom is a fascinating glimpse of history as experienced by real people, rather than events seen through the eyes of historians. It is a portrait of the 20th century compiled from memories of some who lived through much of it. It is a compelling social record that might otherwise be lost to future generations. It celebrates a generation's amazing life and longevity from the relative innocence of youth in the early 1900s, to the maturity and wisdom of their later years, in the 21st century. Some of the articles were submitted having already been written, but never published; some people answered a questionnaire and others were interviewed. All ages can learn from the older generation, all of whom have seen some dramatic and extraordinary changes.

It is well-known fact that people going through teenage years resist advice from adults but hopefully this book might smuggle in advice between the lines. By the very nature of talking about their wishes, regrets, ambitions and observations means these octogenarians can't help but pass on advice indirectly, or impart some sort of knowledge or wisdom. The contributors were aware that some teenagers wouldn't listen; that they themselves needed advice from teenagers; some didn't feel that had anything relevant to pass on or didn't feel qualified; and others had plenty to offer. This book links us to history and shows us why history is so important. There are horrific stories of concentration camps and those who helped the prisoners, which must never be forgotten. There are stories of poverty and mass unemployment, which as a society we should learn from; and the all too common remarks about the pointlessness of wars, which unfortunately we haven't learnt from. The juxtaposition of the mundane and the horror; of the creative and the destructive; the ambitious and pedestrian domesticity displays a true cross section of the lives of octogenarians in today's society.

The reading of common experiences sometimes across continents gives us an insight into why that generation feels as though the current generation have lost a sense of community and miss out on connections with extended family and why they enjoyed the war years, which is something generations since can't understand. Some think themselves luckier than modern teenagers despite the disease, illness, war and poverty they suffered. We wonder if current teenagers will think like this in 60 or 70 years time.

A percentage of the royalties from this book will go to the Royal Hospital Chelsea Appeal Fund (www.chelsea-pensioners.co.uk)

We hope you enjoy reading this book as much as we enjoyed listening to and recording the stories. Please visit the website to find out more about the possibility of continuing this project online. (www.8000yearsofwisdom.com)

Michelle Abadie and Mike Cast

Foreword

by Baroness Lady Thatcher

In the early years of the Twentieth Century much of the world looked forward to the century ahead with growing hope. The advance of science, technology and medicine was transforming people's lives. New discoveries were being made at an ever more rapid rate. Industrial productivity and trade were reaching undreamed of levels. Over the next 100 years people came to expect longer, healthier and wealthier lives.

Just by listing some of the advances we can see how much our lives have been transformed. In the first decade of the last century the motorcar was still a rarity and powered flight had only recently begun. There were no washing machines, no refrigerators – and no air conditioning. Antibiotics and plastics were yet to be developed. The atom remained undivided. Our understanding of genetics was rudimentary. There were no radios, no televisions, no computers. Space travel was a science fiction. The Net was for fishermen and the Web for spiders!

But amidst all this progress the last century also saw the two worst wars and the two greatest tyrannies the world has ever known.

Today, in the first decade of the Twenty First Century, the octogenarians featured in this book recall some of those milestone changes, as well as more humble, but equally significant observations, before they are lost to future generations. These anecdotal and informal accounts give colour and life to more formal, historical social records.

The experiences of a friend or relative in their eighties might seem a world away from the life of our young people today. Yet, their experiences do have a resonance with the modern world and a wisdom which many young people will recognise as their own lives unfold. Wisdom does indeed come with age. I know that you will find in these pages much to inform and much to enjoy.

Acknowledgements

Our sincere thanks go to all the people who gave us their time to contribute to this book and we apologise that we could not include everyone who responded.

We are also very grateful to the following:
Lynne Bentley; Marilyn Dixon; Chelsea Arts Club; Wendy Cope; Szilvia Czingel, Centropa Budapest; Economics Institute; Diana Fowle; Ian Frank; William Hetherington, archivist of the Peace Pledge Union (www.ppu.org.uk); Peter Higginbotham (www.workhouses.org.uk); Dr Phil Hutchinson; Emma Kilkelly; Ivan Kolev, Sofia University; Philip le Grand, Editor of the Bletchley Park newsletter (www.bletchleypark.org.uk); Ruby Lescott; Rosalind Leveridge; Jo Manchester; Andrew Marshall; Karen Marshall; Steven Marshall; Sue Marshall; Brian Moody; The Royal Hospital (www.chelsea-pensioners.org.uk); Edward Serotta, director of The Central Europe Center for Research and Documentation (www.centropa.org); Maureen Sinclair; David Smith, The Sunday Times; Sue Snell; Elizabeth Super, Helen Bamber Foundation (www.helenbamber.org); Louis Theroux; Odette Veazey; Vishvapani, The Friends of the Western Buddhist Order (www.fwbo.org); Roohi K Ralhan Coordinator, Nek Chand Foundation, India (www.nekchand.com); Stephanie Quirk, Ramamani Iyengar Memorial Yoga Institute (www.bksiyengar.com); Carly Whyborn, Holocaust Memorial Day Trust (www.hmd.org.uk); Nick Yapp

We were very sorry to hear the sad news that John Berry died in December 2009, Billy Arjan Singh died in January 2010, Jane Brooker died in March 2010, Avi Livney died in May 2010 and that Lionel Irish also died before the publication of this book. At the time of going to press we have not been notified that any other contributors have died. We would like to apologise in advance for any upset this book may cause in the event of other contributors having died before publication.

Contents

Rosalind Mary Hudson

27 April 1915
Derbyshire, England

Rosalind Mary Hudson age 18 (middle)

I have very fond memories of when I was a child, growing up at Laurel Hill, Repton. I remember when I was quite small, before we had a car, Father and Mother used to take me shopping on a Saturday afternoon to Burton. If the seats with the driver were not taken, Father and I used to sit next to him. There were two long seats down each side of the bus and the other passengers sat facing each other. Jean, the conductress, collected our fares and then stood on the steps just inside the doors, in order to open them at the next stop. In Burton, as a great treat Father would buy me a large bag of sweets or chocolates, but I was not allowed to have any until we were on the bus and I had offered one to Jean. My father taught us that we are all born equal, which has remained a favourite expression of mine. At home Mother reared chickens so that we could have fresh eggs, and chicken. We ate homegrown fruit, such as raspberries, and vegetables such as asparagus. I remember the time when we had gas lamps and then later the excitement of getting electricity to the village, when my husband, a clergyman, and I moved to the Rectory at Burton-le-Coggles.

I was a Sunday school teacher and then an infant and junior schoolteacher in state and private schools. I taught ten to eleven year olds. My first job was at a marvellous school in Derby called Overdale. I was paid ten shillings per week. My last post was at Friargate House School, Derby in 1985 when I retired. Father was a churchwarden and my husband was clergyman – we all had important roles in a small local community so I was very sad to finally leave. I had returned to Repton in 1959 after my husband died and lived there until very recently. It was a lovely, friendly village before the war. But as soon as the public school started taking dayboys things started to change. Parents bought up pockets of land and built executive houses, which spoiled the village. Repton was a lovely church and people from the area used to come to the services. I never really wanted to leave Repton but some of the behaviour of the lay people decided me. I now live in sheltered housing and love it, but I do feel that I came here before I was ready and for the wrong reasons. I was very active in my hometown and since being here I seem to have slowed down. I love gardening, which I can't do here and I loved visiting garden centres, and since giving up my car I can't do that any more without relying on other people.

My strongest memory of World War II was enlisting in April 1939 in Derby and being called up to No7 Balloon Centre, before war was declared on the Sunday at 11 a.m., to call up the RAF men. The Balloon Centre was there to protect the Rolls Royce works. It was a very friendly camp because we were all local people.

I was a founder member of an Abbeyfield Home in Repton in 1966. Abbeyfield is a not-for-profit organization, which helps to make the lives of older people easier and more fulfilling. I have never come across the sort of kindness that I did when I was working there, but I also saw serious cruelty. One of our best housekeepers was a twenty-stone cockney. Many of her childhood relatives had been evacuated to Repton during the war so she had spent many holidays there. When she grew up she left London and moved to Repton and worked at Abbeyfield. She loved the people she looked after and gave them marvellous birthday parties. Everything went well until we unfortunately had a snob voted on to the committee. She could not get rid of Dot quick enough, and unknown to us was hounding her. Eventually Dot retired and, soon after leaving, she had a massive stroke.

Things are so different for young people today. There seems to be much less social interaction on a face-to-face basis and I am sorry that television seems to have spoilt things for them. It is a lovely time of life, and shouldn't be wasted in front of television or computer screens. For entertainment we used to go out with groups of friends to dances on Friday and Saturday nights. On a wet evening Father, Mother, Ernest (my brother) and I played cards.

John McCallum

20 June 1917
Glasgow, Scotland

John McCallum age 19

At the age of fourteen, in 1931, I had the choice of becoming a bellboy with the Cunard Line or a telegraph boy messenger with the Post Office. I chose to be a landlubber, with no regrets. I worked from the Head Post Office in Glasgow, and my wages were ten shillings and six pence per week. My ambition was to achieve the rank of Chief Inspector in the P.O. Engineering Dept., unfortunately they changed the system to a more technical method of grading and I never made it under the new system, and I ended up as a senior technician. By the time I retired I was a BT telephone engineer.

My first salary was not a princely sum, but very welcome in a large family, as we were still living in the shadow of the great depression. People talk about being poor nowadays but the poverty that I remember is something nightmares are made of. My brothers and I walked for miles to the nearest coal mines to glean bits of coal from the shale bins and then trundled our little wooden bogey all the way home again. Every little helped. Things were so bad that I can remember our little grocer shop selling tablespoonfuls of jam to customers who could not afford a one-pound pot. When I attended primary school in Oban, I had to do my homework by the light from an oil lamp which was not good for my eyes. The dry toilet was not good for my nose, and a nice hot bath was a luxury. There have been a million improvements since those days and I appreciate every last one of them. We did have a few treats though: I remember my favourite 'dine out' meal was a nice mixed grill.

When World War II broke out in 1939, we left Scotland to get kitted out in England. Within fourteen days we were in Arras, France, where GHQ Signals were situated. We were there until April 1940 when the Germans came through The Maginot Line, which was a fortification that the French had built in order to protect them from invasion by Germany. However, the line had two major gaps in it, the first along the Belgian border, extending to the English Channel and the other across a huge forested area in the Ardennes. When the Germans broke through, our section was moved up into Belgium to provide support. We were later diverted to St Omer in France, where I was wounded and captured. I remember looking down the barrel of a Mauser pistol, held by a big German sergeant who was going to shoot me, and thinking that no one would know what happened to me. I closed my eyes, because I didn't want to see the flash that killed me. But, instead of pulling the trigger, the big softy tended my wounds, and offered me a cigarette and a piece of chocolate. The nice sergeant didn't shoot me but, believe me, I definitely died a little that day. The John McCallum who came to life again was different.

Months later I was sent to the notorious Stalag 8B in Poland with my brother, Jimmy, and friend, Joe, and then we were sent out in a working party to the Sudetenland. Two years later the three of us escaped, through Poland, stowing away on a Swedish ship to Malmo. From there we were sent to Stockholm, and from there were flown in Mosquito bombers to Leuchars in Scotland, then to London for debriefings and, only after that, home to Glasgow. Because I successfully escaped the POW camp, I was retrained and transferred to Intelligence Corps, until demob in January 1946.

I then returned to Germany as a British Passport Officer and carried on doing the job I had been doing with Intelligence. I finally came home in November 1949 – I will never forget those ten years.

Despite what happened to me during the war the most devastating thing that happened to me is my wife dying after we had been together for sixty years, and then I knew for the first time what the expression 'a broken heart' meant.

My generation has experienced things that today's young people probably can't understand. In my experience teenagers don't listen to old people. In fact very few people listen to old people and I wonder if they will remember that when they become old themselves. I wouldn't have the temerity to offer a teenager advice unless asked.

John McCallum wrote 'The Long Way Home', an autobiography, published by Birlinn.

'Billy' Arjan Singh

15 August 1917
Gorakhpur, India

Billy Arjan Singh with Harriet, one of the leopard cubs that he reared and returned to the jungle. Photograph courtesy of Billy Arjan Singh

I spent much of my childhood from 1923 until 1932, in the princely state of Balrampur of Terai, hunting birds and animals. This area is a belt of marshy grasslands, savannas and forests near the borders of India and Nepal, in the foothills of the Himalayas.

When I left the army, soon after Independence, I started farming in the area that is now the Dudhwa National Park, not far from where I grew up, where the thunder of deer hooves was commonplace. In 1958 I had gone out into the forest on Bhagwan Piari, the elephant with whom I spent 25 wonderful years. At the confluence of the Soheli and Neora rivers I discovered a patch of land that was owned by a politician who had lost all interest in it. I bought it and turned it into a functioning farm, which was inundated several times a year when the rivers were in spate, but which profited greatly from the fertile silt that was left behind. I built myself a basic house and this was the beginning of Tiger Haven where I still live. It is now a wildlife sanctuary and has been since the late 1970s.

In 1960 I ended the life of a beautiful leopard and I was overcome with remorse. I suddenly realised that I had no right whatsoever to destroy what I could not create. I was a bloodthirsty, murderous urchin who shot anything that moved – owlets, hyenas, leopards, and tigers. I am condemned to live with my deep regret for being part of the slaughter of such magnificent creatures. I stopped hunting and started to concentrate my efforts on how I could help protect wild animals, which is the most important decision I have made.

As the years passed, having established my farm as a pioneer settler, farmers began to migrate from Pakistan in large numbers. When a company called The Collective Farms and Forests Ltd. cleared 10,000 acres, I could see the writing on the wall and began to seek a halt to the destruction. I also wanted to protect the area in which the deer lived, as their numbers had dramatically dropped, since I had been living here. I created grasslands, salt licks and water sources to attract the deer. I also submitted a proposal to request that Dudhwa became a wildlife sanctuary so that the deer could live in safety. This was granted and best of all Tiger Haven was right the middle of it, which indirectly made my home, and surrounding grasslands and forests, a protected area as well.

The tiger shikar (hunt) was banned in 1969 and I am proud that I had a small part in this. I realised when the tiger was slipping away from us that sport hunting was a sinful, hypocritical act opposed to all civilised human thought. No one has the right to be entertained by murder. Sadly the virus of sport killing runs deep in the human psyche. Along with several friends we used to reserve the shooting blocks adjacent to Tiger Haven to stop others from using them. Some old shikaris (hunters) used to come and drink with me around my campfire and their loosened tongues would provide me with information that I would unhesitatingly use against them! One way or another we managed to provide a safe haven for wildlife. I was repaying old debts.

When the shikar was banned, the outfitters of the day tried every dirty trick to coerce the Indian government to let them carry on their bloody business. They spoke sanctimoniously then about conservation, but took extra money for guaranteed kills. I recall that the famous safari outfitters, Allwyn Cooper Ltd, actually set up a dead leopard for the famous African hunter, Robert Ruar, to shoot when they could not deliver a live animal. They were an unscrupulous lot and India is well rid of them.

For ten years I shared Tiger Haven and the surrounding areas with tigers and leopards that I rehabilitated and reintroduced to living freely in the forests – I consider this rehabilitation to be my biggest achievement. It started in 1971 when I was presented with a male leopard cub, Prince. Two years later he opted for a wild existence. I was then gifted two female leopard cubs by the Prime Minister, Mrs Indira Gandhi, which had recently been presented to her. However the experiment was handicapped by excessive human presence. One of the leopardesses was poisoned by the Forest Department but the other survived to breed twice. I was then given the approval of the Prime Minister to look for a young female tiger. Eventually one was found at the Twycross Zoo in England (Indian zoos were not able to produce a cub). I hit problems when I was told that I could not bring the tigress to India because she was hybrid, which would pollute the purity of the Indian bloodline. It struck me as an absurd quibble that scientific dogma should wish to preserve the bloodline of a subspecies from the same genetic stock, while perpetrating inbreeding, which would lead to degeneration. Hybridisation is revitalising. I had the Prime Minister's office battling on my side and finally Tara, the cub, was allowed to come to India. By the age of five, she had delivered a total of nine clubs. I claim that the tiger population would have been further depressed without Tara's introduction of genetic diversity. Tiger Haven was designated as part of the Dudhwa National Park in 1977 and remains a wildlife sanctuary where tourists can come and visit.

Environmental conservation is a crucial development of the last century however it still needs great improvement. During the days of the Raj, The Forest Department was commercially exploited; hunting was permitted and huge areas of habitat were destroyed. Commercial forestry has now ceased but there are no budgetary provisions therefore no development procedures came to be made. The unbridled increase in human population is now competing with the tiger for survival and we cannot co-exist, and for animals to have an entity, habitat must be separated. As the master race, we have to resolve this conflict. We are losing our forests, and the symbolic presence of the animals it shelters, before our eyes.

I would tell children of today that animals have an equal right to exist. The air we breathe and the water we drink stem from the biodiversity of the universal environment and its economics. The tiger is at the centre of this truth. If it goes, we go.

Billy Arjan Singh has written many books, including 'Prince of Cats', published by OUP India

Bill Ash

30 November 1917
Texas, USA

Bill Ash when he was a POW in Stalag 111, 1943-45 (back row, middle)

I was born in Dallas, during the Great Depression, and started working when I was ten years old, delivering newspapers. My father, a commercial traveller, was endlessly on the road, and then eventually my mother had to go and join him. I boarded with friends and worked while I went to the University of Texas. I had been studying about the horrors of fascism and when I finished university, Hitler was moving into Europe so, when Britain declared war, I was at one with that and decided to join up. I hoboed my way through America to Canada, jumping on and off trains, meeting the most incredible people. I crossed the border into Canada and enlisted in the Royal Canada Air Force, but, by doing so, I lost my US nationality. I arrived in England, as a fully trained fighter pilot, two months after the Battle of Britain.

When I came to Britain I was stationed on the outskirts of London, in Hornchurch, flying Spitfires. London was such as interesting place to be during the war. All the bombings and difficulties brought the people together so there were no race or class issues – just people trying to get on during a war of destruction. I also got to see some interesting bands and musicians, like Myra Hess, in the National Gallery. All the paintings had been moved out of the Gallery and taken to a quarry in Wales to keep them safe.

In 1942 I was shot down over France, which was quite an interesting experience. I spent a couple of months on the run, getting to know the French people and learning to speak French. I actually quite enjoyed it. Members of the French Resistance helped me find safe places with the aim of getting me back to England, until, unfortunately, I got caught and was sent off to Germany to a prison camp for British airmen.

Before finally ending up Stalag III, which was the main prison camp for British Air Force officers, I had been caught by the Gestapo and sentenced to death twice. While in Stalag III I escaped another three or four times and consequently spent much of my time in the cooler. I've been compared to Steve McQueen, the Cooler King, in the Great Escape, but seeing as I can't even ride a motorcycle, and we certainly didn't have them to help us escape, I find it quite funny.

The prison camp was a remarkable place and we were treated reasonably well. The camp leader was not at all like a lot of the German forces, who were unbelievably vicious. There were rules about the treatment of prisoners and this chap kept very closely to these. The camp was full of air force officers, many of who volunteered to join up. Perhaps this is why many of them had strong attitudes and opinions. Towards the end of the war those of us who were interested in politics used to meet once a week to talk about the kind of Britain that we wanted after the war and I enjoyed these meets very much. They contributed to me wanting to stay in Britain after the war instead of going back to Texas. There were also people who knew about music, literature and history. A friend of mine, Bill Stapleton, had collected a lot of classical records and every night after lights out he would give us a musical performance.

I wrote my first book was when I was in prison camp. They used to supply us with paper so that we could write home and I collected enough paper, by swapping it for chocolate with other inmates, so that I could write a novel. I kept the complete book, written in longhand, in the top of my locker. After one of my failed escape attempts, the soldier who was taking me back to the cooler found the manuscript and questioned me about it. I explained to him that it wasn't about the war but he burned the whole lot anyway.

After the war I studied a course in philosophy and economics at Oxford University, and I secured a job with the BBC, working on foreign broadcastings in the overseas department . I spent three years as the BBC representative in India.

I've always had rather left-wing views and after the war I met Reg Birch, who taught me a lot. He had an important job in the Communist Party of Britain and was a very active trade unionist. Although I didn't agree with everything about the Communist Party of Britain, it was the only communist party in existence, so I decided to join it. However I was not allowed to because some of our differences were too important to be disregarded. I was too left for their liking. Due to some disagreements that Reg was having with the party, he decided to form a new one, which I became involved with from the start, Communist Party of Britain (Marxist-Leninist). This was in 1968. I edited their paper, The Worker, for 20 years.

At that time I was in the external affairs department at Bush House but the upper officers at the BBC had seen my articles in journals and realised that I was a communist.

Bill Ash, a RCAF pilot, in a Spitfire, 1941-42

They couldn't have a communist in their Foreign Affairs department, but instead of sacking me, they made me an outside worker. This didn't affect my position then at all, but it did mean that some years later when I retired, instead of getting a very good pension like those in full-time employment at the BBC, I had just a very small ordinary pension. As an outside worker, I moved into the radio drama department. I really enjoyed this as I was recruiting new writers and working with some of the best drama writers in the world.

I got married in England and had two children and I now have five grandchildren. I met Patricia, a Wren, during the war. But all the time I was changing and by the time I got to India I didn't have as much in common with my wife as I once had. While I was on holiday in one of the most beautiful places in the whole world, Kashmir, now of course occupied by the army, I met this Indian lady, Ranjana and we had a lot in common. I've been with her ever since.

Bill Ash has written many books, read including 'Under the Wire', an autobiography, published by Bantam Books.

Mayie Jardine

1918
Guéthary, France

My ancestors sold some of their land to the railway in 1870, which meant tourists started to come to our town for the first time. It changed everything. It allowed my grandparents and my parents to become hoteliers in Guéthary,, as I am.

I was educated at a religious school as were most children of my generation in this area of France. We are Basque and the church was very important in this region, but not any more. I would still go to church but I can't manage it with my knees, and it is too early in the morning for me but there is a mass on the television, so I watch that. At school we attended church every day and had prayers twice a day, but I didn't like it at all.

My mother sent me to England just before the war to learn English. I went to a college, on the outskirts of London, run by two old ladies who used to stay in our hotel every year. I remember that I was quite nervous about the long journey, which I had to make on my own. I stayed for three months and I had a lot of fun. We had a lot of freedom and were able to go to the cinema, theatre and I met my first English boys who were very well-mannered in those days – I don't know about now.

In Guéthary there used to be a casino on the beachfront, which is now apartments, like many of the hotels, including the beautiful art deco hotel Guetharia, also on the seafront. I loved going to the casino. There was a great orchestra and we would dance in the moonlight on the terrace, which over looked the sea. I loved to dance – the slow, tango and foxtrot, but I don't like modern dance, I like to dance with someone. Many big beautiful cars drove through Guéthary early in the evening, to drop off beautifully dressed people. It attracted great singers and entertainers, I seem to remember that Frank Sinatra played there. Charlie Chaplin, who we adored, used to spend his holidays in Guéthary, allegedly so that he could go to the casino. He also came to see the Joie de Pelote, as did everyone. Pelote is a bit like squash, but mainly played outside. It was played at the Olympics at some stage, but only two teams played so it was abandoned. The people of Guéthary take Pelote very seriously. I had a photo of Chaplin, my family and me watching the game – we were waiting for the game to start when Charlie Chaplin came and sat in front of us. It was very exciting. Only men were allowed to play Pelote, but they have just started training girls. I'm not sporty so I'm pleased I didn't have to play. I preferred the beach and going to parties. I was always known for having many soirees until very recently.

Mayie Jardine age 18

When the Germans arrived in Guéthary in 1940, we were not happy. All the hotels were requisitioned for the German soldiers, including my parents', for which we were paid a small fee. The commander chose the best building for his headquarters, the big beautiful art deco hotel. We didn't make problems for the Germans so they didn't make problems for us – they were very friendly, but also they seemed very young, even though I was quite young myself. Some Germans even came back here after the war, built properties and stayed.

In about 1952, I met my husband, Douglas, while I was serving drinks in the Bar Basque. He was Scottish but was living in Paris at the time and on holiday in Biarritz. He came back to the bar every night before returning to Paris in September, when he gave me his telephone number. I went to Paris later with my niece and when we arrived she suggested that I phoned him. So I did. He couldn't speak French and I couldn't speak very much English then, but he had a French friend with him, whom I spoke to. He invited Nicole and me to dinner, on Douglas's behalf. Douglas and I got married five years later. We had a dog called Ruari that Douglas brought over from Scotland – he always said that Scottish dogs were the best. I've still got the crate that Ruari travelled in. It is said that the dogs around here are descendants of the foxhounds that the Duke of Wellington imported from England, when staying here for the winter; consequently he introduced foxhunting to France. I've been told that Wellington and his armies may have stayed here in Guéthary, and perhaps even in my hotel. After Douglas (and Ruari) died, I was visited regularly by a dog called Bingo. He used to spend his days asleep in the very centre of the crossroads outside the Bar Madrid. We never knew who he belonged to but he was just like an English hunting dog, I'm sure he was a descendant of one of those foxhounds. In the afternoons Bingo used to come to me for ham and to sit with me until early evening. One day about five years ago he stopped coming.

I could not give advice to young people but I could mention some of the most important things in life such as falling in love; to have good friends and a job that you like; to laugh and have fun and to listen to good music, read good books and go to the cinema and theatre.

Kiril Nikolov Vassilev

28 May 1918
Smolyan, Bulgaria

I grew up in the small village of Turyan, in the most ancient of the Bulgarian mountains, the Rhodopes and it was my dream to 'fly out of' the deep recesses of the mountain, read, learn and go as far into the world as I could. Eventually I was able to do this and went to university in Sofia. I had to support myself by doing manual labour because I could not live on the slender means that my parents were able to send me. It was during this time that I was arrested on several occasions for my active participation in the fight against fascism.

At university I read a lot and learnt about Don Quixote from *La Mancha,* and Hristo Botev, who is the greatest and most talented Bulgarian, a poet, thinker and a revolutionary. He lost his life at the age of 28 as the leader of 200 Bulgarian rebels in the struggle from the liberation of Bulgaria from the Ottoman yoke.

During the Second World War, firstly I participated in the underground antifascist resistance movement, then I became a guerrilla fighter, and finally I was the political commissioner of a guerrilla squad. A military mission of three British officers, led by Major Taylor, flew from Cairo and joined the detachment. All the members of the squad put on a British military uniform; and we were supplied with weapons, which were dropped near to us, by planes. On the day of the victory over fascism I wore a British military uniform and a cap of a Bulgarian soldier.

As a scientist and lecturer it was the 1940s when I had my most original scientific ideas. However, I would have liked to have focussed my attention on fewer subjects, but study them more thoroughly. In particular I would have explored the question: 'What is the social nature of the biologically social, and why is his/her biological nature sociologically biological?' I believe that money is the most dangerous temptation, which can damage and destroy the talent of the scientist.

I have reached the age that I have, probably due to the genes my mother and father passed on to me but also studies have shown that the percentage of people over one hundred is higher in the Rhodopes mountains than anywhere else in the country.

I have never smoked a cigarette, have avoided alcohol and I prefer to drink Bulgarian milk and fruit juices. I have always preferred the natural pleasures of life. While I have never been to a football match or even seen one on television, I fully comprehend the significance of sport in contemporary society. It is a way of biological self-defence for the individual and every single person should do a sport. For many years I used to go on all-day excursions in the mountains to the highest peaks, at least once a week, stripped to the waist, even in winter when the temperature was minus 10–15 degrees Celsius.

As well as that I have observed a strict routine of scientific study throughout my life since my youth. As a whole I have lead a healthy way of life. I have been careful about eating meat although I am not a vegetarian. I have always preferred the natural pleasures of life and have never been tempted by the destructive bliss of psychotropic and biological opiates. I have never gambled. I have never been intoxicated by such interests as I consider them to be the mass diseases of civilization.

For decades now I have been doing regular exercises for 35–40 minutes every morning. I have been exercising all the muscles of my body among the trees in the park. As it is, life is a strain, both in a physiological and psychological sense.

The modern world is very exciting due to the latest scientific discoveries that have created unparalleled opportunities for the production of material wealth; for the advance of transport and communication technologies; and by bringing people together from all over the world. However, these unprecedented discoveries, under the current social system, are mostly exploited by a tiny part of humanity, which makes use of them in order to accumulate vast wealth under its control; to increase the exploitation of human labour; to develop weapons of mass destruction and to push the world into wars for global dominance. Without new universal moral principles and without a fundamental humanitarian reorganization all over the world, the apocalypse may cause our civilization to perish. Two discoveries that without doubt are of great importance are the deciphering of the genetic code (DNA), the bearer of human life, and the invention of the computer.

During my life I have seen how a lot of people have changed their ideological beliefs. That fact has strengthened my own belief that a great many people are not as wise and far-sighted as some thinkers claim them to be. Actually most people have a rather primitive, conventional mindset. However, I would not deny that there are wise people among us, but still they are quite few, almost as many as the precious stones in deep waters.

I have always done my work with conviction no matter what that work entails. Young people should strive to become citizens of the world, be less selfish and more altruistic; they should learn to defend their dignity and their personal freedom without threatening the dignity and personal freedom of other people.

Ruth Ive

16 June 1918
London, England

During World War II, I worked in a little known intelligence department called the Postal and Telegraph Censorship. There was no telephone service from this country to America because at the outbreak of war we fractured the Post Office's underwater cable on the instructions of the British and Canadian censorship authorities. When America entered the war a very rudimentary transatlantic radio link was established but it was thought that it would be fairly easy for a determined engineer to unscramble the conversations. Sure enough every call that Churchill made was on Hitler's desk within two hours so we had to monitor every conversation and ensure nothing was said that might compromise national security. Any calls with references to food shortages, air raids and civilian casualties had to be immediately interrupted and perhaps disconnected. Neither could you use the name of the person that was on the line.

The only people that used the line were the War Cabinet, heads of government departments and European royalty. Our royalty didn't use it – the telephone really wasn't King George's thing. In 1941 I was told to report to an office in St Martin's Le Grand, near St Paul's. It was a small dark room with trestle tables and sandbagged windows. I was about 23 when I took the first call and I was terrified. My favourite callers were the Dutch royal family. Queen Wilhelmina and her husband came to London during the war and their daughter, Juliana had taken her children to Canada. It was considered that they would be safer out of Holland. Wilhelmina really missed her grandchildren so she would phone them. Beatrix, who was about eight or nine, spoke beautiful English and was a little chatterbox. These conversations humanized the situation.

I had to cut people off fairly frequently. Robert Boothby (a Conservative politician) was a very charming man who dined rather well so he could be careless at times. However, when I intervened he was very good about it. "Certainly darling, of course", he'd say. However, Lord Beaverbrook, who was also a politician as well as a close confidante of Churchill, was a horror and would refer to convoys and sailing dates. When I interrupted the conversation he was quite rude to me, saying things like, "Get off the line, you silly woman."

Soon after starting the job I got into a row because I wasn't writing enough things down. So I began to write everything down. Churchill used to end all of his calls with KBO. I had no idea what it meant, but I would write down 'KAY BE O'. I worked for a very irritable colonel who told me sharply not to do so. It only meant 'keep buggering on'. I wasn't alone, I'm sure Roosevelt didn't know what it meant either. We've used the expression in my family ever since.

Churchill's working day nearly killed us, we had to work when he worked and he never went to bed. The lack of sleep and working in a blacked-out room without daylight round the clock dominated my life. One day I had heard that Churchill was going on a private visit to the States. It meant I could have time off and rest! Instead, I was given a rail pass by the colonel and told to get a train to Lincoln. The RAF chap that met me from the train wasn't expecting a girl. He was concerned that they had no ladies' facilities, but I didn't mind, I wasn't there for long and there was a bush outside.

I worked in this little Nissan hut and my job was to make everything secure and to leave only one phone line operational. Around dusk, I saw the undercarriage of the Lancaster bomber just miss the top of my hut. I will never forget the noise. It was so low that I could see all the bomb bays. Nineteen planes left for Germany that night and we waited all night for them to return but, as we now know, only eleven came back. I only found out the next morning, when the Dam Buster Raids were all over the newspapers, that I was at Scampton 617 Squadron and had just witnessed that extraordinary departure.

I give talks in school about my experiences and, once the children realise that Mr. Churchill doesn't sell insurance, I can tell them that he really was a great man and tell them stories about how he stood alone and saved democracy in this country. It is because of what I experienced that I hope they value democracy and their freedom. We should safeguard it, fight for it, and treasure it. I also think we seem to have lost our sense of history and with that we seem to have lost a sense of our identity.

Ruth Ive wrote 'The Woman Who Censored Churchill', an autobiography, published by The History Press.

Ruth Ive

Bellur Krishnamachar Sundararaja Iyengar

14 December 1918
Bangalore, India

I was born into a large, poor Brahmin family in Bellur Village, Southern India. My father died when I was nine and I had to go and live with my brother in Bangalore. After that, my mother was dependent on her children so she had no voice, but she was a strong-willed person, and I think I imbibed that strong willpower and that made me determined to make or mar myself through yoga.

I wasn't a very healthy child, and was born during an influenza epidemic, which left me sickly and weak, and later I developed tuberculosis and typhoid. I don't think I was expected to reach adulthood. When I was fifteen years old my life changed dramatically when chance made me go and live in Mysore with my eldest sister and her husband, who was the renowned Sanskrit scholar and yogi, T. Krishnamacharya. After a few months he taught me a few asanas (postures) to practice in order to improve my health. I consider him as my Guru. He not only remained my hero but also became God to me.

Bellur Krishnamachar Sundararaja Iyengar

I first started teaching yoga in 1937 in Pune, Maharashtra, and I have remained as a yoga teacher to this day. Yoga had absolutely no respect from the people of India and I wanted to present it through public demonstrations to bring back its glory and majesty.

Health, which began to shine on me after seven to eight years of yoga practice, changed the way I thought about things. I was a failed matriculate so I would not have got a decent job and the only way that I could make a living was through teaching yoga. So, when I began, it was purely on a mercenary basis. In 1946 my family Deity Lord Srinivasa (commonly known as Balaji), came to me in my dream. He gave me a few grains of paddy and said that I need not worry about my daily wants, but to pursue my yoga practice with both my heart and head. Since that day to this, the grace of God pours down on me like torrential rains, keeping me away from wants and making me a real devotee of yoga. I look upon each asana as an incarnation of God. I use my body as the bow and the asanas as arrows with the target of hitting the soul to merge in the universal soul.

The most significant thing that has happened to me in my lifetime was when the world famous violinist Lord Yehudi Menuhin underwent yoga training in Bombay and then invited me to England and Switzerland. It gave me a chance to expose the value of yoga to the world. Another unforgettable incident was when I had to teach head balance to the Queen Mother of Belgium in her 84th year. She knew that I was very nervous and she asked me whether I had faith in what I do, and if so why was I afraid to teach her to stand on her head. This forceful and powerful encounter, though it shocked me, made me have full faith in what I do. Her words opened my heart and I taught her to stand on her head, discarding my fear.

The highest practical philosophy that I would like to pass on is to give back more than what one charges or earns or at least give back what one takes. I would like the younger generation to build up confidence, zeal, magnanimity, courage, firmness, attentive awareness, to pay respect to the body that is given to us, and lastly to live a lively, graceful, worthy life and leave a good imprint on the coming generation.

Margaret Watson

23 March 1919
Dorset, England

Margaret Watson age 18

When I was young we had wonderful visits to my grandfather in North London from our home in Dorset. We went by steam train and I remember on the journey looking out for the White Horse at Westbury and the Sutton seedbeds near Reading. I fondly remember the smell of Paddington Station; visits to the Zoo and the Tower of London; and being taken to the variety shows at the Hackney Empire. The show was nothing like anything I'd ever seen in Dorset. There were acrobats, dancers and magicians. After going home by train, we would have fish and chips and fizzy cream soda with a pebble in the top – bliss!

I left school at 16 and went to London to work at County Hall for the London County Council. It was exceptionally young to be leaving home but I think my parents thought that I was a bit of a nuisance so didn't mind. I was completely innocent of the facts of life but the Providence of God took care of me – but a little advice from my parents would have been good. I worked on the switchboard in the Care Committee Office in Kensington and at first I was terribly frightened, as I had never used a telephone before. I cut everyone off and never remembered anything anyone said to me. I was called industrially useless on a report so they moved me to County Hall by the river where I worked in a nice big office, mostly with men who didn't make me use the telephone. I lived in lodgings in New Cross Gate and it took me a quarter of an hour to get to work by tram. At lunchtime I only had enough money to go to Lyons where I would have a large coffee and a bun, or small coffee and roll and butter. Sometimes I had enough for a Welsh rabbit which was glorious, but they were few and far between.

I remember the morning that war was declared and the sight from Shooters Hill of the barrage balloons all over London. We were terrified when they starting evacuating children and at the sound of the first air raid siren. We expected a fleet of German planes to arrive and bomb us all to bits. But nothing happened for months. I was a radar operator for the RAF during the war and my job was to give the plots of fighters, bombers and enemy aircraft through to the girls who worked at HQ. These were then passed on to our pilots enabling them to be in the right place at the right time. I was based at various small radar stations up and down the south-east coast of England where we were in a perfect position to pick up many enemy planes as they left Holland. We could track aircraft for up to 200 miles away. Some radar operators tracked our own planes that often limped back from bombing raids. The accuracy of the last plots that they took were essential for picking up any pilots who ended up 'in the drink', to enable the crew to be rescued as quickly as possible. Most of the radar operator's jobs were kept a secret; even our own families didn't know what we were doing.

I used to believe in capital punishment until we started to see people wrongly incarcerated or worse, having been hanged when they were innocent. There was a case in the 1950s, which has always stayed with me, where a Welsh lorry driver, Timothy Evans, was convicted of killing his pregnant wife and baby daughter. It was later discovered that the murderer was the serial killer, John Christie, the Evans's landlord who lived beneath them in Ladbroke Grove. Christie was hanged a few years after Evans. I believe that Evans was granted a posthumous pardon in the 1960s for being wrongly convicted and that the case played a large part in the abolition of capital punishment in Britain.

The enforced abstinence during and after the war gave me an excellent digestive system. This has probably helped my longevity along with not worrying about life but giving thanks to

God for the good things and taking the bad as it comes. I've learnt from my life that loving your family and friends is the most important thing. People should also make the time to stop to smell the flowers before it is too late and to realise that if things do not turn out as you would wish in the long run, they often turn out to have saved you from disastrous consequences.

Anonymous

1920
London, England

It must have been about 1923, perhaps my earliest memory, when I can remember playing on the hearthrug and being gently shushed by my father to be quiet, while he fiddled with one of the earliest radios, his 'Crystal Set'.

I grew up in a purpose-built small block of flats, many of these Edwardian buildings can still be seen in London. There were three flats to each level, the lowest of which was below pavement level but we were lucky to have a top flat below the roof garden. The flat had gas for lighting and cooking but no electricity. There was a grate for coal heating, which had to be black-leaded daily and needed a sack of coal delivered once a week (up three flights of stairs). The weekly washday was a chore. We needed to heat water in saucepans on the stove; have galvanised buckets and bath; and a scrubbing board. The washing was dried on the roof and ironed later with a flat iron that had to be heated on a gas ring. There was a lot of horse-drawn traffic in the streets, which carried merchandise, especially coal.

I started school in 1925 in Hatton Garden, the centre of diamond retailing where men exchanged gems in 'knots' on the pavement. As I grew up I began to appreciate the privilege of living in Holborn, on the edge of the City of London. We had easy access to many London markets such as Smithfield (for meat); Billingsgate (for fish); several street markets, including Leather Lane, which was our nearest, where mother shopped daily. The Royal Parks were relatively close by and were where we walked with my father on Sunday mornings. I remember on one occasion we had a treat, which was a milk shake at one of the new Milk Bars.

I contracted scarlet fever in about 1926 and, in those days, children were hospitalised in isolation wards, which was a traumatic experience for an only child who had never been away from home. I cried for twenty-four hours until a kindly nurse asked if I would like to write to my mummy. She probably thought I would scribble nonsense on a pad but I sat up and described the ward and its rocking horse in every detail. The letter was my salvation.

Public transport was in the form of trams and open-top buses. Barrel organs were a feature that was heard in the streets, often accompanied by groups of dancers who were men in drag.

London however was beginning to change. The trams were disappearing and trolley buses arrived and the open-top buses had been replaced by covered ones. Piccadilly Circus tube station had installed escalators and by this time the men who lit the London gas street lamps with a long pole were disappearing as electric lighting became commonplace.

I had developed a great sense of the history of, and had a deep pride in, the area where I lived. It was certainly a great privilege to wear the flash on my uniform of '1st city of London Company – the Lady Mayoress's Own' with my fellow guides.

During these years we started to notice that Chinese people had started to move into Soho and Italians into Clerkenwell. The annual procession in Holborn and Clerkenwell to the Italian Church was quite a spectacle for those of us who lived there.

During the war years there was a danger of crossing roads because there were no traffic lights. They were covered except for a slit, which showed the light through as a red or green cross. It was very cold in the winter and many women wore knitted hoods. I made a dress from two identical man's shirts, and a pair of slippers from an old skirt with soles cut from a man's trilby hat.

We witnessed the awe-inspiring sight of St Paul's dome ringed with fire, as we watched from the roof, irrespective of the danger we were in. In a later raid in the spring of 1941 our block of flats was demolished in the last great raid on the capital. Only ash remained. Mother was injured and she was in and out of hospital for two years before she fully recovered. We were given temporary accommodation in a small hotel in Bloomsbury, which had been commandeered by the Government. The family unit was restored in 1944.

Tommy Godwin

1920
Connecticut, USA

Tommy Godwin winning outright the famous 'Muratti Gold Cup' at Manchester track – 3 wins 1946, 1947 & 1948

I was born to British parents in Bridgeport, Connecticut. My father was interested in sports, and as a child I recall him asking me if I would enter the Olympic Games, which must have planted the seed in my mind. We came to the UK when I was twelve and the depression in Britain seemed worse than in America. We had nothing, so the family were split amongst relatives and my fifteen-year-old sister was the only one working at the time, as a book clerk. We eventually settled and became very happy.

In America before we left, I had hoped to attend Yale University, but in Britain aged fourteen I worked in a factory, sweeping floors, emptying bins and making tea, which I didn't find very interesting. Then I worked at a large chain store of grocers called Wrenson's where I rode a bike with a basket on the front, delivering groceries around the area. Two of my customers, Mr and Mrs Bolton, were keen cyclists and tandem riders and I remembering seeing their cycling books. I saw images from the 1936 Berlin Olympic Games of Arie van Vliet and Toni Merkens who had both won gold medals.

Wrenson's put on a sports day and I entered the cycling race where I finished third, on a borrowed bicycle, competing against others who were on proper racing cycles. I won a stopwatch that my father used throughout my career while helping me train for competitions. I later worked for BSA (Birmingham Small Arms Company) as an apprentice electrical engineer, and bought myself a cheap bicycle and started entering races. The following year, 1938, my father was so pleased with my determination that he bought me my first proper racing bicycle, which cost £10, 19 shillings and 6 pence and it had wooden rims. I rode in the BSA sports day and had two firsts and a third. The next year I won all four cycling events.

I took part in the 1940 Olympic trials and I won a gold medal at the 1000m time trial. The final Olympic trials were due to take place in London on September 9th with the Olympics themselves in Helsinki the following year. However, war broke out on the 3rd and everything was cancelled. I volunteered for the Navy and Air Force but I was needed as a qualified electrician at BSA which was the biggest munitions factory in the country.

Tommy Godwin riding 1000 metre time trial in the dark for the bronze medal

Great Britain hosted the Olympics after the war in 1948, however rationing was still on, London was still scarred with bombsites and there was no proper Olympic village. The Olympians stayed in schools, hostels and army camps. The runners' starting blocks were brought in from different countries and the diving boards were brought in from America.

The track cycling team stayed in a big house (owned by Bill Mills, editor of The Bicycle), which was adjacent to the Herne Hill track. We slept on camp beds and my mum cooked us our meals, which included spam fritters and toad-in-the-hole. My father picked up some tips from his boxing friends, which were supposed to help with my training. I was to drink down in one swig a new laid egg in a glass of sherry to build up my strength; a jug of water with freshly squeezed lemon and Epsom salts to clear my system; and I had a drying out period from a Thursday to a Saturday where I had no liquids. I must have raced sometimes totally dehydrated which I now realise is one of the worst things I could have done. However I did win two bronze medals in the team pursuit and the 1km individual time trial.

I believe that drugs have been in the Olympic Games since the beginning. Competitors would eat berries or consume stimulants such as caffeine, and way back in history strychnine was used. After Reg Harris, the World Champion cyclist, turned professional he hired a soigneur, Louis Guerlache, and while giving me a massage, he offered me something to help me win gold. I said, "Absolutely not. If I can't win a race with what I've been gifted, I don't want to win." I wouldn't be alive at 87 years of age had I been involved with drugs. One rider I know used to greet any good performance with "Good ride, what are you on?"

In the early 1950s, BSA still paid me while I raced and represented the country. My colleagues at BSA threatened to strike if the boss didn't get rid of me because they didn't think it was fair that I should still be paid, so I was made redundant. After three years of not having a proper job, I decided to buy a cycle shop. My wife Eileen took a lot of the responsibility for running the shop because I was still racing and travelling abroad. I competed at the Empire Games in Auckland, where I won the bronze; it took me five weeks and a day to get there by boat, fortunately I came back by air. I rode until 1953, and retired on the day of the Coronation. In the winters of 1953 and 1954 Eileen became ill and suffered terribly, it was discovered she had tuberculosis and required 53 weeks in a sanatorium and part of her lung removed.

After I retired from racing I was appointed the first National Coach for cycling in the 1960s and became manager of the British National Cycle Team at the 1964 Tokyo Games. In between coaching and managing, I worked at the shop and also spent time encouraging children who showed an interest in cycling, some of whom became champions. My advice to these children was always that, in order to excel in any sport, you need to have ambition, dedication, discipline, respect for other people, and above all make sacrifices to work the body almost beyond human limits.

Tommy Godwin wrote 'It Wasn't That Easy: The Tommy Godwin Story' , an autobiography, published by John Pinkerton Memorial Publishing Fund

Hugh Maw

1920
India

When I was born I was registered as a British subject with an Indian birth certificate. I was the third surviving son of Quaker missionaries, who had a long pedigree in the Society of Friends.

While at school in Reading I was a member of the League of Nations Union (similar to the United Nations Association of today) and I signed the pledge to renounce war of the Peace Pledge Union, and read their paper *Peace News*. From 1938 to 1942, I was at Bristol University studying for a degree in biology with a view to becoming a teacher.

In January 1940 I was notified of the date when I was eligible for Military Service, and knew that I must formally register as a conscientious objector (CO) at the Bristol Employment Exchange, which I did. The application for the Bristol Tribunal had to be at the Ministry of Labour and National Service office by 6 July. Thus I had several months to prepare my statement as a CO. Friends in Bristol and Birmingham (where my home was) were very supportive. Since I had not joined the university Officer Training Corps, I volunteered instead as a university firewatcher, and as a Bristol Royal Infirmary theatre orderly during the worst air raids. In the vacations, to earn money to get me through university, I worked for the Ministry of Agriculture and Fisheries searching for the Colorado beetle in Devon and Cornwall. I also joined work camps in Birmingham, digging air raid shelters and growing vegetables.

My tribunal was on 24 October 1940, before Judge Wethered, CP Brown and Prof. GC Field. My statement, read by all three men, confused them. Judge Wethered asked what religion I was, and I was subjected to a tirade against it. To my intense surprise the matter was quickly resolved, and I was given unconditional exemption and encouraged to complete my teacher training. I am, of course, eternally grateful for the result, because it enabled me to follow a course that changed my whole life. The university generously accepted the decision, and I had no opposition, insults or condemnation from anyone.

After my tribunal, I was a volunteer worker, with two other COs, in the Quaker Refugee Hostel in Tyn-y-Cae, Brecon, caring for the families of Austrian Jewish refugees whose menfolk were interned as enemy aliens on the Isle of Man. We were all threatened by Brigadier Whales, of the local garrison, that we would be shot if any Germans landed in the area, and we were all subjected to continuous searches and indignities.

I finally got a wartime BSc and a postgraduate Diploma in Education at Bristol. I did a series of teaching jobs until 1946 when I was posted to Berlin to take over from the Friends Ambulance Unit team working there, which was disbanding. I worked continuously and closely with Vera Brittain, with the distribution of parcels from Save Europe Now (a campaign to feed people starving in central Europe after the devastation of the war). She used my photographs and some of my reports for articles in *Peace News*.

My main work, however, for the year in Berlin was to carry out a survey, for the Allied Military Government Education Department, of delinquency in Berlin. This was given publicity in Parliament and acted upon. I also started an International Youth Club called the Karolinger Jugend Haus. Though it no longer exists, the Old Karolingers still carry on as a group, produce a journal and are still in communication with me.

In 1948 I was accepted for training on a postgraduate Diploma Course in Remedial Education at Birmingham University.

During the course I did a practice placement at Kingswood Approved School in Bristol (a boarding school for boys in trouble with the law who were sent there by Juvenile Courts). One of the pupils at that time was Derek Bentley, who later became the centre of a campaign for justice lasting 45 years. In 1952, at the age of 19, he joined in a warehouse burglary with a 16-year-old, which ended with the younger boy shooting a police officer dead. Although Bentley could barely read and write more than his own name, and had a mental age no more than 11, he was found guilty of murder and hanged, while the other boy, too young to hang, was imprisoned. In 1998, after years of campaigning, the conviction was quashed, on the grounds, among others, that the trial did not properly consider Bentley's mental age and ability.

I went on to other jobs in remedial education and then in ordinary teaching, ending as headmaster of a Quaker School near Banbury in Oxfordshire. I remain an active member of my local Friends' Meeting, where the clerk happens to be the first woman in Britain recognised as a conscientious objector.

Clara Foldes

17 March 1920
Arad, Romania

My grandmother, Grunbaum, had a summer kitchen with an oven for bread. The oven was very big and behind it there was a special place where a large pot was kept, where the grease was gathered after the rendering of the scraps. One day I was sitting at the table for dairy products drinking my cup of hot chocolate. I was watching the women working at the other table, the one for meat products, and I noticed that they kept going to the pot behind the oven and poured the grease in there. So I took my cup and poured my hot chocolate in the pot, too. Of course, my grandmother couldn't use the grease any more.

My family, including my younger brother Gheorghe, lived in Curtici, on the Romanian-Hungarian border. Before the war we had no financial problems, and lived in a big house, in the basement of which was my parents' textile store.

When I was seven, my mother had just had an operation, so my grandmother Vilma moved in with us to help with the household. In the autumn we bought geese, fed them up and then the best parts were pickled in brine or smoked. They were delicious. We did the same with veal. At the celebration of Purim we used to make a lot of shelakhmones, cakes with nuts and poppy-seeds, and we took these to our Jewish friends. I don't remember celebrating birthdays, mine or anyone else's. As I child I attended religious education and then later the rabbi visited our school to give us classes.

I attended a Red Cross nurse course for two years in Cluj and then I started a two-month voluntary defence course in 1938, where I learned to use a shotgun, as well as having theory classes. After a while Jews weren't allowed to attend any more, and I was sent home; I cried all the way.

During World War II, when Hitler's regime began, many Jews who had gone to Germany to study returned home via Budapest-

Curtici-Arad; due to not having any documents they were made to get off the train in Curtici. My father, the president of the Jewish community was contacted by the frontier guards each time anyone new arrived. The travellers stayed with us a few days, they had the chance to take a bath and change into new clothes, which we had bought for them. Hungarian territory was not safe from the Nazis. This where my paternal grandmother, her daughter and two of her boys lived so they were taken to concentration camps.

In 1941, a law forced all Jews who lived in villages to move into the nearest town. My family were given only two hours to get ready to leave, and had to move to Arad. A year later I went to live with them but this was made very difficult because at this time the only way Jews were allowed to travel was if they had a certificate to prove that they needed to have medical tests in Arad. Once I was there I obtained a job at the Jewish school and worked there from 1942 to 1948. I was the youngest teacher and thoroughly enjoyed it. I met my husband Andrei Foldes at a New Year's Eve party in 1943 and we were married for 44 years. We didn't have children, although we wished to.

During the war, the Germans needed our school building, so we had to move into a community building. The Nazis imposed restrictions, which meant that Jews could not enter certain shops, restaurants or the swimming pool and my father had difficulty in finding a job. Our shop apprentice who remained in Curtici took care of our store, and sent us money from time to time. The Orthodox priest and other villagers also bought us supplies.

In 1950 my parents moved to Israel. After my father died, my mother used to make and sell cakes. She died in Quiryat Yam in 1989, a few days before the Romanian Revolution. Most of my Jewish friends from my youth moved to Israel too but I remained in Romania because the climate would not have been suitable for my health and I couldn't speak the language so I wouldn't have been able to teach. I visited Israel in 1969 and 1988; it is a wonderful country.

Printed with kind permission of Centropa (www.centropa.org). Interview by Oana Aioanei.

John Berry

9 June 1920
London, England

I was born in Hammersmith and my first job was as a paperboy when I earned 3 shillings and sixpence (17½ pence in today's money). I have been an artist for most of my life and my current job is a 48 x 40 painting of foxhounds.

When Hitler started messing around in Europe I was thirteen and six years later the war broke out. In 1938, I won the scholarship to the Royal Academy schools. I was told at midday that I had won the scholarship and was overjoyed, as I had worked so hard to get it. By 3 p.m. the same day I was told by the principal that the London County Council wouldn't give me a grant, the R.A. wouldn't give the LCC the returns for my attendance so I couldn't go.

Two years later I volunteered to join the RAF, which I regret. I wanted to be a fighter pilot, but I had long eyesight so I was rejected. I served as a radar operator in the Western Desert Campaign in the Middle East and in 1941 we landed in Aboukir (Egypt) and were kept in a holding camp, waiting to go to the front line. There was nothing much to do there, except swim. One day I met a priest who was setting up a prayer day for the soldiers and wanted to advertise a National Day of Prayer so I offered to do a poster for it. My superiors liked it so much and Air Marshall Tedder (head of the RAF Middle East Command) wanted to put 'my talents' to better use. When we were called out and put on lorries to go off to the front line, I was called off the lorry and instructed to go to Cairo to see Randolph Churchill, who became my boss. I thought I was in serious trouble, but instead I was told to be a war artist. I was told that my paintings from this time were exhibited in the National Gallery in London during the war. They have ended up in the permanent collection at the Imperial War Museum in London.

After being in the Middle East, I was then transferred into Royal Welch Fusiliers in 1944. I became a marksman, lecturer on art and was asked by the army to start an art class but was demobbed three or four days later.

After the war, I designed various advertising campaigns and created the ESSO Tiger in 1951. I worked for Astral Arts Group who started as War Artists Illustrated (they only employed war artists). I remember it was a Thursday afternoon and I was asked to go to a meeting with McCann Ericksson where I was asked if I could paint tigers. Their client was Esso and at that stage all they knew was that they wanted an illustration of a tiger. They asked for a rough drawing by Monday morning, which I duly did. After initially complaining that 'back legs were a little paralysed'. they asked me to design the whole scheme with the slogan on it, as a finished layout. The slogan 'PUT A TIGER IN YOUR TANK' is mine too, having opened my big mouth in a meeting with the advertising agent. I got paid £25 for the whole job. When the design was finished with my tiger and slogan and submitted to the company, they asked me to paint out my signature and explained to me that I wouldn't get any royalties. As we know now, the whole campaign was eventually used worldwide, up 30 foot posters were produced and the campaign lasted 10 years. It is a shame but nobody knows where the original drawing is.

I have painted many portraits including Queen Elizabeth and Prince Philip, in the early 1960s; George Bush Senior; Prince Charles and Princess Diana at the time of their wedding; also Princess Diana on her birthday in 1986 and another in 1988. I have also illustrated books and book covers for Ladybird books, Corgi, Penguin, Readers Digest, amongst others. If the paintbrush hadn't been invented my life would have been very different. The paintings of Rembrandt and Velasquez have inspired me to continue painting all through my life.

My son says that my favourite saying is "Good old England", meaning that I think the place needs a good shake-up and needs to stop being so wet and indecisive. The world generally needs a shake-up, it has become more greedy and violent and crime is getting worse. It isn't a favourite of mine but I say, "ooh do leave orf", quite a lot.

William Clifford Golding

24 August 1920
Hampshire, England

I was born at an address for unmarried mothers in Southampton. William was the name of the registrar of births, and Clifford was a priest who happened to be a witness.

William Clifford Golding age 19, somewhere in France

At the age of four, my mother and I were admitted to the Stockbridge Workhouse in Southampton. I still have vivid memories of the smell, which was typical of such places, I guess – of a mixture of carbolic soap and stale bread, which seemed to cement the floorboards together. This was more apparent on the long wooden tabletops in the dining hall although the women inmates scrubbed these daily.

From here, things could only get better and fortunately, when I was five I was placed in a Children's Home in Shirley. I distinctly remember that first day there. I was ushered in a side door of this grand old white building into a passage whose walls were painted in a dark chocolate colour, where I met some children about my own age. The games they played were quite violent. Two lines of children faced each other outside on the lawn, then advanced towards each other in turn, singing at the tops of their voices, a ditty which went: "We are the Germans, we're the German soldiers". The opposing line of boys came back with greater force (with fixed bayonets), with "We are the English, we're the English soldiers". Whichever side "killed" the most soldiers were declared the victors. No sissy ball games for me then!

This was the start of a long stay in many different care homes.
At the age of fifteen, I got my first job, which was at Kingsworthy Court Hotel, near Winchester. I was fitted out with my first pair of long trousers, new shoes and a shirt. Upon arriving at work, I was presented with an apron and scrubbing brush and told to clean the front steps. After this my work was mainly in the scullery, washing dishes and pans. I was paid 7/6d per week (thirty-seven and a halfpence). This, to me, was a small fortune and in addition, I was given a half day off on Wednesdays and a whole day off on Sundays. Money, when you have so much at such a young age, means freedom, power, security and status. I didn't let it go to my head, though. I went to the Post Office and opened a Penny Savings Account and have not been short of money since.

It was about this time I decided to pay a visit to a girl I'd been friendly with at one of the homes, who'd given me her home address. I took the train to Southampton and was invited into her home where I discovered that her father was a policeman. However, I was made welcome and I enjoyed the family's hospitality until quite late. I caught the last train back to Winchester. Arriving there I decided that I would take a stroll round the outskirts of town when suddenly a large figure approached out of the darkness. It was the local bobby, doing his rounds. He enquired what I was doing out after midnight in that neck of the woods and I explained that I was just taking a walk. He wasn't satisfied with that and I had accompany him to the police station. Apparently, there'd been an increase in burglaries in the area and he was taking me in on suspicion.

At the station I had to give an account of my movements that night. To verify my story they said they'd have to get in touch with my girlfriend's father. Unfortunately, he had just gone out on his beat and would not be reporting in until six o'clock in the morning. Consequently I was kept in a large iron cage (just like in the movies), all night. I was released, with not even a cup of tea, just in time to be able to start work at 7 o'clock back at the hotel.

After a few years I decided to join the army to see the world. But I was too young. The recruiting sergeant, however, out of the goodness of his heart and as it was near Christmas, said I could get in by adding a year to my age. Consequently, on Saturday, 4 December 1937, I took the King's Shilling and joined the Royal Corps of Signals. A couple of years later, at the outbreak of war, we were already at our mobilisation stations in Aldershot and in the early hours of Saturday 14 October 1939, we marched off to war.

The evacuation from Dunkirk, where the term "organised chaos" was born, is my most vivid experience of the war years. I must say that but for efforts of the Royal Navy, aided by the Merchant Navy and a host of small boats, I, and thousands of others would not have got away. My mate and I watched as men waded in and out of the water in an attempt to reach the boats while a mad British officer fired wildly in the air with his revolver, threatening to kill anyone who disobeyed his orders. Clearly he'd been at some looted brandy. The pair of us didn't fancy any of that so decided we'd make our way down to Dunkirk harbour. We eventually made it on to a destroyer without as much as getting our feet wet and, in addition, we got a tot of rum.

I met my wife, my greatest hero, in 1940 when, arriving back from Dunkirk, I was billeted with her family in Hammersmith (where we enjoyed the London Blitz). I married her after the war and she looked after me and kept my feet on the ground for over fifty years until I became her carer when she became too ill to cope. At the end, 10 May 2003, she collapsed from a stroke and died in my arms.

As an octogenarian I often get asked how I got to be the age I am and for advice based on my experience. Of course there are no secrets. I can only say: walk, don't run; avoid strenuous exercises; hold your shoulders back; take a deep breath and simply get on with it. Giving advice to teenagers is tricky as they seem to have so much knowledge already and for the most part are 'streetwise'. I am proud to say that at the age of 85 I enrolled as a student at a local college – hopefully this would show young people that it is never too late to try something new.

Sheila Donaldson Walters

17 October 1920
London, England

I come from a very good family of Irish Quakers who always seemed to volunteer to help others. My father came to London from Ireland to join the British army to fight in World War I. After the war he contracted MS and died very young so he was unable to ever return to his homeland. I adored and respected him and I still remember his kindness. I treasure his last letters that I received from him while he was in hospital when I was five years old. I had a twin sister with whom I went to boarding school but we were never in the same classes or dormitories so I never had very much to do with her. Even in the holidays at home we led rather unconnected lives, and this continued right through our lives. After the war she married and moved to Chicago. When I was a teenager I wanted to continue my education and go on to Art College and I'm pleased to say that I did follow my convictions and have been an artist all my life. I met and married a rather unusual young Royal College of Art student who also had a twin, but they were very close.

I enjoyed boarding school from 6-17 years of age but having been brought up on traditional English school 'grub', I did not think much of food when I was young. I remember that I always gave my meat to Olivia who sat next to me.

The biro pen, with its continual flow of ink, was the most important invention for me. I was born left-handed and at school we had to write with a steel pen nib in a wooden holder dipped in an inkwell, which was placed on our desks. I had to write with my right hand to avoid slopping ink over my work. If the biro had been invented earlier I would never have been compelled to change to my right hand to do all my written schoolwork.

The most tragic thing that happened in my life was losing our son in a hideous gassing accident in Turkey. He had done very well at university and gained a first class degree in European Studies and Norwegian. He went on to teach English as a foreign language and went to Ankara. In the late 1970s, Turkey was in a rather bad state where extreme leftist groups rioted against the state, taking control of the universities, so all the teaching staff were taken off to Pamukkale in the west of Turkey for a break. During the afternoon a Turkish student told the two teachers, my son and a friend, that he could show them an ancient site where the young priests of the Goddess Cybele received their omens and is dedicated to Pluto, god of the underworld. The site is on a Plutonium spring and still gives off deadly poisonous gases. It is where Apollo met the mother goddess of Cybele and it has been suggested that she descended into the cave without being affected by the toxic fumes. The three of them went to the site and but they had to climb over the entrance in order to get in. My son and his friend went back later that evening, without the student. They did not come out again. At breakfast the next morning, people realised that Justin and Ian had not returned from the site. The principal of the college went and discovered Ian's jacket outside the entrance. He found the two young men stretched out on the ground, overcome by the poisonous fumes.

What is marvellous about life is that we have memories and upon that one calls back extraordinarily happy moments, as well as remembering the sad times. I can say that I have enjoyed life tremendously in spite of some of the awful things that have happened. When I look back I think that fundamentally the world has not changed since I was young, except I think there is a need for greater kindness and humanity towards one another.

Sheila Donaldson Walters – Granny, Mother, Sheila and sister Brenda

Douglas John Huxley

11 November 1920
Lancashire, England

I was born in Preston and my favourite decade was my first one – I liked school and church and I led a life of all pleasure. During the school holidays we were given a jam sandwich, a bottle of cold tea and were told to return before 6 o'clock. We picked bunches of primroses, bluebells, stinking garlic, sticky buds and may flowers so that we could sell them. We also made money from selling the good coal that we collected from the tips. When we returned home, we were fed, bathed and then put to bed. My childhood games included fighting, hoop and stick, spinning top, conkers and leapfrog. We played with a diablo, which was also known as 'the devil on two sticks.' It was made up of a spool, which was whirled and tossed on a piece of string, which tied to two sticks, with one held in each hand. I also played football, rugby, scout stick fighting, cricket; and we went fishing, made catapults and collected birds' egg. My parents advised me to stand up for myself, and to stick together with my brothers and sisters. The remedies that I recall as a child are a kiss on the area that hurt; a bread poultice for boils; mustard bath for colds; caster oil and Parish's food (a tonic) to build up strength; brimstone and treacle to stop spots; hot lemon and honey for colds with goose fat rubbed on the chest; a brown paper vest was sewn on to you for the winter; crushed marigold flowers for swellings and bruises, and a cup of tansy tea for a headache.

My first job was as a farm worker, aged 14. I lived at the farm and was given food and clothing. I was paid 7 shillings per week; 4 shillings in cash, and 3 shillings saved for holidays and Christmas. I would have liked to be a stonemason and a dry-stone waller, but at the beginning of the war I joined the services and always seemed to be on the move, training and sleeping rough. We joined the invasion of Normandy, which seemed a blessing to me, and then I fought with the Guards' Armoured Division in a Churchill tank from 1943 until the end of the war. I still vividly remember when I saw the sky full of gliders and parachutes in 1945 when we crossed the Rhine in Germany and the knowledge that we would win the war. My life-changing experience happened when I witnessed the Germans surrender in droves.

I used to hate the Germans with all my heart, but after I witnessed them surrender, my hatred changed to pity; since then I've found that you don't get anything from hating anyone and it is better to be kind. After the victory I sailed for Japan, but finished up in Palestine, after the atom bomb was dropped in 1945.

I don't know how I have got to the age I have, but I've smoked from an early age, drank more than my fair share and kept my eyes open for a pretty girl. I try to keep within the rules of good manners and I try never to go to bed with a problem unsolved. I also try never to get angry. I think the world we live in today is better than when I was young in some ways. Poor people are looked after better than they ever used to be; there have been advances in medical science and travelling is much easier than when I was younger. However, I think, as a teenager I had a much better time than modern teenagers do. I want young people to have a good time, as they will soon learn that it will be over quicker than they thought.

Molly Rose

26 November, 1920
Cambridge, England

Molly Rose in the ATA age 24 (2nd left)

My brother, Arthur, who was seventeen years my senior, enjoyed his first flying lesson in Norwich in 1927, obtaining his Pilot's A Licence a year later. In 1929 he bought a new Gipsy Moth and his first flights were made from flattened fields behind our home in Cambridge. When I was a little girl he didn't mind taking me up for a flight if I was hanging about. He was very tolerant. I had some very cold flights because if your big brother offered to take you flying, you didn't run in for a cardigan; you nipped smartly in to the front cockpit! The cold certainly didn't put me off flying; in fact in 1937 I started flying lessons myself and a year later I passed my flying licence. When I finished school in the summer of 1938 my father agreed to allow me to do an engineering course at the aerodrome, which he founded, and so I worked as a ground engineer. The chaps were extremely kind to me, despite the fact I was the only female working in the hangar.

With war declared in 1939, I married Bernard Rose in December of that year. He volunteered to serve in the army and I returned to my ground engineering in 1940, working there until my husband was sent to the Middle East at the beginning of 1942, which is when I joined the ATA.

The Air Transport Auxiliary (ATA) was formed in 1939, just before war was declared, with the task of ferrying aircraft from the manufacturers to the squadrons. The ATA was comprised of male pilots who were not eligible to join the RAF and women who had gained their Pilot's Licence but could not, in those days, enlist with the RAF as pilots. The first group of women ATA pilots, of which there were only eight, was formed at Hatfield in January 1940. It was rapidly proved that the women pilots could pilot aircraft just as successfully as their male counterparts.

The ATA had its own system of training because they recruited people with a variety of experiences, from all around the world. When you first joined you were allocated your own instructor and mine was a lovely lady called Joan Hughes. She was one of the original eight women pilots and was one of the youngest female pilots in Great Britain.

I was stationed at Hamble, which was one of the two "all women" ferry pools. As the majority of aircraft we handled at Hamble were fighter planes, we were responsible for delivering aircraft to all the fighter squadrons in the south of England. The most dangerous part of flying was flying in bad weather. Although the planes were fitted with radios, they were strictly for use only in combat situations. So once you were up in the air, you were on your own and had to use a compass and maps, and in bad weather this was a challenge. I was 26 when I came out of the ATA and had flown 37 different types of aircraft, both single- and twin-engine fighters and twin-engine bombers. I think it is rather disappointing that it took 40 years after the ATA was formed for the RAF to accept women as pilots.

My husband, who was in the Royal Armoured Corps, had landed on D-Day at Arromanches les Baines and was taken prisoner seven days later at the Battle of Villers Bocage. He was to spend the next eleven months in the German Brunswick Camp (Oflag 79), and didn't return home until the war in Europe was over. He was a don at Oxford and as educationalists have never been terribly well paid, there was no way I was going to spend his hard-earned cash on flying light aircraft after I'd had lovely aeroplanes to fly with the ATA, so I have not piloted an aeroplane since then. I had flown solidly for three years and felt very privileged to have done so. It was all very exciting and still, on a lovely day, I wish I had a plane to fly and I often feel, when being flown to overseas destinations, that I could perfectly well take over the controls should there be a crisis in the air.

My generation was very lucky, as we were born at a time when we weren't stopped from doing anything simply because we were female, but we were always looked after. I've had a fascinating life and the whole way through I've succeeded to the best of my ability in doing the things that I really liked doing.

I'm so sad for teenagers today and I think they have a jolly hard time. They are expected and they expect to make all their decisions independently but they haven't got the experience to do so. However they often seem to resent having decisions made for them. My generation had tremendous respect for the older generation and we had the opportunity, if we had a problem, of discussing it with them and being helped. It is terribly sad but advice is not a thing that teenagers appear to seek today.

Kate Cast

1921
Lancashire, England

With the help of the local mid-wife, Granny Windrow, I was born in a little cottage in Ormskirk, Lancashire. I remember seeing her around the village while I was growing up, she always wore a black poke bonnet and cape and carried a black Gladstone bag.

My childhood was happy. With hardly any traffic on the roads except farm carts, we were all allowed to play outside on the cobbled road. One day I remember well. The very keen gardener who lived almost opposite to us invited my friend and me to tea. He had a wonderful row of sweet peas, which he had grown in order to put them in for a competition at the local show. On impulse, I cut off all the heads! Rightfully, in a very bad temper, the neighbour almost dragged me home and told my mother what I had done. She promptly beat me with a cricket stump, which actually broke on my back.

During World War II I worked as a chemist apprentice because I wanted to go to the School of Pharmacy in Liverpool. However, I had to forego my place when I caught TB from a sick locum. I was a rebel teenager and probably had a low immune system, due to burning the candle at both ends. I had to go to a sanatorium in the Lake District to recover. During an air raid on Barrow in Furness, we had to go to the shelter and I remember very clearly the doctor in charge commenting that there was enough metal in the ladies' hair to make a Spitfire. He was referring to the metal hair curlers the ladies used. I remember my parents coming to visit me and they told me that when waiting to change trains at Preston station, they had a lucky escape when one of the sandbags behind the seats they were sitting on burst and the whole lot came toppling down. As soon as I was able to return home, fit and well, we went to many dances at the local college which was taken over by the medical unit of the army. A friend of mine was a qualified dancing teacher and I was invited to join her to teach the soldiers to dance. This is where I met my husband, John.

As an octogenarian I can see how important it is to enjoy the years of freedom that comes with being young and to experience other countries and cultures if you can. That is something my generation couldn't do.

Istvan Domonkos

1921
Budapest, Hungary

In 1940 our country joined the Axis alliance, which consisted of Germany, Italy and Japan. Peter, my brother, joined up as an officer, but in 1941 he was ordered to remove his uniform and like so many Jewish men and women, he had to sew a yellow armband onto his civilian clothes. This was the beginning of the Anti-Jewish Laws in Hungary. In the summer of 1942, he was sent to the front, and a year later my father was notified that he had died.

I was forced into a labour camp in October 1942 and the first thing I did was get in touch with my father, telling him what we needed. This became a regular thing so we formed a Care Committee, and used to apply to what became known as, the Committee of Ex-Servicemen of the Jewish Community for what we needed. The committee raised the money for these supplies from wealthy Jews and later they made this a country-wide organisation.

In 1944, when Germany occupied Hungary (in order to keep us as allies) they immediately made my father an administrator for the Jewish Council. He spoke German quite well, but they didn't know he was Jewish The Jewish Councils were set up in Nazi-occupied Europe and were obliged to communicate the wishes of the Germans and the local collaborating authorities to the Jewish communities. Some people considered the members of the Jewish Council as traitors while others thought that they did everything they could to save those doomed to die. The first thing the Germans did was to appropriate all the Jewish fortunes they could. They demanded all sorts of things, for example, 100 blankets, 50 typewriters, a piano for General X, and usually it was required within 24 hours. My father had a good team who knew where to go for these things, but it wasn't a pleasant situation.

In the same year, they also started taking Jewish women from Budapest, my mother included. She was put on a barge on the Danube, which sank into the icy water, and all the women on it perished. At the same time my sister was assigned to a death march. Somehow, my father managed to find out that the march would stop in Borgondpuszta for a while, and entrusted a man called Zoltan Ronai, also a Jew, who had very good contacts with the police, with rescuing her.

Karl Eichmann (SS lieutenant colonel, one of the main organisers of the annihilation of the European Jews) got more aggressive and increased his threats against the Jewish people. Jews were secretly being deported from Hungary, but when it was found out, they were taken back to the internment camps. Raoul Wallenberg, a Swedish humanitarian, was sent to Budapest, having received information from the Jewish Council that many Jewish people had been deported. After Wallenberg's visit, Eichmann summoned three of the Jewish leaders and kept them in detention without food or water. My father might have been among them but I don't know – it was best not to know about everything. Eichmann ordered the deportation of about two hundred people to Kistarcsa Internment Camp from where most were deported to Auschwitz.

On 15 October, the Germans made Ferenc Szalasi, who was pro-Nazi and head of the Arrow Cross Party, Prime Minister. While the tanks were moving down the streets, my father managed to go to the office but nobody else dared to go out. He called Lieutenant-Colonel Ferenczy, the highest-ranking leader of Jewish matters in the Hungarian government, to tell him that they were in very serious trouble. Ferenczy had said in the past that he wouldn't let any more people be deported and they wouldn't be Eichmann's servants. However, now he said that the Jews got what they deserved and he hung up.

When the Arrow Cross decreed the setting up of the ghetto my father was made the security officer. The ghettoes were like small countries – there were districts, a ghetto police, institutional food, and leaders for every block, whose task was to draw up a list of names to give to the Arrow Cross men. They provided medical care, and dealt with the deceased. In the beginning we were able to take the dead to the Jewish cemetery, but then Arrow Cross men forbade it and from then on, the funerals were held in the courtyard of the Dohany Street synagogue. And later, there were so many dead, that the poor things were just piled up in a room.

My father was on good terms with Raoul Wallenberg, so the whole family got a Schutzpass, which enabled us to travel to Sweden where we were protected by the Swedish Royal Embassy until it was safe to return home.

I met Katalin Schwartz, in the ghetto and later married. My parents weren't happy about it because they wanted me to continue my studies, however I couldn't go to university because of the anti-Jewish laws. In 1947, our first child, Judit, was born, and later, our son Peter. We lived simply, but we had everything we needed. We never had a car and we didn't go on holiday. My wife was a trained seamstress and managed our financial life very skilfully. When the war was over, a friend and I started a sound recording company, which unfortunately didn't work out so I got work as an electrician, repairing war-damaged houses. Everything would have been all right, but then when Rakosi, acting Prime Minister of the Hungarian Communist Party, was in power, he didn't seem to want the tradesmen to work, and they set very high taxes, which were unbearable so I gave it up.

In 1947 my father was decorated, and in 1950 he retired. But three years later, after Stalin's death the secret police, acting on the orders of Rakosi, caught him. Similar to Stalin's political purges, Rakosi was arresting, jailing and killing both real and imaginary enemies. The secret police were feared and hated by the Hungarian working class because of their record of torture and murder, and because of the privileged position they held in Hungarian society, receiving between three and twelve times the average workers' pay. They kept my father in prison for more than six months, before taking him to the hospital. Before his imprisonment he was well built but it was a wreck of a man, weighing just under half his normal weight that they took to the hospital. He lay unconscious for days, and he never walked again. Later he told us, that they had taken him to the prison, stripped him and forced him to make a confession. He died soon after he came out of hospital, on the 25 February 1954.

My wife Katalin died in 1990 and she wasn't buried in a Jewish cemetery. She wasn't religious any more. Like so many other Jews, she could not understand how the Almighty could let this happen.

Printed with kind permission of Centropa (www.centropa.org). Interview by Mihaly Andor.

Magdolna Palmai

1921
Nyíregyháza, Hungary

I grew up in Nyíregyháza, with six brothers and sisters in a close loving family, enjoying meals, holidays and walks together. I remember my first experience of anti-Semitism at middle school when one of my friends said, "Let's go to swing!" I asked "Where?" "On the beard of the Jew," she replied. My father worked in a dressmaker's shop, and he played an important part in raising us because my mother was ill after my birth. As a child I always enjoyed reading, particularly Mór Jókai, Kálmán Mikszáth, Kant and Spinoza. At the end of the 1930s despite hating it, I learnt the trade of sewing, following in the family tradition. I worked at a salon where famous actresses and countesses had summer dresses made.

In 1940 I moved to Budapest, my friends and I were excluded from education, and so Professor Ferenc Mérei taught us literature, psychology and politics in secret for three years, until it became too dangerous to meet. I was living with a very nice Jewish family when I learnt from newspapers and the Jewish community that my family had been deported. They raised white flags in the town that they cleared of Jews – the newspapers reported that this had been done in my hometown. Most of my family died in Auschwitz – my parents, two of my sisters and their children, two of my aunts, five cousins and great-cousins, and my father's relatives. I cried very much when I found out they had been deported, but from that moment on, was not able to shed another tear. Many years later, in 1965, I visited Auschwitz and saw through the big glass wall, the hair, the suitcases, and the shoes. In one exhibition there were children's wooden shoes and shirts, and a lamp that they had made out of human skin. I cried for the first time in over twenty years.

In the summer of 1944 my older sister, Jolan, and I cleared away the rubble from bombed buildings for a small salary so that we could buy some food. We slept in a corner of ruined house, until the foreman told us that he couldn't hide us any longer as the front was coming, so we had to leave. We had to join up for forced labour, as the Germans set all Jewish women aged fifteen to forty-five to work, digging ramparts, mounds and roadblocks (approximately 10,000 people in total). Neighbours helped by giving us food, clothes and a backpack. We were given a shovel and spade that had to be carried on marches of up to forty kilometres. At night we were hungry and exhausted, packed like sardines on a concrete floor in any buildings that could be found, we huddled together for warmth due to lack of clothing. In Maglod a little woman said to us: "Don't cry, we will tell our grandchildren about the grandmother who was a soldier…" On another occasion, a former opera singer called Erzsi sang the 'Yiddishe Mame' her voice echoed and was amplified by the hall. The door opened and there stood the gendarme first lieutenant and he was crying. He said, "How can this be done to women? How?" He asked us what we needed, and that night a truck arrived, bringing us more food than we had seen in our lifetime – bread, bacon, marmalade and margarine. We were given warm water to wash and demobilization papers so we could leave. We were liberated but we had nowhere to go. Budapest was still a dangerous place with lots of shootings and Jewish people were told to be careful and run away if possible, using secondary roads.

We returned to Nyíregyháza, but none of my family was there. My family's belongings had been distributed amongst the neighbours. I didn't have anything, but beautiful life. We lived in the bare shell of Aunt Leni's apartment and had help finding some of our family's old belongings to start our life over.

Two of my brothers survived. My sister Fanni also survived Auschwitz, and after liberation in 1945 she went to live in the United States, because she thought all other family members had perished. She found that American Jews often disbelieved her experience of Germans and Auschwitz. My husband, Sandor, who I met in 1942, was liberated from Gleiwitz in 1945 and we married shortly after.

My family and I had many problems with citizenship papers. In 1946 we moved to Beregszasz (then it was in the Soviet Union but today it is in Ukraine) where we lived as fugitives and I worked as an administrator at a garment factory. When my brother visited us, I was afraid for him to speak his mind about the state; I feared he would be put in prison and he didn't believe how bad it was. My daughter was born in 1947 and on her birth certificate they wrote 'yevrei' (Russian for Jew). After many of my family were exterminated in Auschwitz, I became disillusioned with religion, however, my family and I remained Jewish in soul. I wish I could have buried my parents in a cemetery, so I could have mourned and paid my respects.

In 1959 my daughter and I arrived home to Nyíregyháza. My husband arrived a year later and because he was a Russian citizen we had to apply to unite the family. I was a data processor at the Hungarian Central Statistical Office for three years. I then resumed my studies and achieved a librarian degree while working as a librarian at the Institute of Party History. I worked there for sixteen years, until I retired in 1978. This period (1959-1978) was the nicest period of my life. My husband died in 1995 and we buried him at the Jewish cemetery.

I still read novels, go to the theatre, do gardening, play cards with friends, bake and knit for my grandchildren. I am almost never alone; my daughter and grandchildren are daily guests at my house. In my life I have maintained hope in difficult situations, and I never gave up. I tried to remain human even amongst the most difficult circumstances.

Printed with kind permission of Centropa (www.centropa.org). Interview by Zsuzsanna Lehotzky.

Evelyn Richards

9 January 1921
London, England

Evelyn Richards age 20 on the Kenyan coast

My mother was strictly Victorian and her only advice for me was to get married and have children. Any of my own suggestions were vetoed. Although I did get married when I was nineteen, I didn't intend to follow any more of her advice. My wonderful father told me never to be afraid of anything. I didn't see him after he and my mother divorced when I was fifteen. He was killed in the war in 1942 while in the RAF. He was a brilliant pilot, artist, musician, sailor and he was also incredibly good-looking.

The man I married when I was nineteen, at the outbreak of war, was an absentee army officer who then left me and went to Abyssinia. I was living in the Kenya at the time so I took a job, with no salary, managing a 300 acre farm, just to a get a roof over my head. The enchanting little house looked down on Lake Nakuru.

We were all ordered to grow pyrethrum which was used to make flit (mosquito spray) for the troops. It only grew at an altitude of 7,000 feet or more and had a work gang of mostly women and children to pick the daisies when they were at their peak. If you didn't pick them at the right time, which I didn't at first, you only achieved inferior quality ratings for the crops.

I could do whatever I wanted with the land that was not being used for pyrethrum, so I grew vegetables, kept rabbits, chickens, pigeons, and turkeys. I also started a business growing and selling violets. One day I found a few violet plants flourishing under my bedroom window which had an overpowering perfume and glorious colour, evidently planted by the previous owner. I decided to try and sell them in the flower shops in Nairobi. This was a great success as they flowered all year long and were a rarity in Kenya. Various wild animals shared the house with me, as well as my two beautiful Alsatians. They were to guard me although this wasn't necessary in those halcyon days of peace and friendship, when the doors were always left open. However I did keep one of my ex-husband's rifles by my bed, just in case.

I had an extraordinary life in Kenya, in which I learned to survive without electricity, running water, telephone, and of course, not a sign of computers or mobile phones.

My travels throughout my life have made me look at things very differently. I went to India, Australia, Iran, Egypt and New Mexico. I travelled to these places as an individual and not as a tourist so I was enable to meet and communicate with the people of those countries and I learned a lot about them. I wish that I had lived in Taos, New Mexico indefinitely and become part of the art community there. The Indians, Americans, and many other nationalities produce fantastic work and it would have been amazing to stay with them for longer. I read this quotation years ago and it has meant a lot to me ever since. *"It is imperative that the people of the many countries of the world come to know one another better in order to arrive at a universal understanding and appreciation of the many diverse cultures and ways of life that contribute to the world we all share."*

When things got fraught my French grandmother always used to remind me of the three Cs – cool, calm and collected. I have learnt from my life to not be afraid to have a go and remember the apple at the top of the tree.

Bob Godfrey

27 May 1921
New South Wales, Australia

I was born Roland Frederick Godfrey in Horseshoe Berch West Maitland, New South Wales. My parents had gone to Australia after the First World War on an ex-serviceman's immigration scheme. My mother took an instant dislike to the wide-open spaces so we came home to Ilford, Essex when I was about six months old.

I didn't pass any exams, until I got to Leyton Art School when I was fourteen. I saw a lot of films but I particularly loved Popeye, Chaplin and Laurel and Hardy. I wasn't in the least interested in how films were made probably because in those days I wanted to be a painter like Van Gogh. My first job at the age of seventeen was as an errand boy with Unilever Ltd at Blackfriars. Eventually I was transferred to the art studio of Unilever advertising agency where I was still a runner but a white artist's smock came with the job.

When World War II broke out, we moved to Twickenham in Surrey to get a little further away from the bombing (five minutes flying time for a bomber). In 1941 I joined the Royal Marines and served until January 1946 and my strongest memory of those five years was coming out of a cinema in Paris and seeing a crowd of young people with a placard saying "JAPS QUIT!" When I returned to London I got my old job back. It wasn't exactly my old job, as you can't very well be an errand boy at twenty-six, but I was a sub-size layout artist, a very uncreative and boring pastime. Although most of my friends were captured at Dunkirk, I missed the romantic life of a service man.

I went to work for an old Disney director on something that these days is called merchandising – painting rabbits and parrots on shoe boxes, which I found pretty depressing. Eventually I had a meeting that changed my life – it was with Peter Sachs who gave me a job. Peter, being German and Jewish, was interned on the Isle of Man during the war but was released to work on wartime propaganda films. He made me a background artist, working on scenery for his animated cartoons.

In 1954 I set up Biographic with two colleagues and in 1955 we made a 15-second black and white animated ad for the first night of commercial television, ITV. I can't remember now what the ad was for.

I was nominated for an Oscar in 1971, but I believe I was the first British animator to get one in 1975 (*Great*). The nomination came about after I had shown my films to some students in Leicester Square. I was asked by an American guy if he could buy one of my films, *Kama Sutra Rides Again*, to give it to his son as wedding gift. I sold him a rough old 16mm print for £50. The next thing I knew I'd been nominated for an Oscar for the same film. I didn't even know it had been distributed in the States. It was after that film that Stanley Kubrick phoned me to ask if it could accompany the UK general release of *A Clockwork Orange*. I was very surprised to hear from him – and pleased, but Stanley Kubrick was to withdraw his own film from circulation. In contrast to that in 1974 *Roobarb*, the first animated television series to be made in the UK, was first shown on British television, written by Grange Calveley and animated by me. It went on to win various industry awards and has recently been recommissioned.

Georgette Collins

19 July 1921
London, England

Georgette Collins

During the war I lived with Mother and worked in the research labs of the General Electric Company in North Wembley. At first they said I couldn't work for them due to my parentage. My surname was Andreassi (my father was Italian and my mother was German). I was a stroppy 19-year-old, so I argued my case. Eventually they gave in and gave me the job, which in hindsight they shouldn't have. They didn't know who I was and what research information I could pass on.

On 10 June 1940 when Italy allied with Germany, Churchill panicked and the decision was taken to round up all the undesirable aliens who could possibly pose a threat to Britain, despite the fact that many of their sons were fighting in the British forces. Originally the internment age was 18 to 60, but Churchill raised it to seventy years old. My father was 65. He was a tailor and had come over from Italy in about 1907 with my mother. He was president of the Italian Tailors for Ladies in Charing Cross. He was arrested in the early hours of 11 June 1940 and taken to a camp somewhere in England. I don't know where he was held but we heard they were billeted to army camps, hotels and holiday camps; anywhere that could be found, just as long as they were out of circulation and away from the public and their families. According to Red Cross reports, these internees were terribly treated, without proper food, sanitary conditions and medical care. We only had a few words of correspondence from my father and he didn't say much.

They were to be exported to Canada and Australia, unbeknown to the passengers or their families. There were three ships to take the Austrians, Germans, Jewish, Italians (internees and POWs) and the Arandora Star was the second to leave. It was originally a luxury cruise ship, which had undergone changes to convert it to a troop ship. It had been overpainted in battleship grey and had the appearance of a troop carrier; the lifeboats were secured behind heavy mesh; the ships maximum capacity was supposed to be 500 (it was approximately three times that when my father was on it).

The Arandora Star left Liverpool docks on Monday, 1 July 1940, bound for Canada. Then the next day it was torpedoed by a German U-boat. It is assumed that its crew had mistaken the grey ship for an armed merchant ship. Thirty-five minutes after being hit, the Arandora Star sunk. I believe nearly 700 people were killed. I never saw my father again, and we were never told what happened.

My mother was not interned, even though she was German, but she was not allowed out after dark and when my brother, even though he was in the British forces, came home on leave, he had to leave his gun next door.

I don't have a bad feeling about any of it – there was a war on, but I do feel resentful that no one ever wrote and told us that my father had drowned, but it's all in the past now.

'Jack' G H Holsgrove

11 August 1921
London, England

I spent 1938 and 1939 wiring housing estates but then went to work at Stirling Corner where they were building a new factory for a highly respected Dutch engineer, S E Opperman, to re-design and make the under-carriage of the Stirling Bomber.

The Stirling was a four-engined bomber and there was a lot of trouble with the under-carriage because it kept folding up on landing. I was Opperman's assistant on this project and it was top secret.

Soon after solving the problem, I got a new placement but all I was told was that Bomber Command had posted me immediately to 5 Group HQ at Grantham. It was top secret and urgent. I had to leave for Lincoln Station immediately.

When I arrived at Lincoln, I was taken to RAF Scampton not Grantham as I was told. The area was very high security and there were no other personnel around. I was driven to the Flight Hut where I was met by Flight Sergeant Chiefy Powell. Behind the Nissen hut, roped off, with a guard standing beside it, was a Lancaster bomber. I walked around the enormous plane – the largest I had ever seen. It had four enormous engines and I could see that the bomb doors were open and hanging between them was a large barrel-shaped object – the bomb.

I was told that the bomb had stuck but the release gear had fired and my job was to find out why. The only thing that I could do was to get on top of the bomb and have a look at the release gear to find out what had happened.

I discovered that the gear was totally jammed because the carrier was completely distorted due to the carrier not being strong enough to hold such a huge bomb. I explained to Barnes Wallis that they would have to design and make a new, much larger, release gear. I was told in confidence by Barnes Wallis that they needed instant release the moment the firing button was pressed and the weapons would be dropped from very low level, over calm water, and they needed pinpoint accuracy. That was all that I knew about the raids on Germany's dams.

Barnes Wallis told me to get on and redesign the carrier, the way that I had suggested, and was in charge of all modifications. Along the way there were a further couple of problems, which I solved. One of which led to someone needing to fit a time delay fuse-link only minutes before take off. But as soon as the fuse-links were fitted, the aircrews were not safe. If a release mechanism was accidentally triggered, or if the weapon was to become dislodged, it would explode within ninety seconds, with catastrophic consequences. It was decided that the aircrews would not be told that the weapons would be live.

It was the only possible answer and even though it was something that I had come up with, I wanted no part of this unbelievably dangerous solution. Barnes Wallis and Scampton's CO told me that the fewer people who knew about this project, the better, and I was to modify each of the carriers and fuse each of the aircraft before take off. I was told that I was in charge of the whole operation and it would be my decision to send the Squadron away on the night of the raids. I was told that I would work alone and tell absolutely no one.

The day of the Dam Buster raids came. The nineteen Lancasters, each with a crew of seven men, were to fly all the way from their base in Lincolnshire at tree-top height, with just the light of the moon to guide them. They were to destroy three mighty hydroelectric dams in the Ruhr, which were vital to Germany's industrial production.

After the Lancasters were sent off shortly after 9.30 p.m., I was ordered to burn all the drawings and notes that I had made about the project. I was instructed to go to the main mess hall where there was a meal for me and I was to speak to no one and would be under guard, in fact under arrest until all the aircraft returned.

As I walked to the mess hall, I heard the first of the aircraft coming back so I stepped out of the cookhouse to watch. As I stood watching them arrive back, a car approached. In the car I saw a high ranking RAF officer and a civilian in a thick overcoat and a felt hat. 'I just wanted to congratulate you. Very well done.' It was King George VI with Air Chief Marshal, Bomber Harris. Apparently it had been an intentional meeting, but had to be kept secret. I soon found out that eight of the Lancasters failed to return. Nearly half of the squadron were lost, but I was reassured that it was due to nothing that I did. I was told, for my own safety, that I would be banned from European postings and anywhere where I could be taken prisoner by the Germans.

The raid was deemed a success as the destruction of the dams caused widespread flooding and interrupted industrial production. However it came at a high cost as eight of the nineteen Lancasters failed to return, fifty-three aircrew were killed and three survived to be taken prisoner.

Jack Holsgrove wrote 'Dambusters Away', an autobiography, published by Tessera Publishing.

'Jack' G H Holsgrove age 14

The Rt. Hon. Sir Patrick Nairne
GCB, MC, MA

15 August 1921
London, England

I was at University College, Oxford, during the early part of the 1939-45 war, but in 1940 I volunteered to join the army. Serving in the 51st Highland Division, I was wounded twice. On the first occasion I was involved in a night attack and, as battalion intelligence officer, I was making my way to contact one of our front companies which was a few hundred yards away, when I was suddenly hit in the leg by a bullet and I collapsed to the ground. I remember thinking that I was likely to be taken prisoner, but somehow I pulled myself together and more or less crawled back until I was picked up on the battalion front line.

The second occasion was towards the end of the war, when I had become adjutant of the battalion. In 1944 the Germans made a major attack through the Ardennes Forest. At one point I was speaking on a small hand-set phone to the commanding officer, telling him about the front line situation, when a German shell landed very close indeed. It wounded me in the neck and hand. I was evacuated to a hospital in England and I didn't return to the battalion until the war in Europe was over.

I was then released from the army, so that I could complete my studies at Oxford. I had no interest in going into business, but saw my first choice as going into the public service. I was accepted for the Civil Service and found myself posted to the Admiralty.

In due course I was appointed Private Secretary to the First Lord of the Admiralty, Lord Carrington. We got on well and have been friends ever since. After the Labour Government was elected in the 1960s the Defence Minister was Denis Healey. He was the first person to have the position of 'Secretary of State for Defence', with one department responsible for all three services (the navy, army and air force). To my surprise, he chose me as his Private Secretary. Some years later I was promoted to Deputy

Secretary and after three more years to Second Permanent Secretary in the Cabinet Office. After two years I was promoted again, this time to be Permanent Secretary in the Department of Health and Social Security – as it then was. My first Minister was Barbara Castle. I knew that she was not always an easy Minister to work with and it was a relief when I found that we got on very well. I retired from the Civil Service in 1981, at the age of 60.

The Rt. Hon. Sir Patrick Nairne GCB, MC, MA age 17 (bottom right)

My last job was as Master of St Catherine's College, Oxford. There is now a series of annual lectures in my name at St Catherine's, which are intended to relate to the wide variety of appointments and interests I have had during my life. My son, Sandy, who is Director of the National Portrait Gallery, gave a lecture recently on the theme: 'Why do painted portraits still matter?' If I ever had to give such a lecture it would be on the value of watercolour landscape painting.

Both my wife and I are Christians, as are most of our children and my religion has played a significant part in forming my attitude towards most things. However, it was surviving the war that made me feel that I ought to try to do some good with the rest of my life. While I recognise that there is value in getting experience from a variety of jobs, often abroad, I firmly believe that, sooner rather than later, it is important that young people should secure some professional qualifications or become permanently engaged in some particular field of work. I once heard a speaker advise young people that they should aim "to leave a brick behind", meaning that, as if helping to build a wall, you should in your work aim to make a distinct contribution of your own.

John Stanley Shuter

29 September 1921
Oxford, England

In Senio, Italy in 1945 I suffered mass bombing with anti-personnel fused bombs, which destroyed my recce group and my scout car.

The army, generally, at the time was being bombed severely from the air with anti personnel bombs and I was a gunner troop commander with an Indian division who had been hit terribly. We were lined up in a cobbled street when we were attacked. My truck, which was in the middle of several others, had its roof blown off, my driver was decapitated and two gunners in the back were killed. After doing what we could for the injured, I made my way back to my troop headquarters but found to my horror that another load of bombers were coming and the same thing was going to happen again. My new gunners arrived and a strange officer who was a replacement appeared out of the top of the Sexton, and as I went to shake hands he suddenly bowed down out of sight and I found that we were being bombed again. I dived under the tank with the thoughts of countless people I had already seen killed up the road. I thought I was marginally safer under the tank than in the street, until I found the tank was turning and the tracks were coming nearer and nearer. If I had moved from under the tank, I would have been bombed. I was very frightened. But the tank stopped moving and I could escape in safety. My one coherent thought was that if I survived that I will never be so frightened again. I never have been.

I was in London as well for part of the war and it was very exciting. I remember there was this propaganda cartoon character that the government had brought out called Billy Brown of London Town. He was one of these insufferable characters who did everything properly. He was dressed as a city gent, in a pin-striped suit, bowler hat and carrying an umbrella. He was used to give the public little pieces of information on the tube or on buses. For example, the glass on the tube trains was gauzed over to reduce the risk of casualties from bomb blasts and people used to pick at it so that they could see what station they were in. One day Billy Brown appeared, pointing to where the gauze was peeled off and in a speech bubble next to him, it said, *'I trust you'll pardon this correction, this stuff is there for your protection'*. Somebody I remember had written underneath, *'I thank you for the recitation but I can't see the bloody station'*.

After the war, I went straight from the army into colonial service and worked for Crown Agents, until I retired at 60 years old, and thus travelled, worked and lived extensively in over 70 countries, overseas. Crown Agents is an international development company whose job it is to help the growth of the developing world and my job was mainly marketing but I had a whole range of roles. Although I went to many countries, I was only in four countries for long family postings of two or three years each –

John Stanley Shuter age 19

these were Uganda, America (Washington DC), Saudi Arabia and Barbados. But other than those long posts, my visits were usually quite short. I was in Nigeria for four or five months at a time, including during the civil war. Nigeria was never much fun, it was a strange place – strangely foreign. Most colonial territories had a very heavy English influence but Nigeria never did. It is a very big country and much divided amongst its own people both religiously and ethnically.

In the 1970s while working in Sierra Leone, after its independence, I was arrested as a suspected mercenary. On one of my trips, I took a colleague who had worked for years in the Crown Agents but had never been abroad. The hotel was directly opposite government house and one morning when leaving the hotel we saw a ceremonial sentry in a pillbox, standing at the gates of the building. He was wearing the distinctive parade uniform of the The West African Frontier Force (a force formed by the British Colonial Office), which comprised of khaki drill with red fezes, scarlet zouave style jackets edged in yellow and red cummerbands. I suggested to my colleague that he ought to take a picture of him, as I didn't think it would be seen for much longer. So he did. The next morning the same thing happened except the soldier was in camouflaged greens so my colleague took another picture. We continued on our way into the town but as soon as we arrived, we were arrested as suspected mercenaries. There had apparently been a revolution during the night and the airport that was only a few miles away had been surrounded by men with machine guns. Due to this, there was sheer panic, which is why we were arrested. We were marched into a cell and kept there for half an hour. Luckily I had only just visited the chief of police a few hours earlier so I asked if I could see the commissioner and soon we were sent on our merry way. But it was a stroke of luck that I had come to know him otherwise it could have taken several weeks to get out.

'The hardest thing for age to learn is that it is now an observer and no longer a player' is a saying which I very much relate to as an octogenarian. It's no fun getting old but if you have to have aches and pains you may as well be an In Pensioner at the Royal Hospital in Chelsea as anywhere. I've been here for four years and it really is marvellous. There really are very good to us here. We don't pay for anything and get whatever we want. Whatever

the army is paying you, i.e. a war disability allowance or long service pension, the hospital take from you and you no longer get the pension once you are accepted as an In Pensioner. You normally have to have an army pension but I think they are in the process of modifying the rules a little bit so that you may be able to pay towards your stay here.

My advice to a teenager is hard work and application will probably enable you to win promotion by doing your job well but after that, far more important is how you can get on with people i.e. how well you can persuade and encourage people to work for you. But I think it is important to add that unsolicited advice should be proffered sparingly.

'Johnny' George Johnson

25 November 1921
Lincolnshire, England

I grew up in a farmhouse in the rural area of Hamingham. My mother died when I was three years old so my father raised my four brothers, one sister and me. He was strict and sometimes used the force of his razor strop on me as punishment. I couldn't wait to leave home and go to school.

When the war broke out, I volunteered but failed to make the grade as a pilot but retrained as a bomb aimer. I had just qualified when I was selected to join the crew of Flight Lieutenant Joe McCarthy as part of 97 Squadron flying in a Lancaster bomber. We had made approximately 30 trips when I joined the new squadron that was being formed for only one trip. It was 617 Squadron and the mission was top secret, even our phonecalls were monitored. I was due to get married to Gwyn and although all leave had been cancelled they did allow us time off to get married but no honeymoon was permitted.

The first we knew about the bouncing bomb was the night before the raid when Barnes Wallis showed us a film, which caused much speculation amongst us, as to the target of the raid. It wasn't until the day of the raids that we found out that our targets were to be five of the main hydroelectric dams in the industrial Ruhr valley in Germany. Our crew was informed that our specific target would be Sorpe dam, which was very different to the other dams. It was built of earth covering a concrete core, which would absorb more of the shock waves created by the bomb, and reduce the intended effect so we knew it would a difficult dam to break. The raid was by moonlight during the early hours of 17 May.

Our aircraft behaved perfectly during training but that day it developed a hydraulic leak. Joe, in his hurry, caught his parachute as he left the aircraft and it was billowing out behind him as we ran to the reserve plane. Joe wasn't going to bother replacing it, but Flight Sergeant Chiefy Powell managed to get a replacement for him before we took off.

On the way out, south of Hamburg, the front gunner asked Joe if he could fire at a goods train he had spotted. Joe reluctantly agreed. The gunner opened fire with little 303s, however, the goods train was armoured and retaliated with rather more than 303s. We felt the plane take a hit, but didn't know where. It didn't seem to be causing a problem so we pressed on. It wasn't until we got back to RAF Scampton that we discovered where we had been hit. When we landed at Scampton, it was fairly bumpy, as it was still only a grass airfield at that time; but we were starboard wing down, trundling along. The flight engineer looked out of the window and informed us that we had a flat type. We had been shot through the undercarriage and it burst the tyre. If the shot had gone a couple of feet in another direction, it would have hit the petrol tank. The plane would have exploded killing us all. Bomber Command lost something like 55,000 men in the end. I did 50 trips and didn't get a scratch. I was extraordinarily lucky.

When we arrived at the dam, we flew down the hills one side, levelled up and then flew along side the dam as close as possible to try and hit the target. It was extremely difficult and took ten runs to try and get it right. On the last run, we dropped from 1000 feet to 30 feet. The explosion sent a huge tower of water into the sky, but when we flew over again we could see that while we'd damaged the parapet, the wall had survived and the dam didn't burst. Five aircraft were briefed for that particular attack, but when we got to the target, none of the other aircraft were there and no one had been. It wasn't until we got back that we discovered that two of them had to turn back, one had flown into cable and the other had been shot down. We, and another reserve aircraft, were the only ones of the five planes to reach the dam. Barnes Wallis thought it would need at least six bombs to only crack the concrete, which was all we needed to do as the water pressure would do the rest.

I recently returned to the Sorpe Dam and I was glad we didn't succeed in breaking it. If we had, the valley would have been totally destroyed. It could have been rebuilt, but it wouldn't have been the same.

I feel that the best and most accurate book written about the Dam Busters is by John Sweetman. The book that was used for the film had a number of inaccuracies, including putting my character in the wrong crew. I met Peter Jackson, the film director, at a reunion dinner about three years ago and he mentioned they were thinking of remaking the Dam Busters film and they wanted to ensure they get it right. To make an accurate film of the raids means more to me than anything else. Later Steven Fry, the scriptwriter, came to my home to interview me. The new film will bring the story up to date for the younger generation, instead of them having to watch an old 1955 black and white, inaccurate movie.

'Mimi' Eva Jirankova

27 November 1921
Prague, Czechoslovakia

I lived with my family in Prague during the winter, but from May to October we lived in our country house, in Revnice, which is thirty kilometres from Prague. Throughout the war we stayed in Prague mainly because we had no cars to take us to our villa. On 15 March 1939 my father received a phone call from a man at the foreign ministry to warn us that the Germans had crossed the

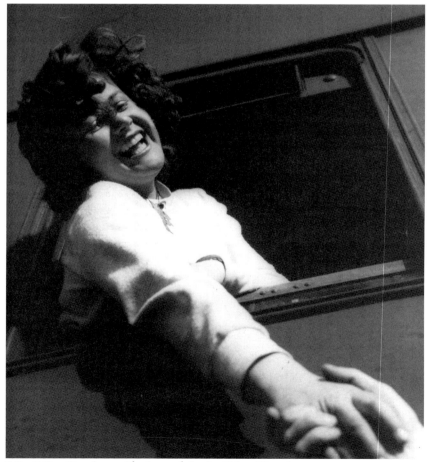

'Mimi' Eva Jirankova. Photograph by Ladislav Sitensky

border and would arrive in Prague in two hours. I was seventeen years old when I stood at the living room window, with my father, as we watched the tanks roll past our house. The man who phoned us was later shot.

On my wedding night in 1942, the Gestapo stormed in at 3 a.m. and arrested my husband. He spent a month in prison in Prague and then he was sent to a concentration camp. In January 1945 my husband and fellow prisoners were ordered to march from Breslau, near Auschwitz, in Poland to Dachau, near Munich. They had to walk at night, so the planes didn't see them, often through thick snow, and during the day, they hid in the woods. It took them four months. Many of them died along the way, and those that survived were starving and freezing. They were liberated from Dachau by the American army in 1945 when I finally was able to see my husband again.

Between the end of the war, in 1945, and the Communists taking over, in February 1948, we had a very privileged life in Prague. My daughter was born in May 1946 and my husband was the managing director of his family's publishing house and a newspaper, "Lidove Noviny" which still exists. We had two and a half wonderful years before we had to flee the country and leave everything behind. In May 1948 when we tried to cross the border, by foot, we were arrested. They kept me in prison for only a few days, as I had a small baby, but my husband was kept for four months. They held him in the same prison in which he was held during the war. Eventually there was an amnesty for the prisoners when the new Communist President Gottwald was elected and my husband was released.

In November 1948, we managed to get our immigration passports, but at great expense. We arrived in Paris only speaking a little French, with nothing, except a little bit of jewellery that I had managed to smuggle out, which I could sell. We lived in a tiny room in a hostel in the Latin Quarter, which was full of refugees who had fled the country. We lived on bread, pancakes and wine. We had permanent residence in France, we never got permission to work but we were happy to be free. Many of my friends who couldn't leave ended up in prisons or were made to work in uranium mines and died of leukaemia. Their only crime was that they born into bourgeois families. My brother finished studying law, but was never allowed to practise and had to work as a labourer for all of his life.

We arrived in London in November 1951 as penniless refugees. I spoke four languages but not a word of English, but luckily my husband did. We lived in a flat in Hammersmith, which we found with the help of the Czech refugee trust fund, where we paid a small weekly rent. My husband was a doctor of law, a journalist and as he spoke a few languages he was able to obtain a job with the Foreign Office where he stayed for twenty-five years, until his retirement.

I secured a job selling ladies hats at Woollands in Knightsbridge, on a weekly wage of £7 plus 1% on commission on sales. This was the first job I had ever had and I loved it.

In 1961 I worked in the millinery department at Liberty's. After a year of selling hats there, I was sent to the fashion shows in Switzerland, Italy and New York to look at the new collections with a view to buying for Liberty's. I was at the first collection of Yves Saint Laurent in Paris when he left Christian Dior. It was an exciting time to be in fashion. I was now going to Paris about four times a year which was such a contrast to when I was in Paris the first time – now I was staying at a very grand hotel instead of the refugee apartments in the Latin Quarter.

In November 1989 there was a revolution in Prague and Václav Havel became the new president of Czechoslovakia, but unfortunately my husband died exactly one month before this. In January 1990, I went to the Czech Embassy in London, to ask for a Czech visa so that I could go home after all those years. I cried when I received it. Our house, in Prague, became the East German Embassy during the communist era and at the fall of the iron curtain, we got our house back with the help of the British Ambassador. Now I go to Prague sometimes six times in a year.

I would say to young people: be polite and caring, it does not cost anything. Also that sport is very important, it keeps one healthy and out of mischief. I also think that one year of military service would be good for discipline and to see the world.

Zsofia Tevan

1922
Békéscsaba, Hungary

One of my aunts, an uncle and both my grandmothers died in Auschwitz. Only four Jewish girls from my class at school survived. The others also perished in Auschwitz. Of the surviving four I still keep in touch with two. My father was taken to Bergen-Belsen and a man who he worked with in the camp told us that he had died of the spotted disease. His death was never confirmed but I do understand how that was not possible. When the Americans liberated the camp they couldn't do anything else, but bulldoze huge areas. It was impossible to identify and bury the prisoners one by one. There were many awful experiences of the war but three particularly stick with me. Soon after Germany invaded Hungary the Jews had to move into the ghetto and we had to wear the yellow stars. As a breadwinner I was allowed to leave the ghetto for two hours a day. A Polish girlfriend from Krakow convinced me that I had to flee. All of her family had been taken away and killed so she was too scared to come with me but she passed her one-year old daughter over the wall of the ghetto to the wife of a textile engineer. Later they were able to escape to America. This little girl is still alive today. The other terrible memory I have was when I had to say goodbye to my grandmother, with whom I had lived as a child, knowing that I would never see her again. She was in the House of Jewish Old and when I last visited her, I couldn't tell her that we would flee. She was not that old, she was younger than I am now, she was about 78. The last memory that I find hard to recount is when we were hiding in an apartment, which was very near the railway station. I heard the boxcars shut at night; the German commands; crying and screaming. I had to listen to it, which was very hard. I tried not to tell the others in the apartment in order to avoid the loss of hope.

After the war I went to university to study architecture, which was a great thrill for me, seeing as before the war, being a Jewish woman, I was not allowed to go to Architectural college or any technical school. My partner was drafted in 1943 and died in forced labour but I didn't know at the time. Once the hope of him returning had faded, I became seriously involved with someone whom I met at university who became my first husband. Perhaps, it was not a mere coincidence that he was studying electrical engineering just as my previous partner had done. However, it wasn't long before I met my future second husband. He immediately wanted to marry me, but I couldn't. He was married at the time but his wife was living in Paris with another man, a Hungarian sculptor. In the end his wife returned to Hungary and our relationship was terminated.

Luckily there was a great demand for engineers when we left university so in 1949 I started work as a structural engineer. In the same year, my future second husband was arrested in connection with the trial of Laszlo Rajk (the Hungarian communist politician) and was sentenced to life imprisonment. As a consequence, I became directly 'unreliable'. However, not everyone knew that we were having a relationship, which meant that there was an informer, which we were used to in my country, but I was still surprised.

For the first time in my life I stepped over the Hungarian border in 1953. I was sent to Copenhagen for a women's international congress. Although I was not directly involved with women's rights, I was able to go because of the Hungarian Women's Democratic Alliance. I remember vividly admiring the shop-windows where the undergarments on show were made of nylon. Of course, we didn't have money to buy such things.

I went to Budapest in 1954 but it was very difficult to find a job as an engineer. I found a position, as the head of the technological department of a cement factory but I wasn't respected at all, in fact I felt ridiculed. My chief engineer didn't have a diploma in engineering and the director was a drunkard. I had a weekly meeting for construction clerks to check whether the previous week's work had been done. It hadn't. One day I suddenly flew off the handle and cursed like a man, shouting at the workers. I explained that if the work wasn't done by the following week that they would be sacked. From this moment on, because I could curse in this way, I would be recognised as a building professional. They wanted to assign me chief engineer, but due to many arguments because I condemned our firm for spending too much money, I was fired.

My son was born in 1955 during the days of the Russian occupation, so I didn't dare do anything revolutionary but I was terribly concerned about it and would have taken part in it for sure if my son wasn't so young. However, I felt as though I did a little when together with the other people in our house, we pulled up the paving blocks to cause an obstruction when the Russian tanks came. I also found a way to get milk, butter and anything that the local dairy produced and distributed among those who had children. I am proud of what I did, even though it wasn't very much. It still wasn't safe in the streets. I remember queuing up for things in front of a pharmacy in our street when the Russians fired guns at the buildings.

I met my second husband again in 1967. We divorced our respective partners and got married. My second husband and I lived a very happy life together. There were difficulties, of course, because it frequently happened that I spent Christmas alone because he had to go to his former family but I found it natural.

My husband collapsed and died of a heart attack in 1992 after a walk up Liberty Hill. We had been talking about our grandchildren and how they would come up here on the following day and we'd take them for a ride on the sleigh. Soon after he died I entered into being a full-time grandmother and I took great delight in it. Maybe this was because I didn't feel that I had been a full-time mother.

Printed with kind permission of Centropa (www.centropa.org). Interview by Balazs Merzaris.

Sir John Herbecq K.C.B

29 May 1922
Moray, Scotland

Sir John Herbecq in his early teens

Growing up, I can remember my father saying: "If a job's worth doing, it's worth doing well," this is advice I would happily pass on. As an octogenarian I would also like to pass on to younger generations that they probably have another 60 or 70 years to live. It is important to try to look beyond the next few weeks or months.

I have several strong memories of World War II: the day it broke out, the London air raids, seeing the devastation caused by our own raids on Germany and nuclear bombs on Japan. During the war, I was at home, and working in London until October 1941; then five years in the RAF, in various places in the UK; also in Canada, North Africa, Malta and Italy.

Spending a short time advising the Malawi government, as part of the aid programme gave me a new outlook on the lives of ordinary people in Africa. Hastings Banda was the president at the time, and he was greatly criticized. He was an old democrat and governed the country well; and although we locked him up, as we did most African leaders, he was very pro-British. He ordered a review of the Civil Service and when an international group was suggested, he refused and said instead that he wanted all British. I was asked to lead this and we produced a very thorough substantial report at the end, which suggested things to be implemented in a wide range of operations. I thought Africa was run very efficiently; what particularly impressed me the most was that Africa was free from corruption, and this was a considerable tribute to Banda himself. When we presented the final report to him, and I mentioned about the lack of corruption, he pounced on me and said: "What's that?" When I explained, he said: "Good, Good." His own Civil Servants seemed quite timid, when they looked at him, he said: "I don't expect to have a Civil Service better than the British, but we can have one as good as the British." You can't generalize from any country and apply it to everyone, but I can say that the African people I met in Malawi were very pleasant, gentle people and a joy to work with.

To consider how the world has altered over the years is impossible. It is too large and hugely varied. However, if I had to say how this country has changed, I'd say that medical care has improved; there is fairer treatment of women; and there is a greater realisation of the extent and evil of child abuse. But there has been a decline of religious faith and the growth of violence.

Lionel Irish

2 October 1922
Cornwall, England

Lionel Irish

I was one of nine survivors of HMS *Kite*, which was sunk by an enemy U-boat, in the Barents Sea in Russian waters, only twelve days after I got married.

On 20 August 1944 we had been spotted by German aircraft while we were escorting two aircraft carriers to Northern Russia and at 6.40 the following morning we were hit on the starboard side, by two torpedoes from a German U boat and heeled to that side immediately. The stern broke off, floated for a few seconds before sinking and the bow remained afloat for a short while and then sank. The whole ship disappeared in 90 seconds. Once I was in the water, I was surrounded by shards of splintered wood and other debris. I attempted to swim to any large pieces to use them as floats. I climbed onto a reasonable sized plank of wood, which disintegrated immediately, leaving me with splinters in my chest and legs. I eventually found a block of wood about a metre wide, with three men hanging on to a corner each. I climbed onto the last corner. One by one the men died. I said to the last man alive that I couldn't hold on any longer and he told me to try as he could see a ship coming. I craned my neck to see behind me and towards the HMS *Keppel*, the ship that eventually rescued me, but by the time I had turned back to the man, he had slipped into the grey icy water and died. At this point I saw my wife, in her wedding dress, walking towards me on the water, holding her wedding bouquet.

The next thing that I remember was an almighty splash in the sea near to me. A grappling iron had been thrown into the water for me to grab but I was too cold to be able to hold onto it. I decided to take hold of it by wrapping my arms around it when I heard a voice shouting to be careful otherwise 'his guts' will be ripped out. Finally a boat was lowered down to rescue me, but I was only picked up for dead. I absolutely, without a doubt, was between two worlds when I was rescued. I had been in the freezing water for nearly an hour without any clothes on. I thought I was dead. My rescuers certainly thought I was dead. After that I remember nothing until I woke up weeks later when I realised that I was paralysed due to the cold. I regained the use of my legs six weeks later. Apparently there were about 30 men in the water when HMS *Keppel* started to collect survivors, but only fourteen were rescued. The temperature in these Arctic waters was near freezing point. A human being could not survive long in those conditions. Of the fourteen picked up, five died aboard within minutes and nine of us survived, but two hundred and seventy-one perished in total. Those who died aboard were buried at sea. The German U-boat did not get away with it. The following day a Fairey Swordfish, a torpedo bomber from HMS *Vindex*, piloted by Gordon Bennett, sank her. The boat went to the bottom with all her fifty crew.

After convalescing I went on three more stints including the liberation of Guernsey and the D-Day landings. I loved every minute of being in the Royal Navy.

James Proctor

16 October 1922
Lancashire, England

James Proctor age 37

I was born in Wheelton, a small mill village between Chorley and Blackburn in Lancashire. As a teenager, I enjoyed playing football, cricket and tennis and my favourite food was homemade broth and dumplings and a barm cake. I remember many remedies I had as a child for example, the local street shop sold Ipecacuana wine which gave the patient a very high temperature, put them to sleep, and allowed them to awake the next morning, fit and well. Iodine was in constant use to treat cut fingers and grazed knees. Goose grease was in great demand to rub on chests for the relief of heavy colds.

My first job was as a counter assistant at a Dunlop Rubber Company warehouse in Preston, with a weekly wage of 13s 6d. Throughout my teens my main ambition was to ride and work with horses and I applied to join the Indian Mounted Police, but the war put a stop to this.

During World War II, I was a RAFUR pilot for almost five years, stationed in the UK, North Africa, British West Indies, Australia and the Pacific. My strongest memory was of taking part in the Battle of Arnhem, considered by some as one of the most terrible battles that happened in the war. However, it was a split-second decision during the first few minutes of the D-Day landings that I consider the most important decision that I ever made. I was only 21 years old and an RAF Volunteer Reserve Warrant Officer. I was selected to drop thirteen paratroopers into a field in Normandy at 00.02hrs on D-Day. The French Underground had helped us by clearing the Drop Zone (DZ) from mines and they were to assist the arriving paratroopers. We had been briefed to remain in tight formation with other aircraft throughout this, particularly the lead aircraft, in order to drop all the paratroopers together in safety. The flight was conducted in total darkness, each aircraft was fitted with three hooded white lights on the wings to assist pilots with their formation. It was the pilot's responsibility to tell the paratroopers when it was safe to jump. As the subsequent planes were following the lead aircraft, everything depended on him making the initial correct decision. On the way it became apparent that the lead pilot was not up to the job, his timing wasn't right and the planes were badly drifting off course. With just seconds to spare, I manoeuvred my plane into position and flicked the 'Go' switch over my head, which gave the signal for the paratroopers to start jumping; this was against instructions, but was necessary in order to save lives and to allow our operation every chance of success. I then flew the plane very low, and dropped all their equipment from under the fuselage – small motorcycles, arms and ammunition wrapped in thick rubber packages. The result of this operation, plus other infantry attacks later in the day, saw the destruction of the Merville Gun Battery (the Germans formidable defence of continental Europe from Allied invasion), which commanded a clear view of the Allied Beachheads which were developed later that day.

Two months later I was summoned to the Wing Commander's office and questioned as to why I chose, against instructions, to drop the paratroopers where I did. After I had told him the full story, he congratulated me on my decision. Two weeks after my interview with the Wing Commander I was awarded 'The King's Commendation for Valuable Service in the Air.'

I've always had a keen interest in writing children's literature, and in 1961 I had a book of short stories privately published. The book is called *Bridges and Skies* and is partly autobiographical with some flying stories included. Flying has played a big part in my life. My last job was an airline captain with British Airways, operating from Heathrow Airport. Because of my career being a pilot, the inventions of jet engines, aircraft pressurization and aircraft-borne weather radar made a huge difference during my thirty-six years of flying, although I think nuclear power is also one of the most important developments in my lifetime.

There have been several occasions, while serving in the RAF or working for civil airlines, when I have challenged my superiors, mainly on safety matters. I have always been polite and well informed by researching my argument thoroughly. This sometimes made me enemies with those in positions of authority because their knowledge was sadly lacking; but I made a lot of friends in the lower echelons. It is because of this experience that I think it is important for people to always be their own person, obey their own conscience and not to be influenced by their peers.

Nicholas Parsons

1923
Lincolnshire, England

Nicholas Parsons age 16

I was born in Grantham, Lincolnshire but grew up in London and Glasgow. I am an actor, broadcaster and comedy performer and am currently Chairman of *Just A Minute*, which is still going strong after 40 years. Also I perform in a One Man Comedy Show on tour and cruise ships and a one-man show about Edward Lear at arts festivals and cruise ships. I was back in Edinburgh in August 2008 with the Nicholas Parsons Happy Hour for the 8th year.

At a very young age I decided to become an actor, I particularly wanted to be a comedy actor. Although my parents strongly advised me not to, I have never regretted it. It was against all that they wished for me, and they did everything to stop me so to please them I became an engineer before I took up acting. At a tender age of 16 I went to work in the tough and demanding world of Clydebank. I was an apprentice engineer at Drysdale's Yard, making pumps and turbines. My first week's salary as an apprentice was 9 shillings 7 pence (9s 7d) equivalent to approximately 50p today. My parents paid for my lodgings at the YMCA so I could buy my extras on my salary if I was very economical.

I came from a secure background of a professional middle-class family and working at Clydebank meant that I met the most amazing and interesting people. In other words, I experienced both sides of the social divide and it has always helped me to keep everything in life in proportion. This is the best lesson anyone can have. I spent my early teens in London, where I experienced the Blitz and then towards the end of the war I was in Glasgow where I was in the Clydeside blitz. Though this was frightening and challenging, the lasting memory was the severe rationing for a hungry teenager.

The 1960s was a fun and exciting time. Everybody was expressing themselves in different ways, within music, comedy, clothes and attitudes. Also great cultural changes were taking place as young people were rebelling against some of the archaic attitudes of the past. It was also when I met a comedian called Arthur Haynes. It was a chance association in professional terms and the show, which resulted, became a top comedy show on Independent Television in the 1960s and established me in my profession. I always feel everything I have done since then stemmed from this success.

I wish that I had not continued in *Sale of the Century* for as long as I did. I should have left at the peak of its success. By continuing, I have been labelled by this show to the exclusion of the more interesting, challenging and creative things I have done in my professional life. I must have other regrets, but after I had realised the mistake I tried to learn from it and move forward.

My heroes are Winston Churchill, Edward Lear, W S Gilbert, Danny Kaye, Lawrence Olivier and Garfield Sobers. All of them are from different walks of life and have all faced every challenge courageously and never gave up. My favourite saying is "never give up". When one door closes another usually opens. On occasions it can be slammed in your face but it is important you do not give up and persevere. Cast your bread upon the waters, and just hope it does not come back soggy!

My advice to teenagers would be work hard, apply yourself to what you have set your heart on and if you are really industrious you will become successful and might even become famous. Fame is not important. Achievement is everything, and that will give you satisfaction and hopefully make you happy.

Iolo Lewis

19 January 1923
Glamorgan, Wales

In the general strike of 1926 I was three years old and I remember going to the village school where they handed out hot soup to the village children. On Sunday mornings the grown-ups sometimes held "grudge fights", and as we grew up, the young lads went to see the fights on the mountainside. Once the grudge fight was over, the young lads were encouraged to go a round or two with someone of equal age and build. It was worthwhile because if the miners thought that you were good, they would throw coppers at your feet. One sure thing was when it was known that you had taken part in these Sunday bouts, nobody bullied you!

We had no place for swimming other than the rivers, which were ice cold, even in the middle of summer; and they were dangerous. As we grew older, we used to go on bicycle rides. We had an old dog called "Chum" , a smooth-haired terrier, who used to follow us, arriving at the river panting and exhausted, and his only reward was being thrown into the icy waters. It sounded cruel, but he lived to a very old age.

On my way to school in the mornings, I often came across old miners, sitting on the school steps resting, as they struggled home from the colliery, coughing and spitting from clogged lungs. It stuck in my mind, and I was determined that I would never go underground to work.

In the 1930s the rate of suicide was high, with throat cutting, hanging, drowning, and even using dynamite. Disease was lethal, with tuberculosis rife, and my mother would ply us with cod liver oil and malt, from huge jars, to keep us healthy. It worked.

In 1937 King George VI and Queen Elizabeth came to visit our school in Neath, and with them the two princesses Elizabeth and Margaret. I was in the choir that sang to them only 10 yards away from the platform where they sat.

In April 1944 my dear wife Gwladys and I decided to elope and marry without telling anyone, as I had my orders to go to France and we wanted to marry before I left. After I was married I went to Normandy with the 11th Armoured Division in a tank crew as a wireless operator / loader and went all the way to the Baltic Sea, being wounded twice in the process. My division took terrible casualties from Normandy to the Baltic, but that was a sacrifice that we had to make in order to go and release those poor people from the horror camps.

On 27 January 1945, the Red Army liberated Auschwitz, and in April 1945, Bergen-Belsen was overrun by the British 11th Armoured Division, and being the first to get there, my regiment played a leading role. I had been wounded some days previously, and flown to hospital in Brussels, where I spent a month. I returned from England, following sick leave, in a Lancaster bomber and was then travelling in an army truck, back to my regiment, who were then on the Danish border, when it crashed, killing six out of twenty men, all of whom were returning to their units after being wounded. That was near Belsen, and so I saw (and smelled) the aftermath. I stood on the Belsen site in shock at the knowledge of what had happened there. I was absolutely horrified to find out about the inhumanity of man against man. I have never been the same since. It has never left me, so much so that on the 50th Anniversary of the liberation of Belsen, I wrote a poem. The Yad Vashem, the Holocaust Museum in Jerusalem, accepted it for their archives.

It is because of my experience at Belsen that I would tell teenagers of the importance of being tolerant, to avoid racism, and try to understand their fellow beings and they will discover that 'hate' has no future in their lives. I believe that throughout history, it's hate that is the root of all evil, not money.

I had no idea I would meet the Queen, who had been Princess Elizabeth in 1937, again in 1995, as I stood sweating, in the shadow of Buckingham Palace, awaiting the march down the Mall, for the VJ Parade. She stopped in front of me to say that she believed that it was the last big parade, and I nodded, thinking, God I hope so, I've stood here for over three hours in this heat. Many of the British Legion veterans fainted, and one died, however, she was very gracious.

We were milling around in Birdcage Walk when we heard the Guards Colour Sergeant shout *"PARADE"*, and in a flash, thousands formed ranks and at attention. The discipline never goes away. I couldn't believe I was marching down the Mall, with thousands cheering, then passing the saluting dais, with the Royal Princes, Princesses, the Prince of Wales, and Diana, with Harry and William, standing each side of the Queen and Prince Phillip. It was a memorable occasion, and for me, the circle was complete, from that sunny day in 1937, to the sunny day of 1995.

Iolo Lewis age 19

Barbara Hall MBE

3 February 1923
London, England

Barbara Hall age 17

I am a journalist, and currently work full-time as the Crossword Puzzles Editor, for the *Sunday Times*. I have probably published several thousand puzzles – I like to think it keeps the Alzheimer's away. My first full-time job was a railway clerk for one frustrated year in 1940 – the salary was only £1.25 a week.

During the war, I served in the WRNS in the Nore Command on the east coast of England. I worked with codes and confidential books until 1946. But my strongest memory of WWII, alas, is seeing bodies of drowned sailors and airmen, British, German and Polish, laid out together in the courtyard of a naval hospital where I worked. Some, I learnt, were covered in mussels (the scavengers of the sea).

My most important decision was to marry in 1947, and begin a new life as wife of a journalist and as one myself. My husband was also in codes, a sailor, and we met at Borstal naval depot in Cookham camp.

In the sixties we moved with four sons, with another arriving later, to North Rhodesia, then later to Zambia. There, we both worked as journalists: my husband founded the Central African Mail and wrote books about Zambia and African explorers, I wrote articles and was the first agony aunt in Central Africa ("By mistake I have married my mother-in-law"). We were closely involved in political affairs, meeting world leaders, including Mrs Gandhi, most African prime ministers – and entertaining Louis Armstrong! Becoming a freelance journalist in 1969 was the most important thing that has happened to me, I haven't stopped to this day and was awarded an MBE in 2007 for services to the newspaper industry. Writing about the wars in Congo, Africa, generally, and in Quemoy when Mao and Chinese nationalists were fighting, changed my outlook on life.

My heroes are Julius Nyerere, my mother and father, who both won medals in the services abroad in the First World War, and Nelson Mandela. I have never been arrested though came near to it during demonstrations against apartheid in Trafalgar Square.

The world has changed for the better in that it is more cosmopolitan, we can meet people from all over the world in our hometowns, but it has changed for the worse in that we have a more violent society.

Sir Patrick Caldwell Moore CBE

4 March 1923
Middlesex, England

When I was a child, I remember being given a concoction of equal quantities of essence of ginger, essence of peppermint, and sal volatile. It was mixed with sugar, heated up and given to us to drink when we were feeling sick or faint – it soon pulled you round. It was a recipe given by Queen Victoria's cook to my grandmother's cook.

I joined the RAF when I was only seventeen years old. I had lied about my age and the powers that be thought that I was nineteen. The best thing that I remember of the war years was my first flight, as an air cadet, in a Moth. I went on to fly in many aircraft including Wellington bombers. I received my flight training in Canada and while on leave in New York, I met Albert Einstein and Orville Wright (the first man in a powered aircraft). When I met Albert Einstein, I could well believe that he had come from another planet, but he was utterly charming to everybody. Einstein was a talented violinist, and on the occasion of our meeting, he had a violin with him. When pressed to show his skill, he said that he needed someone to accompany him and there happened to be a piano to hand. So there was Einstein playing Saint-Saens' Swan to my accompaniment.

I wish I had been more serious about my music, particularly composition, but I never had the time. I enjoy cricket and chess, and have played for the Lords' Taverners charity teams. I'd like to take all ten wickets in a good class match (I have got nine three times, but never ten) and make 100 runs in a season. This is beyond me – the archetypal number eleven batsman!

I would have liked a wife and family, but it was not to be. My fiancée, a nurse, was killed by the Nazis during the war. Anyone else would have been second best, and that is no good for me.
I am delighted to know, or have known, many of the Apollo astronauts, headed by Neil Armstrong and Buzz Aldrin, both of whom I have met many times, and with whom I have broadcast.

Sir Patrick Caldwell Moore age 17

Buzz Aldrin paid me the compliment of flying over to England, in 2001 to present me with a BAFTA Award. I did indeed feel honoured. He and Neil will never be forgotten. But they are not alike – Neil is not fond of publicity, whereas Buzz is, and is still very much in the public eye. Long may he remain so!

Since 1945 I have been self-employed, as an astronomer and author and to be a writer had always been an ambition of mine. Deciding to spend my life as a freelancer rather than as an employee was a wise, and probably my best, decision. I would have been a hopeless employee, I never pay any attention to what I am told to do and what not to do – perhaps this has helped me reach the age that I have.

I would consider the most important thing that has happened in my lifetime is the development of space research, and the strides in medical treatment. I couldn't imagine a world without the telescope. The 1960s was such an exciting decade for me because so much was happening, particularly the moon landings, and I had so much to do.

Allen Saddler

15 April 1923
London, England

Allen Sadler age 18 (left)

The summer of 1943 had all the usual ingredients – scorching days, record temperatures, cloudless skies, and yet unreal in every other way. Margate beaches, which were sea-washed twice a day, remained unblemished. There were no indentations of children's feet, no donkey droppings, no sand castles, in fact no sign of habitation at all.

Along the promenade there were no cockle stalls, no rock shops, no holiday novelties, no saucy postcards, no holidaymakers. In fact there were no normal residents. They had all been banished to 20 miles inland, and their houses, B & Bs and hotels were taken over by swarms of men in baggy brown suits. The owners however need not have worried about their property because floorboards and stairs were scrubbed every week. The fact was that there wasn't much else to do.

With only the Channel between Margate and the German Army we were in the front line. It was a Garrison Town and I was trained as a signaller. We had our own telephone system, our own lines, and our own exchange, which had to be manned at all times. During the day we wandered the town with a field telephone box. If anyone wanted to know what we were doing, all we had to say was the magic password *"line testing."* Then we could get onto the flat roofs of hotels and bask in the sun, only coming down for meals, which were served in Dreamland, a large entertainment and dance hall complex that had been boarded up, with just the marble steps outside, showing its past glories. We were able to rewire the field telephone so that we could listen in to Generals and Camp Commanders discussing vital military issues such as the date of the next ENSA concert. ENSA was the Entertainments National Service Association set up to provide entertainment for the armed forces personnel during the war. It was also known as Every Night Something Awful due to the substandard entertainment we had to endure, and quite often they only had an audience by direct order from the Commanding Officer.

Our purpose in being in Margate was to repel the invasion, although it had been so long coming that we were beginning to see that if they wouldn't come after us that we might have to go after them, and paled at the thought.

One day I was left manning the switchboard while all the other signallers went for their mid day meal. When they returned I went for mine. I was blissfully strolling along the prom, carrying two china plates and my knife, fork and spoon, with nobody in sight, when I saw two German Focke Wulf planes travelling towards me within spitting distance of the ground. I climbed up the outside steps of Dreamland, with my back to the boarded up window while the German machine gunner fired a type of rocket shell that made great scars in the road in front of me. It all happened so quickly that I hardly had time to register the terror the occasion demanded, but in that split second I clearly saw Jesus in his nightshirt, helping out with the loaves and fishes. When the planes soared upwards there was still no one in sight to have noticed my ordeal, so I calmly climbed down from the steps and went in for my meal, thinking I was lucky not to have dropped the plates. Apart from missing me the German soldiers also missed the pier, which they were trying to destroy, no doubt with the idea that an invasion might start off from the end of a pier as it was that much nearer to France.

The last time I was in Margate there was a statue of a soldier in full battle dress. He was sited on the prom, opposite Dreamland. I don't think it is meant to be me, as I didn't have a Lee Enfield rifle and ammunition pouches, but the statue would look silly carrying a knife, fork and spoon and two china plates.

Jean MacColl

May 1923
Lincoln, England

When I was about two years old I was sent to see a specialist because I stammered. After checking all my reflexes by tapping my knees, he told my parents to encourage me to dance. It worked. I was cured but also I became absolutely besotted with it. I remember the very first day that I went to have lessons. I was barefoot and I wore a silver tinselly top with a rose pink skirt and a rose pink flower at the waist. I thought it was wonderful but I must have looked like a strawberry sundae. This dream came into the room, Marianne Woodman. She was a willowy, pretty woman, with brown hair in a bun at the back. I was desperate to show willing even though I couldn't reach the barre. So when I went into the 'plié' I kept my arm up as though I was still holding the barre. I was then asked to go into the middle of the room and dance for her. When she said it was over, I was very disappointed, as I hadn't finished my repertoire. I was very keen to go back and I knew then that dance was going to be important in my life. Marianne Woodman taught me to dance for 10 years.

In 1930 when I was seven I took my first ballet exam. The examiner was Edouardo Espinosa, a very famous classical ballet dancer and who had just retired and was now President of the British Ballet Organisation. He was a very sweet elderly man who wore white tennis trousers, red kid boots and he had white hair, which fell onto his shoulders. He offered me a scholarship at his ballet school but it fell through because my parents thought I was too young to leave home and also there seemed to be little provision made for general education at the school, which concerned my parents.

When I was 12, I had a new ballet teacher who was very good but I didn't feel like I was progressing with her. She had a young man which I thought was a waste of her time and as regards my future I thought she hadn't got her mind on the job. So I thought I'd better look out for myself. I started to read everything about dance that was in Lincoln library. I started with the Russian ballet because I thought that was where I was going to go next. I learnt all about Russia and its history just from studying the Bolshoi and I was so keen that I began to privately learn the Russian alphabet from a book. I did get to Moscow in 1957 with my own dance group and won a medal for choreography at an International Dance Festival.

One day while looking through a book on modern dance I came across a photo of Rudolf Laban and Kurt Jooss. Rudolf Laban was a crystallographer, artist, architect, dancer and philosopher who shunned block ballet shoes, which I was pleased about, I found them painful. I was very intrigued and needed to learn more as soon as possible. Kurt Jooss was Laban's most famous pupil. He ran his own modern dance company and had just won an award for his great piece of anti-war choreography, The Green Table, which is still performed today.

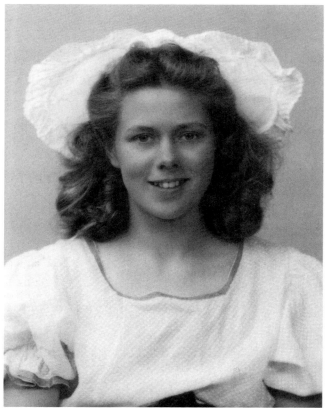

Jean MacColl age 16

The war clouds were looming in my early teens but I was determined to continue with dancing so I carried on with the exams – ballet mostly. I was getting to the stage, because I started early, of taking classes with senior girls so I could go through their exams. I eventually started to help teach the younger girls and that began to really take over my life. For one of my exams I had to do a Russian dance and my mother made me a lovely costume but I needed these red Russian boots to go with it, which cost about £4.15. The price of them utterly shocked my father, which is probably the reason why I still have them. I couldn't get rid of them. They were so expensive and so precious. I don't wear them of course.

The war started when I was 16 and a year later I found out that Jooss was in Cambridge. I contacted him to ask if I could audition for him. After going to Cambridge without telling my parents, Jooss offered me a place as a student dancer with the company. I was so excited, however my father advised me not to go. He was very much afraid for my safety. Firstly the war wasn't going well and in fact it only got worse and many foreigners were being interned. Secondly I only had a year left before I finished my education and things might have improved significantly by then so he thought it prudent to wait.

In 1941 I heard that Rudolf Laban was staying at Dartingham Hall in Devon, as a guest of Dorothy and Leonard Elmhurst, convalescing from one of his many bouts of illness. The trustees of the hall were looking for someone to be in charge of the 300 women on the estate and this person would spend three months with Laban, training to do some movement exercises which would be passed onto these women. I wrote to them telling them of my experience and I was shortlisted for the role. I didn't mention my age. I went off to Dartington to an audition. I stayed at Totnes overnight and found myself digs and was very careful not to get a chill before the audition, I even put a mirror in the bed to check for damp – there wasn't any, so I was OK.

Finally I got to Dartington and met with Laban in the audition room. I was so thrilled. I felt I had worked towards this for 17 years of my life. However, I didn't get the position that I had applied for, as I was considered to be too young to be in charge of so many women, but a new one was created for me. Laban asked me to be his personal assistant and in no time I was joining him in training in Manchester.

FC Lawrence, a trustee of the Dartington Estate and a factory consultant and an engineer was fascinated by Laban's movement theories and thought it would be brilliant if he and Laban worked together to increase production in the war effort. His engineers would rearrange the factory if necessary and Laban would apply his theories of movement. Many women had taken on the heavy work that was done previously by men and I became a pioneer in helping women improve their skills and increase production in factories. The first job that I had was for Mars – they supplied the armed forces with Mars Bars so this was considered an important factory to start with. As well as improving skills, I would also take them for exercises for 45 minutes, regularly – exercise for the eyes, legs, fingers and to keep them moving in ways that perhaps they wouldn't be moving for most of their repetitive day. The workers were very keen and output increased tremendously.

When I was young my parents encouraged me to be independent, by giving me an allowance, which had to cover my clothes, my travel pass and my pocket money. I thought it was brilliant. I had the best velour hat at school and in the summer I had the best straw panama. One day I saw a gorgeous coat, which I adored, but I couldn't afford it. So I asked them to put it aside for me and I paid for it over several weeks until I got it. It was the first time that I had a coat other than one for school. I managed very well on the allowance. I was very lucky and free to pursue my interests. I wanted this for my daughter, Kirsty, too. I was so one track and directed my own life in some ways and I think she did the same.

There are many parallels between my father and me, but there were more between Kirsty and me. All three of us were offered scholarships, which none of us accepted. My father won an art scholarshop as a boy, which he hadn't been able to take up, through no fault of his own. Kirsty had an IQ of over 168 and was offered a scholarship at Millfield at the age of seven. However the children at Millfield looked after animals like gerbils and rabbits. But Kirsty had inherited asthma from her grandfather, Ewan's father, and was very poorly with it. Medically it was not acceptable and I also felt she was too young. I nearly lost her many times when she was young. Neither did I want her to go away at that age; it seemed so young. I was suddenly in the same position as my parents. It is difficult because if your child has a great talent or determination, you don't want to hold them back. However Kirsty must have been very determined, as I was. Kirsty was a voracious reader and learnt very young, as I did. One time she had run out of things to read so she read a book of mine by Margaret Mead, an anthropologist, *Sex and Temperament in Three Primitive Societies*. It became a major cornerstone of the feminist movement but I'm not sure it was very appropriate for her age. Early on in her career she suffered terribly with stage fright and I said that if it upset her that much she shouldn't do it and I suggested that she should do something else. With tears in her eyes she said that there wasn't anything else that she wanted to do. Her determination paid off as did mine.

Jean MacColl wrote 'Sun on the Water: The Brilliant Life and Tragic Death of Kirsty MacColl', published by John Blake Publishing Ltd, 2008. As Jean Newlove she wrote 'Laban for Actors and Dancers', 1993, and 'Laban for All', 2004, both published by Nick Hern Books.

Charlotte Cox

2 May 1923
London, England

Charlotte Cox age 18

I was born at home in Hoxton N1 and when I was growing we really knew what poverty was, although we never went without. It is strange how things change – Hoxton is very upmarket now.

Since the age of fourteen I always worked as a dress machinist, except for the war years, until I retired at 68 years old. My latest job is being part of the pop group, the Zimmers, which has an average age of about 78, I think. I have been part of the Hoxton Singers for going on eleven years and one day these people came to see us. They were going to choose six of us to be in a band and I was one of them. Our first concert was at Abbey Road. There was a lot of hanging about, but it was a laugh. I never thought I'd be doing something like this at my age. I sort of pretend it's not me so much so that my friends tell me that they saw my double on the telly.

The whole group went to Germany sometime back but I didn't go because I would have found it too tiring. I know my limits. We often have to do things, which have to be kept a secret. For example a few years ago we had to record something which would go out on Graham Norton's New Year's Eve show so in March we had to pretend it was December and not tell anyone about it.

The organizers make us learn the songs, which is difficult at our age, as we have no memory and what makes it worse is that they change the songs frequently. Times have changed and the songs are too quick today, which can make it tricky to keep up.

During the war I was called up at the age of 19 and was registered for munitions, I didn't want to go into the services because I didn't want to travel overseas. I wanted to stay at home – there's no place like it. After sixteen weeks of training I became an oxy-acetylene welder on the wings of Lancaster Bombers. Whenever I looked up into the sky and saw a Lancaster, I felt proud.

After my training I went to Brinsdale in Hertford and worked there for about two years before I was released due to getting bronchitis because of the work I was doing. It was a man's job so I'm very proud to have done it despite having burns all up my arms. If I went out for a meal or something I'd have to cover up because they looked so terrible. I had a sister who wanted to go into the Land Army but they said she wasn't strong enough, they wanted her to go and work in a hospital looking after the elderly. A lot of people chose to go into the Land Army, of course, because of the uniform. My uniform wasn't very glamorous. I had to wear a big leather apron with a turban on my head. I quite enjoyed it even though I'd have to be at Liverpool Street station at 6.30 in the morning. Also we worked in Norfolk where all the Yanks were stationed so we had some fun. I think I had been out with people from all over the world, and then finally I ended up marrying the boy next door.

I was a part-time air raid warden as well. I did that locally and if there was a raid I had to go out and check how many people were in the shelters within five streets of where I lived. Sometimes the raid would happen in the middle of the night and I'd have to go out into the street with my hair in curlers.

Being on the edge of the city we were right in the thick of it, but you still had to go to work even if it meant walking over all the exposed water pipes. I remember coming home on the tube after an evening out, and having to tread over the people who would be sleeping on the platforms. Sometimes we went out for a drink in the local pub and when we came out there would be flames everywhere. My mum used to ask where we had been when the raids had gone off, but we hadn't heard a thing. At the beginning of the war we had an idea of what was happening as you could hear the planes and the bombs but when the rockets and doodlebugs came, you couldn't hear a thing.

I still know a lot of people that I did back then and we often sit around chatting and laughing about the old times. I think the majority of people my age enjoyed the war because we didn't know what was going to happen so we made the most of everything. Our lives were so different from young people today and they know that too. They wouldn't take any advice from my generation. I'm sure our advice wouldn't mean anything to them even if they asked for it.

Derek Haken

17 August 1923
London, England

Derek Haken age 15

I retired to glorious Devon twenty-three years ago after forty-three years working with a life assurance company. These retirement years have been some of the happiest and most exciting of my life. I recently remarried for the third time; I am Barbara's second husband and we are very happy together.

I'm proud to be a Londoner, having been born in Lewisham Hospital. My pocket money, always earned from jobs like shoe-cleaning or chopping firewood, was three pence a week. I was able to augment this by collecting horse manure in buckets from the streets. My father gave me three pence a bucket, because he wanted to feed the roses in his tiny back garden. I went out to find the hard stuff, squashed very flat by car and wagon wheels, which was more pleasant to scrape up with my shovel than the freshly dropped stuff.

It was 1939, with the War imminent, I went up to the centre of London accompanied by my mother, to look for work. We first went for a post in Paternoster Row, near St. Pauls, as a "printers devil". My mother didn't think they were paying enough, so we went to a life assurance company in the City, who offered a salary for a junior clerk of £100 yearly. My mother was impressed with the salary so I took that one. I was a salaried employee of the company for forty-three years until I retired.

In those days, many people stayed with one employer for a lifetime, which was not considered a sign of lack of ambition, as it sometimes is now, but a sign of loyalty. My company was an excellent employer. When war broke out, they followed the practice of most employers in wartime and made up our salaries during the four to five years we were away. I am sorry that young people nowadays don't get this opportunity for adventure, and I have always believed that bringing back compulsory national service would help create better and stronger citizens.

I chose the Navy. Three years later my brother chose the same, but was unlucky because the number on his calling-up papers finished with the figure 9, so at that time he was drafted as a "Bevin boy" to work in the coalmines in the Midlands. He consistently had worse luck than me, all his life. He died two years ago.

I found the war very exciting. For most of my service I was on "the lower deck" as a telegraphist, including a year on a destroyer on Russian convoys, when we rounded the North Cape of Norway in the Arctic to escort merchant ships, which were taking weapons and other goods to our allies. We often needed to combat submarines and aircraft to get there. Fortunately my ship, *Matchless*, never got torpedoed, though our sister ship, *Musketeer*, on the other wing of the convoy, sank in those freezing seas with only 3 survivors. Our most exciting action was when we helped to sink the pocket battleship, the *Scharnhorst* off the North Cape on Boxing Day 1943. We were sent on missions to Newfoundland (escorting Churchill), Iceland, and the Med. But most of the time it was the awful stormy winter seas of the north. I was sick every time I went to sea, which lasted three days till I cured myself by drinking nothing and getting thoroughly constipated. No one was sympathetic, and I was never allowed to miss any watch and retire to my hammock. The P.O. Tel, a sneering individual who called me "Dorothy", gave me a pair of headphones, a Morse buzzer, and a bucket, and told me to get on with it.

I am so grateful to have the blessing of good health. I love life, and divide people into the constructors and the destructors. I would urge young people to aim for the pursuit of happiness, which comes not through money or possessions, but through trying everything life has to offer, thinking positively and being determined to tackle every pursuit with energy, always aiming for the best in oneself. I believe that anyone can do anything. At the moment, I am writing my first trilogy of science fiction novels at the age of eighty-three. One last thing, more than important than all I have written – always love others and never hurt anyone.

Dorothy Hope Hughes

7 October 1923
Swansea, Wales

Dorothy Hope Hughes age 18

At the age of ten I contracted diphtheria along with thirty other children in my class and within forty-eight hours twenty-five had died. The rest of us spent twelve weeks in an isolation hospital. When I returned home I was unable to walk mainly because our movements were restricted for so long. I stayed with my aunt and uncle who lived on the Mumbles near Swansea, right next to the sea. My uncle was a garage owner and one of his customers was a Swedish masseur who advised him to get me swimming and this is what he did. My uncle carried me out into the sea in a thick towel everyday for about 18 months and helped me get my muscles working. We would have done this in a swimming pool but there weren't any available in those days. The hospitals had nothing like physiotherapy in those days and they weren't that hopeful of me walking again.

In 1941 Swansea was heavily bombed for three consecutive days, and our house was blitzed, which left us with nothing at all. We had an Anderson shelter, a corrugated iron structure, in the garden. One night a high explosive bomb was dropped and it went under the shelter but didn't go off immediately. Three days later, it went off, fortunately during the daytime, when no one was in it but it took our house with it. My mother was buried in the rubble of our destroyed house for about six hours before she was rescued. She had been on her knees scrubbing the larder from all the debris that had fallen due to the incendiary bombs that had hit our roof on previous raids, when the explosion happened. She happened to be under a marble shelf in the larder, which is the only thing that saved her life. The house collapsed around her. It was terrifying. The whole of the war was terrifying. Everyone had a completely different attitude to that of today; you lived from moment to moment. However the neighbours rallied round, gave us somewhere to stay until we were found temporary accommodation and they shared their rations with us. We relied on them.

Extraordinary things happened as well. While I was still in Swansea, I was a messenger for the Air Raid Precautions and one of the command posts got bombed so I had to cycle to the next one to tell them. While I was cycling along a street of terraced houses, a land mine hit one of them. Suddenly, a bath came hurtling out of a window and landed in the road in front of me. There was still a lady sitting in it, and perhaps more amazingly, she was still sitting in some water. I remember thinking about the amount of bath water she had (we were only allowed five inches) while she was screaming at me to get her some clothes. Luckily, she wasn't hurt, but the blast destroyed the house and the other people in the house were all killed. There were many freak blasts like that.

Just before I joined the army in 1941 when I was 18, the coordinator of Air Defence for Britain had just discovered that he was very short of guns and gunners for this country, as they were all sent overseas. So against the Ministry of Defence's wishes, he decided that he needed women in competent positions, not just as cooks and clerks. Regiments that had been together for donkey's years had to be split up and sent overseas and women took their places on the guns, which caused a great deal of friction.

I was in Heavy Anti-Aircraft in the London division from 1942 until 1946, which involved using a basic computer to point guns in the right direction and evaluate where the plane was so that the shell could reach it as accurately as possible. We had six girls in a team and the other five had information given to them by telephone. I had to check that it was right before I switched on to the guns, which then automatically ranged themselves. We had to prove we were as good as the men were, or better. It was hard going. I know one sergeant who was desperate to get us out; he used to unplug the equipment so we would think that something was wrong. He didn't do it on actual shoots, only when we had practice runs, but I learnt early on to check all the plugs were in place before we started.

After the war I went in to Army Operational Research Group, developing a high proximity shell, which went off when it met metal, which were used against V2 rockets. At the end of the war most of the girls were told that they had a fortnight to leave and weren't asked to stay on because we were only employed for the duration of hostilities. However I was allowed to continue because the research post covered similar things that I had done in the artillery. I was eventually discharged from the army in 1946. After this I was moved to a space research group where we measured the cosmic rays, which were sent back. It was really the beginning of satellite.

Having spent the beginning of my career in a male-orientated environment, I am now one of two ladies living alongside more than 300 men at The Royal Hospital Chelsea. I was the first lady to be admitted. About two and a half years ago when I applied for a position at the hospital, I didn't know that they were intending to allow women. When they broadcast the first showing of *Once a Soldier* I was watching it and thought 'why shouldn't I?' Then I heard the qualifications that one had to have: i.e. be 65 years old; or have an army pension, either a long service army pension or war disability pension and I had the latter. I didn't hear anything from them for about a year and suddenly a letter arrived out of the blue asking me if I would like to go and have my four-day interview. So I went. I was interviewed by the adjutant, chaplains, the matron and the doctor and was shown around by an In-Pensioner. I had my meals with the men in the Great Hall and all the rules were explained. Then I had to sign a rather fat agreement when I accepted my place. One thing that I was asked, which baffled me, was whether I was forced to come here. I replied, jokingly, oh yes, my daughter horsewhips me every day. And then I giggled. He responded quite sternly that it was a very serious matter as quite a lot of families force relatives to come here so they don't have to look after them. I was shocked.

To me it is a new life, I had been on my own for eighteen years and friends that I had made after my husband died had all popped their clogs. I kept thinking that I'm fit and healthy so now is the time to move. It has been wonderful. I've never had so much TLC in my life. Being back in an army all-male environment is like a second childhood, it's like being 18 again. In the army you get a real sense that people are looking out for you, which I have never had in civilian life. And here it is the same.

My advice to young people today is to have faith in what you want to do and not be led on by anyone, not even adults because they can be wrong too.

James Gifford

17 October 1923
Gloucester, England

For two and a half years during the war, I was an assistant steward in the merchant marine, trading on the coast of South Africa. In 1939, at 16 years old, I deserted a merchant ship at a South African port with a dozen other sailors. There was a problem with the ship's boilers and it simply kept going round in circles; we were in danger of being torpedoed by submarines, so it was a lucky escape. A friend and I slept rough before looking for somewhere to eat. When we found a place, someone thought we looked out of the ordinary and called the military police. We were arrested, and after questioning were taken to an immigration detention centre where there were some men who had been rescued from a torpedoed ship. At the centre we awaited a ship to deport us back to England. My Norwegian friend was put on an oil tanker, but was sadly killed when the tanker got blown up. I returned to England and was dismissed from the merchant marine service. Approximately two weeks later, a brown envelope arrived through the post with HMS stamped on it. It was my call-up papers, and my military service commenced. I was in the Armed Forces for four and a half years and travelled throughout Europe, India, Thailand, Malaysia and Burma. I was in Montgomery's 21st Army group; then under Mountbatten in India and Thailand, both of them were good leaders and fine soldiers. In all my travels, Thailand was probably my favourite place because the people were so friendly.

I remember about three months after D-Day, in France, we slept under hedges and had to wait until aeroplanes dropped containers of food, which we then had to collect. The war made me realise how life is so precious but very fragile and although I grew up in a Christian miner's family and always went to church (and still do), it was my experience in the war that makes me want to tell modern teenagers to be at peace with each other.

James Gifford in the 1950s

Stella Lily Owen

26 October 1923
Buckinghamshire, England

As a child I played puzzle games, children's card games and jigsaws. I never played with dolls, although an aunt bought me a large doll from Gamages. As almost all my teenage years were spent during the war, and everything was rationed and in very short supply; favourite foods were not on the menu. The only ambition I had was a domestic one, to be a housewife like my mother; to have a commercial career was never on the cards.

My first job was in 1939 at 16 years of age, as a shorthand typist for the buying department at Yardley Perfumers. I was paid £1 per week and had 11½d deducted for national insurance.

Between 1939 and 1942 I was in Forest Gate at my parents' house. From December 1942 until August 1945 I was in St Albans. I was called up at the age of 18 for civilian war service. The most significant thing that happened to me in my lifetime was World War II; it was catastrophic with far-reaching consequences. My strongest memory of the war was the deaths of my grandparents and their daughter, my aunt; they were killed when a bomb directly hit their house. My mother never fully recovered from the loss.

My most important decision was to get married, aged 20. My favourite decade was the 1950s without a doubt. Life was returning to normal after the war. Good quality items were again in the shops and there were very good film and theatre productions. Radio broadcasting (wireless) has never been equalled since; there were always top class presenters. Newspapers were getting larger again following wartime paper rationing. Lastly, halfway through the decade food rationing ended, making life much easier. All electrical gadgets and any labour-saving devices have made a difference to my life, such as, irons, washing machines, and vacuum cleaners.

I believe that the world has changed for the better in some respects, for example the benefits of widespread use of greatly improved medicines and pain-killing drugs. But, it has changed for the worse in other ways, for example violence and serious crime that used to be unheard of, has now become 'the norm'. I believe it could be true that: "money is the root of all evil".

I worked as a secretary and shorthand typist until I retired. The secret to my longevity is simply being blessed with good genes. I've never had the inclination to smoke or drink alcohol. I keep busy and I have lived in the same house for 61 years, so I've had no stress of moving house. I live on top of a hill and I am always walking; I've never had a car. I fear I would not qualify to give a teenager any advice, more likely they could give me some!

Captain Richard McNeely

27 December 1923
New Orleans, USA

After a second year of college in June 1942, I joined the US Merchant Marine Cadet Corps. This consisted of eighteen months of training (including six months at sea on a small freighter, dodging German submarines in the Gulf of Mexico and Atlantic Coast) and then I graduated from US Marine Merchant Marine Academy in New York, with a third mate license and ensign in US Naval Reserve.

I worked at sea and ashore as Port Captain with Sykes Lines, raising my licence to Unlimited Master in 1948. This meant I could work on any ship in any ocean.

While sailing as chief officer in 1948 I met a passenger, Marigold (Margot) Bostock-Wilson on a trip from Houston, Texas to England. We were married by the end of that year.

In 1950 I was able to fulfil a life long ambition to become a river pilot on the Mississippi River between New Orleans and Pilottown (near the Gulf of Mexico). My job as a river pilot meant that I had to guide any and all ocean-going ships some 90 miles on one of the longest, most treacherous routes in the world. At the beginning of my career the ships were relatively small and slow, whereas now many of the ships are 800-900 plus feet long and 100,000 to 150,000 tons, drawing 45-47 feet.

I have only piloted a paddle steamer once and that was as a passenger on the Delta Queen. It was an old cruise boat on the river, the captain allowed me to pilot her through the harbour. I loved the old steam whistle and blew it at every boat I met.

I worked as a river pilot for 37 years, retiring at the end of 1987. During that time I served on the Board of Directors of my pilot association, and was President of the Crescent River Port Pilots Association from 1962-66. I was also a founder and president of the Louisiana Maritime Museum in New Orleans.

While president of my pilot group I was instrumental in introducing the Bridge-to-Bridge radio communication system on the river, allowing all vessels to be able to speak to one another for improved safety.

In 1993 (two months after by-pass surgery) I was awarded the Outstanding Professional Achievement Award on the occasion of my 50th reunion at the US Maritime Academy.

Captain Richard Neely age 21

Every March the river nears its flood stage in New Orleans and consideration is being given to opening the 'spillway' – a diversion of river water through Lake Pontchartrain, a tactic to relieve New Orleans and the lower Mississippi of excess water.

The river water still provides drinking water for, possibly, millions of people and still is increasingly serving foreign and domestic trade. Much of the trade now is in containers, tankers and bulk carriers and relatively less general cargo, consequently, the many freight drops on the river are idle. Ocean-going ships go up river as far as Baton Rouge, but they cannot go any further as the channel is only twelve feet beyond it.

After my many years of retirement, living on a 'farm', I do still miss the good parts of piloting, but not the slow tedious, and fog-bound trips.

We have raised cattle, quarter-horses, Great Dane dogs in the past, but now are limited to ten chickens. We moved to this rural area north of New Orleans in 1976 after living all my prior life in New Orleans.

Pierre Grimes

1924
Belgium

My mother, who was Dutch, married my Irish American father in Java in 1919; my twin sisters were born in China in 1922 and I was born in Belgium in 1924. My mother raised three children on her own, because my father was in jail. After entering the USA illegally she lived in constant fear of the US immigration authorities.

One of my early jobs was being the soda jerk at a drug store who could, in one full sweeping gesture, flip a soda glass in the air and dump a scoop of ice-cream into it without messing up anything. At that time, my family was devoted to tennis and, instead of church, we were out slapping a ball around the public tennis courts in Central Park. My sister, Betty, was the tennis star, but I had the record of drinking 13 Coca Colas at one sitting.

I was a rebellious youth and without ceremony was kicked out of high school at 16. I studied painting and spent time envying people who could drive out of NYC, stroll safely and breathe the fresh air in the countryside. It was around 1940 when we watched in fear and awe as the Nazi war machine gobbled up nation after nation. When Pearl Harbor was hit I volunteered for the paratroopers.

I went through the mud and mountains of Italy; was at Casino and Anzio; was part of the breakthrough to Rome; and ended the war having gone through six campaigns and two invasions. After I was hit in the hand with a grenade, I contracted malaria and then spent a short time in an Italian hospital. I then returned to my unit and was present at the opening of the Nazis' factory of death and horror that they called a concentration camp. Clearly, this topped all the blood-soaked days I experienced in the infantry and it brought together in one day the horror and the stupidity of man. I had noble and good friends who died around me, tears and a mountain of grief was all I experienced, and I felt there had to be something somewhere real, it just can't be all meaningless. At the end of the war our unit was assigned to the OSS (Operations Support Squadron) and we ran down some of those war criminals who started it all. I ended the war returning to NY on the majestic Queen Mary.

Back in the States I discovered Huxley's *Perennial Philosophy* and Plato's dialogues, amongst other influential books. I often returned to these books, to look deeper and puzzle over what they were saying. I was told that this kind of philosophy was now dead. However, I got into Eastern thought, did yoga and enjoyed reading Socrates' *Apology*.

Pierre Grimes age 16

In 1952 I was having coffee with Joseph Campbell, a writer and lecturer, in Greenwich Village, who had just published his *Hero with a Thousand Faces.* We discussed philosophy and he mentioned that there was a new graduate school at San Francisco State College whose faculty were practitioners of what they taught; a Tibetan Lama, a philosopher from India, a Chinese Taoist, and a French Islamic thinker were included on the staff. I took my wife, my one-eyed dog and drove across the country in a '34 convertible La Salle to finish my degree in philosophy there. I did my M.A. and Ph.D. at the American Academy of Asian Studies, while working as social worker at a rehab centre with a caseload of mostly alcoholics. I gained a teaching fellowship as a Lecturer in Comparative Philosophy at the American Academy of Asian Studies.

Around 1955, Bill Swartly (a psychotherapist), Chris Lovejeff (a friend of mine) and I led discussions on philosophy at San Quentin State Prison. At that time a group of friends started meeting regularly on Friday nights to discuss philosophy, sex and drugs. That tradition of Friday nights talks is still going on today in Southern California.

After getting my PhD I moved my family to New York City so that I could study psychology and in order to pay the bills, I worked as a motivational researcher. I didn't take to psychology as I thought I might so I returned to Southern California to teach and explore philosophy.

I took the first teaching job I was offered and I stayed in it for 40 years as Professor of Philosophy at a community college. In 1978 I started the Noetic Society for the study of dialogue and dialectic. Often people could not recall past dialogues, however when tape recorders became available this made a real difference; we could talk, listen, play back and review. Another gift of technology was the video recorder, which enabled me to tape my lectures on comparative philosophy and share these. With the arrival of the Internet we had the largest audience ever. I published articles and a book on philosophical midwifery. I began to give lectures, papers, and demonstrations on dialectic as philosophical midwifery. This is a golden age for philosophy.

I believe the most important things are to act with integrity and truth, for there is nothing nobler than to act decisively. I think that life is too short and unpredictable to spend one's life energies and talent chasing more money than you need to survive. I have taken many risks; I plan on taking more, and it is better to live well than merely longer and with more money. I would tell teenagers that time is a curious thing because that which you really are doesn't change or grow older, for time is always now.

Charles BA Ford

14 January 1924
Somerset, England

Charles BA Ford age 37

One of my earliest memories was when my sister, Ivy, took me and a playmate of mine called Bobbie Langdon next door to the schoolhouse for a pram ride. After going down the Church Close steps she lost control and the pram went careering down the hill and eventually hit the bank on the opposite side of the road and turned over. It truly frightened us. After my mum and dad had examined our cuts and bruises, they took us to see Nurse Sharot. She said that Bobbie had a broken thumb and I had a badly sprained right shoulder. My dad, not satisfied with the nurse's diagnosis, took me to see Doctor Brimblecombe at Stoke-under-Ham. He diagnosed that the collarbone of my right arm was broken. I am forever thankful to my dad for not accepting the nurse's diagnosis. The doctor put a pad under my right armpit and strapped my right arm across my chest and said that in about 6 weeks the fracture would have mended.

During this time I played outside of school with the local kids, but before I could do this Ivy and I had our chores to do. We had to fetch water in galvanised buckets from the spring opposite the school (we had no running water); fetch milk from the Kempster's Farm next to the school; gather dry twigs from the local hedges for fire lighting; and run errands to the two village shops.

We had no flush toilets, just one open earth toilet, a plank of wood with a shaped hole in the middle to sit on. Toilet paper consisted of daily papers cut into squares on a piece of string and nailed to the wall of the toilet; this toilet served 3 families. We had no heating, other than open coal fires. We had no electricity and used stinking paraffin stoves and lamps. We had refuse dumps at the bottom of our gardens, but usually most of the rubbish was burnt. There were only very basic cooking facilities and we had no fridges, just cold slabs and the village baker would cook us a Sunday Roast. There was a Rag and Bone man, Johnny Hibbs, who came around selling second-hand clothes.

My father worked on a farm owned by the Clark family. His job consisted of thatching hay and straw ricks; making spars to hold the thatch on the ricks (occasionally thatching roofs of private houses); cutting and laying hedges; hoeing and singling beet and mangles; pulling flax; and milking cows. There were no safety regulations of any kind, so if you injured yourself in any way, you just lost work and went on the Parish Relief. Farmworkers wages were very low and to get a few more coppers, my dad used to trap moles. He would skin them and then peg the skins on a board, when dry he would parcel them up and send them to a Mr Cohen in London, for a price that was worth his effort. He used to trap in a field called Bottoms Mead and the farmers paid him a sixpence for every mole's tail.

My mother used to work as an outworker, making gloves at home for the Southcombe Gloving Factory. Monetary awards were extremely small for work completed and if you couldn't beat the deadline, you were not favoured with further work, and what is more sometimes the work had to be done at night on an old treadle machine under the poor light of a smelly paraffin lamp.

Chinnock Feast was held annually, when a pig was roasted on a spit in the field called Close. There were the usual side shows such as Coconut Shies; Topping the Topper; Skittles; Lucky Dips; Flying Canaries; etc. We also had a badger feast, which was also held annually in the Half Moon Public House. Mr Charles Axe was given the job to supply the badger. Mr Axe was a shepherd and worked for Mr Marks, the farmer. I can remember tasting badger meat and it was very dark and strong.

Down the road, on the premises now called Court House, was the butcher's shop and slaughter house owned and run by a Mr Roberts. He used to slaughter all his animals for meat preparation and sale. I watched him slaughter his animals on a few occasions. The cows were pole-axed or put to sleep with a humane gun, as it was called, they were killed immediately. The sheep and pigs were also killed by the humane gun, firing a spike into their brains. Pig's throats were cut immediately and the blood ran into a tank, which then congealed and would be sold for various purposes such as fruit and vegetable fertiliser. The pigs would be put in into a large bath of very hot water and their skins scrubbed to remove the hairs. Mr Roberts removed the pig's bladder and gave it to us. When it was dried and blown up, it made a good substitute for a football.

The advice I would offer to teenagers of today is to be trustworthy; willing to work for a living; be of good manners; be loyal to those who deserve your loyalty; respect has to be earned not commanded; allegiance to Queen and country; respect the laws of nature and of your country.

William 'Henry' George Bond

16 February 1924
Northamptonshire, England

Father always said I would not "make old bones" because I had a poor start. I was born in an old thatched cottage, which was damp and had stone floors. I suffered from chest problems, so much so I was sent to a sanitarium on the Yorkshire coast, near Scarborough, for three months. This put me right but my parents then moved to West Sussex where the air was better than in Northants. As a boy, I was always active, and living as I did in a small farmhouse three-quarters of a mile from the nearest road

William 'Henry' George Bond age 19

one cycled or walked everywhere. I spent a lot of my time fishing. All the boys fished usually with their homemade rods (bamboo and a cotton reel). In my spare time, I made battery-operated radio sets. This was before transistors were invented and one never bought the necessary items, they came from the local rubbish dumps or from similarly minded friends. One was always making things, not buying "off the shelf".

My first job was as a junior in the Midland Bank at the Petworth, West Sussex, branch while waiting to join the RAF as aircrew. This was in 1941 and we used ledgers, pens dipped in ink and had gas lighting. If the door was slammed, the mantles could shatter. Heating was one coal fire, which I had to maintain. There were five staff and we all had to stand most of the day. For this I started on £50 per annum (old money).

By the time I was 16 or 17 I saw other boys, a little older than me, leaving for the services and appearing in their uniforms and I felt I should join up as soon as I could. I did not want to be left out and one always felt that one would survive (and we would win). When I left home to join the RAF at 19 years of age, I remember my father saying, "Make sure you have a clean pair of socks and keep your bowels open". That and "Manners maketh Man" was the only advice that I remember from my parents. When I enlisted I trained at various stations in the UK and finished up on a Lancaster Bomber station (Scampton) in Lincolnshire. My strongest memory of the war is flying in a Lancaster in a bomber stream.

As a teenager I was very fit. I believe plain food, fresh vegetables from the garden and home cooking could have contributed to my longevity. Delicacies were few. A treat was tinned pears or peaches with cream for pudding following a Sunday Roast, which was sometimes pheasant and two rabbits for a family of six. I was allowed the use of a 22 calibre air rifle and this helped with stocking our larder with rabbits and pheasants during the food shortages. Our food in the RAF was excellent, which ensured growing up with few medical problems. A stable family life meant an untroubled mind and two happy marriages have contributed much to my longevity. Also enjoying my job and retiring early have been major factors in helping old age. I gave my company 35 years of my life and retired at 58, since then I've been doing what I want, when I want, but always keeping busy. I have been and still am active in charitable work.

My most important decision was joining British European Airways in 1947. I had to decide whether to stay in civil aviation or take up a new career as a potential company secretary. The airline won (it seemed young and dynamic) and work colleagues were mostly ex-servicemen like myself. There was also the possibility of travel and working overseas. During the 1960s I was based in the USA and was the Manager for BEA with the USA, Mexico and the Caribbean as my territory. I started my commercial life as a temporary bank clerk and if I had not joined the RAF and flown with Bomber Command I might have spent my life as a bank official, probably in the countryside. As it happened, I left the RAF and joined a civil airline, living in London and travelling the world – a much more broadening experience.

My first wife who I met when only 17 suddenly became sick in her 50s and I was told that I was lucky she was still with us and that she could go any time. My wife knew this and accepted it well (much better than I would have done) and we had two further years together, but our philosophy at that time was to live each day, which we did. Every day was a bonus.

To today's teenager, I would say this: the way of life may have changed dramatically but the way the young look at things compared to their parents has not. For example, I recall my father couldn't stand the singing of Bing Crosby and preferred Clara Butt and likewise I find today's rock and roll groups hard to handle. However, try to be tolerant with the elderly and, for example, offer your seat on a crowded vehicle to an old person. They may not accept but they will appreciate the gesture. Listen to advice and consider it. Don't reject it out of hand. Store it away for a later day. We, who have survived since the 1920s, have seen momentous change – ask us about it. One golden rule I would offer to the young is "Follow your instinct, don't ignore it". I have once or twice and have lived to regret it.

Elizabeth Browning MBE

19 March 1924
North Yorkshire, England

My first job was as a cook for a Red Cross home for bombed babies and my salary was £18 per week. The mothers had been killed in the London Blitz and the fathers were serving in the armed forces. Six months later, I served in the ATS (the Auxiliary Territorial Service – the women's branch of the army) on standard army pay.

During the war it seemed as though we were always hungry so we smoked and the hunger coupled with being cold made us very tired. I remember losing my brother and my first boyfriend, both of whom were lovely people and I loved them very much. We had to black out every night so that there was complete, or almost complete, darkness in the city – this was exhausting. We had no petrol, very little transport, very little in the shops and there was endless queuing for what there was. Anybody who had space in their garden kept chickens and even though we were grateful for their eggs, I remember the awful chore of having to feed them in the blackout, at the end of the day. It was all massively boring.

One time I remember going home on leave and finding desperately burnt airmen, convalescing on our farm. They were the men, mostly from Canada and New Zealand, that the pioneering plastic surgeon, Dr Archibald McIndoe, had operated on. My mother agreed to look after them, because she had space at the farm, before they went back to him for further reconstructive surgery.

During the 1960s I sent my specifically speech-impaired 5-year-old son to a special boarding school for children suffering from speech and language disorders, which was paid for by the local authority. For the first time in his life he started to show signs of development. At the age of three and a half he was neither talking nor understanding speech, we began the long process of trying to find out what was wrong and how to help him. Finally someone recognised what the problem was and we were told that it was a straightforward case of aphasia. It is because of this that I am executive chairman of AFASIC (Association For All Speech Impaired Children). It was also during the 1960s that the invention of the pill occurred which brought about women's liberation. This was a really important time, however it did bring about massive social problems.

By the 1970s my husband had set up a hugely successful one-person mail order business, War Books, and sent catalogues worldwide; I wrote a book called, *'I can't see what you're saying'*; our elder daughter was in sick children's nursing training; our second daughter was reading Spanish and French at Edinburgh University and our son had decided on farriery training, and we found a master prepared to apprentice him in Gloucestershire. He emerged 4 years later as a qualified registered shoeing smith. It was a marvellous, happy time with everyone growing up and living to the full. I recall frequent days when 14 people sat down to supper. It is strange to think of this compared to my memories of my parents which were nearly the opposite. They used to say things like 'speech is silver, silence is gold' or 'no one drinks or smokes until they are earning their own money'.

My advice to a teenager would be to read, always have a book on the go and be aware of national and international current affairs. I think learning to think for yourself, based on your own experiences and observations is important.

Painted by Elizabeth Browning while in the ATS, travelling south from Scotland in June 1943 while on duty in old LNER train. This young man 'caught it' on plus 6 the following summer on D-Day. His mum found our correspondence and wrote to me. It still makes me cry.

Mervyn Howell

July 1924
Bristol, England

I remember, in about 1934, a young friend of mine bought an egg for his mother for her birthday because he said they hadn't had one for some time. It wasn't a chocolate one; it was a real chicken's egg. That shows you how things have changed.

In my youth, I played rugby, cricket and swam quite a lot. I continued to play rugby and ended up playing for the county until I was 31. My travels and postings, while I was in the army, were almost all related to rugby rather than my professional qualifications. When I played for the County, I used to reckon that if I was fit enough to run around the pitch twice and finish with a twenty-five yard sprint just before the season started, I would be as fit as everybody else.

During World War II, I was in Bristol and later at college in Ipswich. In the latter part of the war, I was in digs with a fellow

Mervyn Howell (front left)

student and friend. We would stop our studies during the evening if we heard a "doodlebug", also known as a V1 or Flying Bomb, going over and go outside to watch. In the dark, they looked like small aeroplanes with flames roaring out of the back. When the noise and the flames cut out you were safe if the thing was directly above you, because it would come down a couple of miles away. When, later on, the V2's were developed, they travelled too fast to be seen, but you could hear the whistling screech of their jet engines, and if that suddenly cut out overhead, you knew you were in trouble.

Since World War II, there have been some striking changes in the world, especially in social conditions. The availability of healthcare; employment conditions; and aid for the disadvantaged and elderly have become human rights issues throughout much of the developed world. Due to easily available world travel and information technology, those rights might just be creeping towards the more desperate areas of the world, albeit slowly and haphazardly.

Some of my regrets could be summarised in advice: if you feel seriously grateful to somebody, be sure to tell him or her! If they die in the meantime you could be stuck with a niggling frustration for a very long time!

I think the reason I have lived long enough to be an octogenarian is due to one the greatest discoveries in my life – antibiotics. I doubt I would have reached my age without them.

Irene Samain

27 July 1924
London, England

Irene Samain age 17. 'This photo was taken to send to my then boyfriend who became my husband. He carried this with him all through World War II. He was in the Royal Engineers.'

I was born at 75 Herbert Street in Hoxton, London. When the weather was fine, I remember playing hopscotch in the street outside our house and when it rained I made patterns with coloured beads and made outfits for my dolls so that I could dress them up. When I left school, I started work as a machinist in the rag trade, which I did until the end of the war when I got a job in Archer St in the West End, where I worked for a small outdoor bespoke tailoring firm, Mr Jones's. We made men's trousers for Maurice Angels and Savoy Guild Tailors. When I retired I was a clerical officer in the National Health Service but I am now one of the Zimmers, which is a rock band that is made up of about forty old age pensioners – I think the youngest is seventy years old. We have recorded a few singles and go travelling quite a bit. I really enjoy it but it can be tiring.

In 1940 I was sent to an engineering factory (G.J. Worssam) where I worked a lathe machine; I did a small amount of welding and made range finders for the ships. I got married in July 1947. It was such a long time ago when things were very different. We worked very long hours, with very low wages; we had no telly or a bath; we only had a cold-water tap on a wall in the yard; and we couldn't afford carpets. I remember the first wireless that we had, the Relay, and when I heard the voices and the music coming from a speaker, I thought it was the most wonderful thing I'd ever heard.

Nobody had holidays abroad but we did have coal on the fire and we never had to lock our doors, as there weren't any burglars but neither was there anything to steal, in fact you were rich if you had a couple of bob. Children could safely play in the streets or the park and old folk didn't feel so vulnerable. Milkmen and paperboys would whistle while they did their rounds, and a night at the flicks was a wonderful thing. We all had our fair share of troubles but we just had to face them and we cured our pains with a good cup of tea and a chat with friends. It seems as though people were kinder in those far-off days, possibly because we were experiencing similar problems, which makes people pull together, rather than isolate them, which is what seems to happen today. World War II was devastating especially when you lost people that you grew up with but we also had some very funny moments and out of tragedy does come friendships, happiness and laughter.

Angela Mary Cavill Highmore

15 September 1924
Bristol, England

My strongest memory of World War II is seeing the bombed streets of Bristol and I vividly remember the acrid smell of burnt-out buildings. We all felt the loss of the much-loved shopping centre and the high class shops in Park Street. But I also clearly remember the trains, which kept running through the war, they were overcrowded and smelt strongly of smoke (both tobacco and from the steam engines). I remember when the troops returned from Dunkirk, we stood on the streets, giving them cigarettes and sweets.

The war restricted people's ability to participate in sports, but I used to play badminton, tennis, hockey, and rounders. We also played deck quoits, hide and seek, and card games such as snap, old maid, and patience. There were also board games like Monopoly and bagatelle. In those days, there was no such person as a 'teenager', this did not happen until the 1960s but when I was younger, my ambitions were to leave school, become a 'grown-up' person, buy a 'little black dress', fall in love, and have a husband and family. In fact, when I eventually got married and had children I did suddenly grow up, I hadn't realised how immature I was until then – in fact it changed my entire outlook on life, more so than I could have thought.

After World War II, many of the class divisions which had existed disappeared and I think the world changed for the better. Since 1947, we have had the National Health Service, and information technology has given us a much better understanding of the world with its warts and all.

The 1950s was my favourite decade, because the war conditions, such as rationing, were coming to an end. Attractive clothes became available once again and there were parties! The taste of food after rationing was fantastic, this was before the age of the supermarket and there was no frozen food. I loved ice cream, new potatoes, fresh peas, lamb and mint sauce.

There were many new inventions that have made a great difference to my life. Up to the end of the war, we still had to heat up flat irons on the stove and only had iceboxes not electric refrigerators. Electric irons and washing machines made a huge difference to my life.

The advice I would give to today's teenagers is, don't sit in front of a computer all day – there is more to life! Be polite, think of others, work hard and don't take drugs.

Verena Rosemary Quinnell

27 September 1924
London, England

Verena Rosemary
Quinnell age 17

I was born Verena Glencross in Wimbledon and was the ninth of eleven children. We were middle-class but always hard-up, as we were all privately educated. Clothes were always handed down and I used to long for new ones. Nowadays, you can't keep me out of charity shops.

I started out as a teacher but, when my husband left me with small children to bring up, I took up market research in order to have a bit of adult contact. In my 60s and 70s I wanted to make up for lost time and see the world, so I worked part-time to subsidise my foreign travel. Most of this was solo, which is the most interesting way to travel. I had quite a few adventures but, being elderly, always felt perfectly safe.

I have made so many mistakes – the most shattering was allowing the adoption of my three-month old daughter. I had no say in the matter. I was offered a chance to keep her, and my biggest regret is being too pathetic and scared of my mother to accept it. After fifty years we were reunited – I discovered that I had grandchildren and great-grandchildren. I had three sons from my marriage. The oldest died recently and I miss him terribly. The middle one lives in Hong Kong but the youngest lives with his wife and two little children in the same city as me.

The 1980s were brilliant. The kids were off my hands and I was able to spend my hard-earned money on seeing the world. But the 1970s really stand out for me. I think I was born a feminist: the girls in our family were considered very substandard compared to the boys, and I never could understand why. So I threw myself into the women's movement. They were heady times. I devoured *The Feminine Mystique*, *The Female Eunuch*, *The Second Sex* and many other books. We met in each other's homes, talked, called each other 'sister', read magazines such as *Spare Rib*, of course, and the American version, *Ms*. Our husbands were roped in to look after the children while we demonstrated. I used to do Pregnancy Testing, which at the time was considered quite controversial. Now, of course, one can buy kits at Boots. The great thing about the women's movement was the realisation that there were others out there who also resented society's treatment of women and were prepared to do something about it. This is why I think it is important for teenage girls to be independent and not to be pushed around. If they achieve this I think the world will be theirs. I think boys should cultivate their gentle side and stop trying to be so macho.

The second Women's Liberation Conference was held in Bristol, where I lived. I put up four young women who wandered about the house topless, much to my young son's surprise. They invited me to a Pot Party, but I gave that a miss. Some of the women were very bossy and quite scary, but we never burned our bras. Nor did we reclaim the night, alas. I have done few demos in my time, too – the most successful was to Parliament, which resulted in the One Parent Family Allowance. At the time I belonged to Gingerbread, which was the only lone parent family organisation, run by lone parents, for lone parents. The last demo I attended was in 2003, it was opposing the Iraq War.

My regrets? Where can I start? Obviously having to give away my daughter is a huge regret but I most regret my almost complete lack of confidence until middle age. It was such a waste, but I have made up for it – it's wonderful to know that I am not rubbish and am in charge. I also regret not doing more for my son who died last year. He had problems that I never felt able to fully discuss with him. This makes me feel so sad.

Morton A. Reichek

2 November 1924
New York, USA

I find that one of most interesting features of blogging is exchanging comments with other bloggers. The result has been a sort of "pen-pal" relationship I have developed via e-mail with several people I would never have otherwise known. I doubt very much whether we will ever meet, but the opportunity to exchange ideas and experiences with them makes the Internet so fascinating. The situation reminds me of "pen-pal" experiences I had during World War II.

Before my induction into the Army, I worked briefly as an office boy for RKO Radio Pictures, where I voluntarily joined a labour union, the United Office & Professional Workers of America. I was an idealistic kid who was highly sympathetic to the labour movement.

After I entered the Army, the union continued to mail me its newspaper. Each issue contained a plea for the members to write to "our boys in the service" so I sent my military address to the publication, updating it each time I was transferred to a new location. Like most other lonely young soldiers, I was eager to receive mail, especially since I had been shipped to India after only eight months of service. Frequent letters from my mother were not enough to satisfy my desire for links to the outside civilian world.

I didn't have any regular girl friend at the time. But, while studying journalism, I began to write occasionally to two girls who were college night-school classmates I had dated briefly.

The volume of mail zoomed after my name and Army address were published in the union newspaper and I became the envy of the guys in my outfit. Because my civilian address was also listed in the paper, virtually all the letters came from single young women in the Metropolitan New York area. Invariably, the letter-writer included what presumably was her own photograph.

It was obvious that the wartime shortage of young civilian men had produced many lonely young women eager to know a man in uniform, even if it was only through the mail. I responded to every letter that I received, but I eventually narrowed down my regular correspondence to about a dozen girls who were the prettiest and appeared to be the most interesting.

In addition to the single New York area girls with whom I became pen pals, I began to correspond with a middle-aged woman who lived in Glendale, California. She had a son who was an officer in the Navy and her husband was an insurance agent who belonged to my union. After seeing my name and address in his union's paper, I assume she thought it was her patriotic duty to write to a lonely young soldier stationed overseas.

Her frequent letters were often accompanied by fruit cake or other gifts. I believe she developed a special interest in me because I told her that my ambition was to become a writer. She had formerly been the secretary to Upton Sinclair, a popular socialist author during the 1920s and 1930s. She shared his extreme left-wing political views. Indeed, they were so ardent that she seemed particularly interested to learn that my mother was born in Russia. At that time, of course, the Soviet Union was our wartime ally. Sympathy for the communist state was not yet regarded as subversive as it became only a few years later.

I informed the lady that my mother had been brought to the U.S. from Russia as a child and had no emotional or family connections with the Soviet Union, which she was disappointed to learn. But she did send me a copy of an Upton Sinclair book that was personally autographed to me.

Foreign policy and domestic politics, of course, never figured in my correspondence with the bevy of female pen pals. After a durable postal relationship was established with them, a handful of the more adventurous types began to write in slightly erotic terms, which strengthened a libido that really didn't need a boost.

I was inhibited from responding in the same tempo because all our outgoing mail was censored. In my case, the censor was my company commander. I was the company clerk and sat at a desk only a few feet from his. I was highly embarrassed that he was reading all my outgoing letters. I found it difficult to get too personal with my long-distant girl friends, knowing that the captain sitting next to me would enjoy reading any romantic sentiments that I might want to express.

My letters were usually devoted to exotic, rather than erotic, material, for example descriptions of the Taj Mahal and the streets of Bombay and Calcutta and innocent details of my military life that were not subject to censorship. I always wondered how my unknown female correspondents reacted to my failure to respond to their postal romantic advances. They would have to wait until I came home.

None of the postal romances ever developed into serious relationships. Most of the girls were as pretty as the pictures they had mailed me, but none were as sexually aggressive as their letters had suggested. They had taken poetic license to satisfy a lonely soldier overseas.

Percy Hawkins Tilbury

18 November 1924
Hereford, England

Percy Hawkins Tilbury (far right)

I was born in the Hawkins Ward of Hereford General Hospital. I was an illegitimate child. When I was two years old, my mother took me to Hay on Wye station to hand me over to my granny (my father's mother) who I lived with from then on. I never knowingly saw my mother again, although she only lived about twenty miles away. My father came round to see his mother, but he never let on that he knew me or recognised me. At the age of 14, my granny told me to take my own name, show respect and don't get pushed around, I have always tried to follow this advice. She was very good to me.

I am currently a farmer/forest craftsman, but I started my working life as the handy lad to the local vicar. The vicar and the squire visited the local school to select people to work for them and my granny always told me that I should not turn down a job from the vicar even though the squire would pay more money. I left school at 14 years old and earned 10 shillings per week and worked for twelve months. A twelve-month reference from the Vicar was worth an awful lot when looking for another job in those days.

I used to go to church twice on a Sunday but I stopped going when I went into the army, probably because no one made me go. They did issue all soldiers with little pocket bibles, and I still have mine. I'm not ashamed to admit that I'm a god-fearing man.

I used to go *'beating'* and would receive a pie, a pint and a crown as payment. This involved beating the long grass to scare out the game birds so that farmers could shoot them as they flew into the air. I also went rabbiting. They would harvest the fields in a spiralling circle and by the time we got to the centre, we would find all the hiding rabbits and chase them. If we were quick we were able to hit them hard over the head with a big stick. We would pay the farmer a set amount to be able catch rabbits, but we would be careful not walk through his farm on the way home because if he saw that we had caught a lot, he would charge us more next time. Then we would take the rabbits to the market to sell.

I used to work on the farm after school to help my grandparents who must have found things very difficult financially My grandfather was very unlucky. I don't know when it happened but a horse had trodden on his foot and the doctor had to operate with an open razor but it went gangrenous and he lost his toes. His foot was permanently curled up which made it difficult to walk.

During the war I was a farm worker before working as a stud groom in 1943 for Lord Brockett, who had bought the local village estate, which included a huge house and acres of ground. After a while he decided to move the stud down to Bramshill, near Reading, where a whole train was used to transport it and I had to go with it. During the war, the Lord was a very important man and so his horses were considered important too, which meant I was classed as working in a reserved occupation, so was not called up, I volunteered anyway, it felt like the right thing to do.

During the war, I spent two to three years in army service in the Royal Signals; I was a dispatch rider for the home service; and I also served in Calcutta during India's fight for independence. Before going home, I was sent to Deolali Transit Camp (just outside Bombay) to wait for a ship home. The camp was light-heartedly nicknamed Doolally Tap by British soldiers, who were showing signs of mental wear and tear due to the long wait for a ship!

G Johnson

7 December 1924
Meerut, India (British Military Hospital)

G Johnson

I was a roller skating fanatic to the extent of using them as transport to and from school. Raleigh Cycle Works employed me at the age of fourteen, for four months, while waiting to be called to join the RAOC (Royal Army Ordnance Corp) as an apprentice. I worked for 48 hours a week de-burring pawls for three speed gearing and was paid one penny per 100. It was piecework rate. Then I went into the army and was in an apprenticeship programme at 18. I went onto the ranks and at 19 I spent my birthday on a troop ship.

World War II changed everyone and their lives. Everybody's plans had to be put on hold and so many people did things unnatural to their beliefs. Had the war not occurred, I would have taken higher trade qualifications. I turned these down immediately after the war's end because I couldn't bear the thought of going back to school after the high activity of the war years. I made many new friends in the army and they eventually became my family. In fact I would suggest to anyone if they wanted a career and needed to get out of a rut or situation, to join one of the services.

The most important decision I ever made was to emigrate to the USA after leaving the Army. I had to uproot my three children from their school and friends, and my wife from her family and friends of over 25 years. I did this because I was always in trouble with the trade unions for working too fast. I was thoroughly dissatisfied and disillusioned with British working practices and decided to try my luck in a different environment. We were in California for 24 years and 19 years in Washington State. I worked in a variety of posts within the manufacturing and engineering business. I returned in 2005. My wife had died and I entered the Royal Hospital Chelsea.

The computer has made the greatest difference to my life. I worked on the core memories of guidance and control systems for the Space Shuttle, military aircraft, naval vessels, classified weapons systems and covert communications systems, so obviously the computer played a significant part in my career.

I have changed because I have grown to dislike governments and heads of states that make and enforce laws for the masses but exempt themselves and their families. These are the politicians who cannot answer the simplest of questions but have to give prepared statements and speeches.

Nek Chand Saini

15 December 1924
Barian Kalan, India

Following India's independence from Britain, the Act of Partition divided the nation and as a Hindu, my family and I left our village, which was now in Pakistan, and moved into the Indian Territory.

I took advantage of a Government programme to employ refugees, and my wife and I moved to Chandigarh in 1947. Three years later I started work as a road inspector as part of the Chandigarh Capital Project. This project was the planning of India's first city. French architect Le Corbusier was redesigning the city to be able to house innumerable refugees and to provide an administrative seat for the newly formed government of the re-defined Punjab, created after the chaos of Partition.

Around 1958, I began to clear a little patch of land to make myself a small garden. I set stones around the little clearing and before long had sculpted a few figures recycled from materials I found at hand. There were many discarded materials and things that I could use from all the buildings that they were demolishing around the city. I worked secretly at night and at weekends while I still worked during the day as a transport official, constantly fearing the authorities might find out what I as doing. The garden had now grown considerably and I was now trespassing on land that was a publicly owned forest reserve and any building was forbidden. I used rocks, broken crockery, coloured stones, and a few primitive tools. It wasn't until 1975, nearly twenty years after I had started the garden, that the authorities stumbled across the garden, which was now a complex site of interlinked courtyards, which stretched about 12 acres and was filled with hundreds of pottery-covered concrete sculptures of dancers, musicians, and animals. The officials wanted the garden destroyed but as word spread, more and more people came to see it. Eventually in 1976 in front of a crowd of thousands the Rock Garden was officially named and opened to the public. I was then given a small budget and a group of helpers by the local government and I have been encouraged to continue to this day. The now 25 acre Rock Garden of Chandigarh, of several thousand sculptures, is based on the fantasy of a lost kingdom. It is set in large mosaic courtyards linked by walled paths and deep gorges. The entrance leads to a variety of doorways, archways, streets and lanes of different scales and dimensions. It creates a dream world of palaces, soldiers, monkeys, elephants, village life and temples with concealed gateways, waterfalls, pools, and an open-air theatre.

Ever since I was a young man I wanted to *Hawa main Urta tha'* (fly in my imagination), and I suppose I did that with creating the Garden. I have been very lucky and only done things in my life that have come straight from the heart. I would urge people not to consider anything as waste material and, like the Rock Garden, create your life and beautify it.

Jeanne Pelletier-Doyhenart

1925
Guethary, France

I received his first letter four years ago – it was in written in French. I was astonished. I didn't even know who he was. I had apparently met this German soldier when I was 18 years old but we had both now had our lives. He was one of the many German soldiers who were stationed in my hometown in the 1940s. The letter started by saying that I was the first love of his life and that he wanted to come and see me in Guethary. I agreed although I didn't remember him at all and I hadn't seen him for sixty years. He arrived carrying a gift for me, which was a painting that he had made for me when he returned to Germany after the war. He also brought me a dictionary because he wanted me to write to him and I don't know German and he doesn't speak very much French. I had also invited a few friends who were also in Guethary during the war and we all had lunch together. We spent the time talking about how things had changed.

When we first heard that the Germans were coming to occupy our town we were afraid because we had heard that the SS were cruel and dangerous but we didn't know anything about the Luftwaffe. My father was the mayor of Guethary and our house was occupied by soldiers. My mother and I had the small apartment below our house, while three German soldiers resided in the bedrooms. They turned our sitting room into their office. When I was perhaps 15 or 16, one of the Germans in our house told me that I could marry a Prussian, because I was Aryan. I didn't know what Aryan was.

Everywhere in Guethary was occupied – the hotels, guesthouses and big houses. The Germans didn't seem to do very much while they were here except go to the beach a lot. I think they had a nice time. I know that after the war a few Germans came back here to live. The Luftwaffe were very nice. They had lots of concerts and parties, many of which were held in our garden or in the garden of the Juzan, a restaurant. I vividly remember all the beautiful music that they played.

The villagers didn't mix completely with the Germans. But the soldiers were young and made it clear that they didn't want to be in this war – they were only in it because they had no choice. There was one soldier who didn't want to wear the uniform and so he bought a suit, which he wore when he came to see me. When he left to go Russia, he gave the suit to my mother to look after, and said that when he was no longer fighting in the war, he would return. I remember that he used to bring us cakes and chocolate. He wrote to me after the war and told me how the war had been terrible for him and he had become an atheist because of it.

Charlotte Richardson

1925
Rostock, Germany

I was born Charlotte Boas in Rostock, north-east Germany. My father was Jewish, which meant that by the early 1930s life was extremely difficult under the Nazi regime. For those who were fortunate enough to be able to escape, the doors were open through the refugee organisations, and I was one of those children who came to England in 1937, when I was 11 years old. I left behind five sisters who were in the middle of their education and were therefore not accepted by the refugee organisation. The goodbyes on Berlin Station one night seemed a great adventure to me. I did not realise that I would not see my family again for many years. This was certainly the most important thing, which has happened to me during my lifetime.

Being unable to speak English was a big handicap when I arrived at Milton Mount College, a girls' boarding school at Worth in West Sussex. I was there from 1937 until 1942. My heroes in life are the many kind people who helped me – especially when, during the war, I had no family nearby to support me. There were many who were so hospitable during school holidays, and had me to stay. The only regret I have is that perhaps as a child I might not have been sufficiently grateful to all those wonderful people who helped and sheltered me when I had no one else, and nowhere to go.

One family in particular took me under their wing. Together with his niece Barbara Hayes, Sir Norman Angell ('NA') – a Labour MP from 1929 until 1931, and winner of the Nobel Peace Prize in 1933 – gave me many happy holidays and later helped to pay for my wedding. NA and Barbara feature in one of my strongest wartime memories, which was when we sheltered during an air raid in the crypt of the Temple Church in the city of London. NA had a flat in King's Bench Walk, Middle Temple; he also owned an island in the Blackwater Estuary, Essex, which was a wonderful sanctuary and a happy place for holidays.

Charlotte Richardson age 15

Another of my strongest memories of the war is that, when travelling by underground, one would see all the beds on the platforms, in preparations for the public sheltering there during the air-raids. I also remember the 'doodlebugs', and the frightening moments when their engine stopped and one knew that they would then come down and explode.

In 1942 my school was evacuated to the Imperial Hotel in Lynton, Devon, where we spent idyllic carefree years experiencing little of the war – apart from looking across the Bristol Channel at night and seeing the Welsh coastal towns being bombed or burning.

The wartime rationing left much to be desired. Memories of my favourite food while at school were peanut butter sandwiches (or sometimes peanut butter eaten from the end of a ruler, dipped into a jar beneath the desk!) I also enjoyed dried bananas sent from America. Games I played while still in Germany included hopscotch, whipping a top, and rolling a hoop along the road. At school in England we played tennis, lacrosse, rounders, netball and cricket.

After school I had little choice in terms of a career. As an 'alien' I was only able to go into domestic service or nursing. I chose nursing, which gave me some of the happiest times of my life. During the war, as an alien, it was my legal duty to report frequently to the police station. If I was going away for a weekend, I had to tell the police where I was going and when.

In 1942, I started work as a student nurse at Winifred House, a children's convalescent home in Barnet, Hertfordshire. I then took the General Nursing Training at St George's Hospital, Hyde Park Corner, from 1944 until 1951. The starting salary was £7 a month; this included board and uniform, but left little money for extravagances. One great perk was getting free tickets for all the West End theatres. Lyon's Corner House for coffee or meals was a great treat and just about affordable.

On VE day, I joined the crowds outside Buckingham Palace – this was in the middle of the night, during a meal break while I was on night duty. I travelled from Hyde Park Corner to Buckingham Palace on the running board of a passing car. I remember too seeing the Victory Parade from the roof of the hospital.

In spite of the war, the years between 1940 and 1950 were certainly my happiest. I much enjoyed the comradeship of hospital friends and the great wartime spirit of the last years of the war – and these were followed by a happy marriage and the birth of a daughter.

I attribute my longevity to the fact that I keep very active (especially by gardening), to the wonderful support I have from my daughter and son-in-law, and to the frequent contact I have with old friends, even from my schooldays. I think the invention of cordless and mobile telephones is the greatest help to all of us – and a lifeline to an octogenarian.

Ronald John Graham

6 January 1925
Surrey, England

Ronald John Graham age 18

My first earnings were, at the age of 11 years, for delivering fried fish and chips for a local store. I worked three evenings and two lunchtimes a week and was paid a shilling per session, of which I was required to give Mum half. That was my first lesson in paying for my keep! This job lasted a few months until the 'school board man' caught me one evening at around 9 p.m. and put a stop to it. At the end of each evening session I was usually sent home with a parcel of fish and chips for some hungry mouths.

Mum was a dab hand at cooking and with nine children she had to be, and her steak puddings were always delicious and was a favourite dish when I was growing up. Another was omelette made from the dried egg, which was a common food item during the war years, especially served on a slice of fried bread.

My teens were spent during the war years and as my older brothers were being called up for service one of my ambitions was to get into a service before hostilities ceased. At a young age one of my eldest brothers, Sid, who was nine years my senior, was my hero even though he liked to give me 'Chinese haircuts' with the knuckles, and various other tortures.

As my two closest friends were musical types, and could play piano quite well, another ambition of mine was to learn to 'tinkle the ivories' to some reasonable standard. This I achieved due to considerable coaching, so that by the time I became a soldier I was able to knock out a tune on the N.A.A.F.I (the organisation which provided leisure services to the forces) piano of an evening.

Before I joined the army I was living at home and I remember one time when the family huddled in our Anderson shelter in the garden when a bomb fell quite close. This was the night that Dad had decided that he had had enough of the shelter and had opted for his bed instead. Mum immediately came to the conclusion that it was our house that had taken the hit and that Dad was no more. After a few moments of waiting, the sacking covering the doorway parted and a dusty white-faced Dad appeared. Apparently the bedroom windows had been blown in and he had beaten a hasty retreat. In June 1944, I joined the invasion of mainland Europe and was wounded by mortar fire during the Normandy campaign. It is probably due to the invention of Penicillin that I was saved from gangrene, the scourge of World War I soldiers.

My first regret is that I didn't insist that I sit the 11 plus at the age of 10 years, which would most likely have allowed me to progress to a Grammar School. The headmaster of my primary school had written to my parents to ask that I took part but I was not encouraged to due to the likely expense. My second regret is that I didn't continue with a correspondence course in electrical engineering, which I began in 1948. My third regret is that when I was working with BT I didn't try hard enough to reach a higher level, which was easily within my grasp. It is because of my regrets that I would advise anyone to get the best education that they possibly can and make the most of any opportunity that comes their way. People will only get out of life what they are prepared to put into it and it is important to remember that the world does not owe anyone a living.

I am a strong believer that fate plays a great part of life, and having survived some tricky situations during the war and a heart attack later in life I believe that when it is your time to depart this life, you will go.

George Harold Rawson

6 January 1925
Derbyshire, England

At the age of 14, I volunteered to join the Police Auxiliary Messenger Service (PAMS), delivering messages when the telephone lines, which were damaged by the Luftwaffe, were down. At the age of 16 I trained in the Air Training Cadets but I failed the eyesight test.

On my eighteenth birthday, I volunteered for the Royal Navy as a Radio Operator. After three months of sea training I was posted to H.M.S. *Cranstoun*. I would describe escorting Atlantic convoys as weeks of boredom and days of panic, with a fair share of both.

D-Day came along, and we escorted the Normandy convoys, the priority being to blockade the western end of the English Channel from U Boats. Our primary task was to prevent vital supplies reaching the German troops ashore in France. The sea was so crowded with ships that the sonars weren't able to distinguish a U boat. I strongly remember when a German U Boat torpedoed HMS *Capel* on Boxing Day 1944 while it escorted an American convoy through the Scapa Flow bound for Russia. I also remember the crippling of HMS *Affleck* by torpedoes, off Normandy, on the same day. There must have been 100 plus casualties.

After D-Day I become part of a Naval Shore Party destined for island hopping up to the mainland of Japan. But the atomic bombs were dropped, the "show" was cancelled and the parties disbanded and instead I was posted to H.M.S *Saumarez* which hit a mine in the Corfu Straits, before I got aboard, with considerable loss of life. My last spell at sea was on H.M.S *Atheling*, an aircraft carrier. It was converted from its job of escorting convoys into a troopship by removing the aircraft and converting the hangars into massive dormitories. *Atheling* set off for Australia with repatriated Australians, New Zealanders, and replacement troops for all points East of Suez. Compared to previous seagoing trips it was a holiday cruise. A swimming pool was rigged up on the flight deck, there was space for deck hockey and other sports, and after the hazards of war the peacetime atmosphere on board can be described as euphoric.

I remember walking out of the demob centre where I was immediately accosted by a spiv who offered me £5 for the demob suit. Life was no longer a team game, the danger and protection offered by the Royal Navy was gone, replaced by the dog-eat-dog of civvy-street. I was twenty-one and it was 1946, the need for paid employment was a priority. The policy of subsidised training courses for ex-servicemen should have allowed me to obtain a recognised qualification for employment as a Merchant Navy Radio Officer. However I was informed that such a course was only available to those who had previously occupied such a position in peacetime. My three months demobilisation leave was nearly over when I obtained employment with Government Communication Headquarters. It lasted for 38 years, except for two periods of secondment to the Communication Department of the Foreign and Commonwealth Office.

During this second secondment, aged 58, the administrators kicked in with an act of character assassination in order to protect their backs. In 1983, after 43 years of service to the Crown, which involved hot and cold wars, in war and peace, I was accused of treason; the worst possible crime in any book. There was not a scrap of evidence to support their actions, which were based on the ramblings of an ego-tripping member of staff.

I was responsible for a Communications Room in the British Embassy in Helsinki. A member of my staff reported to the Head of Chancery that he had seen my car outside the Swedish Theatre. When asked to explain the significance of this, he said that it was next door to the Russian Intourist Office and signals were missing from the Office.

From this single statement, without any attempt at verification, the administrators arranged for my "extradition." A colleague from the U.K. arrived unannounced with a persuasive yarn that I had to return to the U.K. for a meeting on technical problems. I swallowed the bait to find that on arrival in the U.K. I was confronted with the following. "You have been brought home under false pretences. Serious charges of misconduct have been levelled against you." I had been removed from the matrimonial home by trickery. The excuse for this, that I received years later, was that they had to prevent me from being whisked across the Finnish border by our Soviet friends.

I was ordered to go to a hotel and was detained. After two days of stressful isolation, all was revealed. My accuser could not justify his statements; spy mania had taken him over the top. His reprimand was that he was 'retired' with extra salary, his pension made up to the age of sixty, and he was awarded the Imperial Service Medal (l.S.M.) There was to be no disciplinary action. Without an apology, I was asked to return to post. This event made me mistrust people for the rest of my life.

George Harold Rawson age 19

Stress-related ill health finally led me, without choice, to opt for early retirement, which meant the loss of salary and part of my pension. My working life ended on 5 December 1943. I spent eight years trying to obtain justice and eventually received an apology and a cheque for £12000, explained as. "To add substance to the apology." The money had to be spent on privately funded heart surgery because a G.P. blocked my treatment.

After all I have been through I would tell teenagers not to expect their parents or the state to carry them through higher education or gap years. I think they should contribute to the economy before they are twenty years old.

Guy de Moubray

15 March 1925
Selangor, Malaysia

I am a former senior official of the Bank of England, Adviser to the Governor of the Bank of Morocco and for some years a management consultant. I was born in Kuala Lumpur, then the capital of the Federated Malay State of Selangor. My father was in the Malay Civil Service. Like most European boys born in the colonies I was sent back to Europe at the age of five. Between the ages of five and twenty I was with my parents for no more than about eight months in total. I was brought up by a widowed aunt and went to day school in Brussels from 1930 to 1933 and then to boarding schools in England and Scotland until 1942, when I won a scholarship to learn oriental languages at the School of Oriental and African Studies in London. I entered the competition because it was already clear that the Japanese were winning in Malaya and that Singapore would soon fall and my parents would become prisoners. It is for that reason that I became a soldier and was in the Intelligence Corps. In the summer of 1945 I was stationed in Bombay preparing for the invasion of Malaya, which was to take place in September. In August the atom bombs fell in Japan and the war was over. The invasion was still going to take place but unopposed. I didn't want to wait until mid-September to get to Malaya. I sought an interview with General Roberts, Commander of 34 Corps and pleaded to be allowed to get to Singapore as soon as possible so that I could find my parents. He immediately agreed and transferred me to 5th Indian Division and gave me priority to fly immediately to Rangoon to join a troopship. I got there just in time and on the evening of 3rd September we set sail. We anchored off Singapore on the morning of the 5th September We scrambled down netting into landing craft and set sail for Singapore dockyard. I was in the very first landing craft and was actually the first British soldier ashore. I fastened the ropes to a bollard. The dockyard was absolutely deserted. My Colonel wasn't convinced that the Japanese would surrender without a fight. He called out, "Take up firing positions". So I lay on the ground with my machine gun trained on the dockyard gates. We then witnessed the most extraordinary sight. The great wrought-iron gates slowly swung open and a fleet of Japanese staff cars drove in. They stopped. The drivers got out and bowed to us, inviting us in. My colonel said, "It could be a trick, de Moubray. You and I are going to walk". We walked across the dockyard and over the road into Singapore's main railway station. There was still not a soul to be seen. Suddenly we entered the main concourse and a great crowd of people began cheering and thanking us for liberating Singapore.

I was the interpreter for the battalion – a young lieutenant of 20 years old. I had told my colleagues, interpreters to other battalions about my parents. On the third day one of them rang me on the field telephone to say "Guy, get into a jeep and come to the Sime Road Internment Camp. I have found your parents". It was a very special reunion. Very emotive for them; they had been in different camps and had been reunited only the day before after three and a half years apart and they had not seen me since 1939 when I had been a schoolboy of 14. It was not as emotive for me, because I hardly knew my parents.

I enjoyed the war. We all knew that life had a purpose, the Germans and later the Japs had to be defeated. Spending the night in an air raid shelter at school while Glasgow was bombed gave a strong sense of camaraderie. London in 1942/3 while I was a student was a vibrant city. The streets were thronged with people in uniform, British army, navy and air force, US soldiers in their thousands, Free French, Poles and many others. Fighting the Japanese in the teak jungles of Burma was a satisfying equivalent of the modern gap year. The monsoon was over and we were frequently stripped to the waist in the blazing sun. We were fired on by Japanese snipers and strafed from the air, but as a teenager one has no fear. Oxford University was also exciting.

In a strange way the 1990s were also satisfying. My wife was diagnosed with cancer in 1990 and was seriously disabled from 1995 and died at the very end of 1999. You would think that would be sad, but she was so brave and we became closer than at any other time in our marriage and I cared for her for all but the last five weeks of her life. However I have one regret. I loved my wife and she loved me, but I was so self-regarding that it took me nearly thirty years before I realised that her 'difficult' moods were that she suffered from a form of agoraphobia that shows itself in panic attacks and irrational fears. I so devoutly wish that I could have been more sensitive and imaginative in the early years of my marriage, I came to marriage too ready to take rather than to give.

We had not entertained, for many years, although I had cooked for my children and their friends, who were frequent visitors. When Daphne eventually died I was absolutely shattered. After about six weeks my children took me abroad to stay with them in a Palladian villa in the Veneto. I began to calm down. I decided that I was not going to mope and was going to make up for the lack of entertaining by making new friends and having guests to lunch and dinner. Living in such a beautiful house I felt I should share it with others and I joined a scheme, which was then confined to country houses in Suffolk called Invitation To View. Houses that are not usually open to the public open a number of days a year and the owners give guided tours of the house and garden. Over the last few years I have welcomed hundreds of visitors. Quite a few guests asked me for recipes of my dishes and this inspired me to write and publish two cookery books – *Dinner At Eighty* and *Dinner for One*. I have also undertaken a lot of lecturing. I must have spoken to at least two dozen WIs and various local history societies. I lead a busy and satisfying life

My advice to a teenager would be whatever you do, always strive to do what is right because it's right and not because it gives you any advantage. "Do as you would be done by" – Kingsley's Water Babies – is still a jolly good slogan.

Guy de Moubray has also written 'City of Human Memories', an autobiography.

Bill Nankeville

24 March 1925
Surrey, England

I first got the taste for running when I was at school. I came third in the All England 880 yards championship representing Woking District Schools and Surrey Schools. I was a founder member of the Walton Athletic Club in 1942 and I ran alongside Alan Turing, who famously went on to break the Enigma Code. During the war, my first major win was when I ran in the European Armed Forces in Berlin.

After the war I stayed in the army for an extra year so that I could afford to train for the 1948 Olympics. If I had come home immediately and got a job I wouldn't have had the time or the money to do this. I was very lucky and received full pay and got a month's leave for training. Once I was picked for the team, the maximum training that I ever did was 1½ hours every day, six days a week. I went to the RAF camp in Uxbridge where there were Nissen huts that had been put up for the men to live in. The women were put into various schools and convents in and around London. Things were very different back then. We trained at the running track at Tooting Bec – it was filthy, it was like a dustbin. It was open to the public and kids used to get in our way while we were training. We also used Herne Hill where we had rusty old showers, stone floors and cold water. We had to get public transport to Wembley Stadium, which we had to pay for ourselves, and the track was a temporary cinder running track. It was all very makeshift. The food, which was quite good, was supplemented by food parcels from Canada. I had never seen such huge hams.

My greatest running achievement is when I won the British Championships after a thunderstorm in 1949. I broke the championship record and I got the Harvey Memorial Cup for the best performance in the championship. My biggest disappointment was in the 1952 Olympics when I got flu and only reached the semi-final. The other disappointment was being beaten in the 1950s European Championship, in Brussels, when I was beaten by about two feet, but I did get a bronze. Later in my career I won the Amateur Athletics Association mile four times. In 1953 I broke the records in both the 4x1 mile event with Roger Bannister and Christopher Chataway and the 4x1 500m races.

The 1948 Olympic Games was very successful because I think the whole games only cost £732,000 and I think they made a profit of about £30,000. All the amateur athletic clubs supplied most of the officials for nothing and the Olympic committee who weren't getting huge salaries, weren't really professional. It's very upsetting for me, and others like me, who were in the 1948

Bill Nankeville

Olympics to hear that they are spending billions on the new stadium. When they built the new national stadium at Wembley, which cost around £750 million, they should have put down a running track so that they could make good use of it in 2012 and spend the Olympic billions on hospitals, old age pensioners and building athletic tracks and swimming pools all over the country. The track, which was put down four years ago for the Athens Olympics, is surrounded by wires and security men. No one is using it and it's fallen into disrepair. The Montreal Olympics, in 1976, are still being paid for. It's a worry to think about what will happen after the 2012 games. I think the Olympics should be held in Athens, where it began, every four years.

I think the money stakes are too high these days. If you win the 100 or 200 metres, you can easily become a millionaire and with that kind of money at stake, it's no wonder that people take drugs to win. The closest thing to drugs that we had was a spoonful of glucose and maybe a glass of sherry with an egg in it.

Tony Benn

3 April 1925
London, England

I was brought up on the bible as my mother was a bible scholar and every night we read bible stories. She said something to me that makes more sense to me now than ever when I heard it. She said the bible is a story of the conflict between the kings who had power and the prophets that preached righteousness. She taught me to support the prophets against the kings, which has got me into a lot of trouble in my life!

Tony Benn

Jesus was a teacher but I now see Jesus as a prophet really. He was a good man, who said love your neighbour and blessed are the peacemakers. But then as years go by and what Jesus taught us gets misinterpreted, religion becomes distorted. The Holy Ghost, the Kingdom of God doesn't interest me. If people want to believe it, it doesn't upset me, but the message is there which is important and has helped me.

My father said 'say what you mean, mean what you say' and 'don't attack people, personally'. Once he said to me, when I was about eight, 'never wrestle with a chimney sweep'. For years I didn't know what he meant but I realise, now, he was saying was if someone plays dirty with you, don't play dirty with them; otherwise you will get dirty too. My dad used to say something else, which was based on another bible story, Daniel and the lion's den. This very good man, Daniel, was put, into a den of lions by the emperor Darius, in order to test his faith. The lions didn't eat him. So based on that, my dad said to me, 'dare to be a Daniel, dare to stand alone, dare to have a purpose firm, dare to make it known'. My parents greatly influenced me, as did my older brother, who was killed in action, and of course, I was influenced by the war.

My father and brother were already serving in the Royal Air Force when I joined in 1943. I served in Rhodesia, when it was a British colony, learning to fly. In 1897, Cecil Rhodes went in, stole all the land from the local people, and gave it to the white farmers. When I was there not a single African was allowed to vote and it was a criminal offence for an African to have a skilled job; and now we lecture Mugabe on democracy. It helps to understand history.

I could mention many things that have changed my outlook on life, but if I had to choose one, I suppose it would be the war. I was born in Millbank in London and was 14 years old during the Blitz. We were in the rescue shelter every night and we would come out of the shelter every morning to see areas of London burning. I especially remember seeing the docklands on fire. I was terrified. People were being killed around me.

I remember Hiroshima. Later I went there and saw the hideous destruction there. There was one little mark on the pavement where a child had been sitting and it had been vaporized. Next to it was this twisted metal lunchbox.

When I hear now about our pilots bombing Iraq, I don't think about the pilots, even though I was one, I think of guys as frightened as I was while I was in London during the blitz. I hate war but World War II really focussed everything for me. War is 99% boredom and 1% real danger. When you're bored you talk and what we said to each other was very simple. We had mass unemployment in the 1930s, we didn't have mass unemployment during the war, if you can have full employment by killing Germans, why can't we have full employment by building schools, hospitals and having a health service. The same argument applies to Baghdad, with the Iraq war. For a fraction of the cost of the Iraq war everyone in Africa with AIDS would have free drugs.

When I came back in the troop ship in 1945, I heard the words of the charter of the United Nations. "We, the peoples of the United Nations, are determined to save succeeding generations from the scourge of war, which twice in our lifetime has caused untold suffering to mankind". That was the pledge my generation gave to next generation, and we tore it up in Iraq. It made a big impression on me and was an aspiration, a hope and a commitment that I've never ever forgotten.

I'm not an academic, but when I look back on history I can't say I'm terribly interested in kings, presidents, prime ministers, dictators, that kind of thing. They come and go. The people who I'm interested in are the people who explain the world. A politician will shine a torch down and say, 'This is the road we are following, you get in behind me'. But a teacher explodes a pyrotechnic into the sky and all of a sudden you will see just for a second where you came from, where you are, where the dangers are. It's the teachers that matter. Moses was a teacher; Jesus was a teacher; Mohammed was a teacher; Buddha was a teacher; Galileo was a teacher; Darwin was a teacher; Marx was a teacher. It's the teachers plus self-organization that change you. That's my philosophy.

I'm not sure about the sense of advising people. I think encouragement and hope are the key to everything. Almost everybody in the world is paid to tell you what to do. People who encourage have a special quality of their own. You want to encourage hope. It is the fuel of progress.

I deeply distrust those who gallop on to the stage on a white horse and say, 'Vote for me and I'll solve all your problems'. You have to encourage people to have confidence in themselves, to do it themselves. My experience is that all progress comes from underneath. What people need at every age is encouragement and it is the responsibility of the old to encourage. I've benefited enormously from people who have encouraged me and when I'm passing on encouragement, it has to be more than just 'Oh you carry on, it'll be all right'. You have to help people to see what they want to do, and help them do it. I learnt through all my weekly surgeries when I was a Member of Parliament, which I was for 51 years. My education has come that way. I have learnt from listening.

Wisdom is passed on through encouragement and hope; and one obtains wisdom by listening.

Helen Bamber

1 May 1925
London, England

My childhood was not a happy one. I was an only child in a bleak non-practising Jewish household. During the thirties my father became increasingly obsessed with the dangers of the rise of fascism and the outpourings of hate. My father saw the rise of fascism as a universal problem. He anticipated early on the carnage that was to follow. It was a difficult and dangerous period of unemployment, deprivation and racism.

Through his work he was able to help a number of people leave Nazi Germany before the onset of the Second World War as the Nazis were already conducting their machinery of destruction. Refugees visited our house en route for various places. They recounted stories of persecution and cruelty. Some had suffered beatings and worse, some had lost members of their family.

When I set out in the way that I did, 60 years ago, I didn't have a plan or any clear aims except this one overwhelming feeling that there must be something someone can do in such catastrophic disaster. I was 20 years old when I worked in the former concentration camp Bergen-Belsen in Germany and I did feel quite overwhelmed by what I was hearing and witnessing. I had worked for a year in the National Council for Mental Health, working with returning soldiers, who had broken down in the war. I was aghast to find that we were intended to patch people up to send them back again. I didn't understand that as a civilized society we were able to do that. I had also trained for a year in the UK with the Jewish Relief Unit. I then went to Germany as an assistant to the director of one of the units that was sent to help at Belsen.

Belsen and other camps did not just disappear after the liberation. The German guards and others taking charge did, but the people who had been held in the camps had nowhere to go. The Iron Curtain had fallen on Poland, Romania and a number of other eastern European countries. A lot of Poles who tried to go back to Poland, which was illegal, were set upon and some were killed, others were forced back across the frontier to Germany. Belsen didn't close until 1950. It became a transit camp for those who had nowhere to go. until 1951 when the UN convention on the status of refugees was established to address the needs of future refugees.

The reason I decided to go to Germany was partly because of my father and partly a way of dealing with my own fear. I felt that surely there was something that people can do in the face of, and in the aftermath, of such dreadful cruelty. I think it was in some ways disappointing for my father that I went. He wanted me to go to university. He felt a sense of inevitability but I'm not sure he ever felt proud. I didn't feel that either of my parents were pleased that I was going. My mother, particularly, was angry.

I did learn something in Belsen, which has stayed with me all my life. I learnt from a woman with whom I sat on the ground and we rocked backwards and forwards. As she dug her fingers into my back, she rasped. She was like a piece of material sitting on the floor – that's what people looked like, bits of material. She rasped out her story and I realised that she probably would not live long. I remember I was able to tell her in a sudden flash of realisation that I would be her witness, I would tell her story and people would listen. It sounds a rather lofty statement but to bear witness is probably what we're doing here at the Helen Bamber Foundation, where we work with survivors of cruelty from around the world, and what I've done most of my life. But at that time I didn't see it as a clear aim. It still is hugely important that we continue to bear witness. All the stories that I heard were so horrific that it was difficult for me to absorb the enormity of what can happen to people.

When I was in Germany I was able to do my job as many people do when there is a catastrophe – they rally. I learnt a lot in a very short time. But I did come back with some hate in my heart. It was a strange time. There was still rationing and the people I returned to in England had been blunted by war. Understandably individuals, who had suffered many loses, didn't really want to hear about the concentration camps and about people from other countries who had been subjected to the most appalling acts of evil.

When I returned from Germany in 1947, I worked with concentration camp children and orphans who came to this country in 1945. I was appointed to the Committee for the Care of Children from Concentration Camps working with a psychoanalyst, trained in looking at the traumatic effects of young children who were torn from their parents, who were exposed to grotesque events and the loss of family members, most of all their parents.

I met my husband before the war. He was a refugee from Germany. He had seen his father beaten to death on the night of the Kristallnacht, 10 November 1938. He'd been badly beaten, and injured himself, and eventually his mother persuaded him to join a special agricultural scheme to come to this country. His mother and all his other relatives were killed. His mother and his paralysed grandmother were taken to Majdanek, in Poland, where people were thrown into the furnaces alive. So I lived with a man who never really forgave himself for leaving his mother and the rest of his family, who were all killed, behind to their fate. This guilt is something I see every day in the consulting room.

I worked for Amnesty in the early sixties, about the time of its inception and the work I did there was about bearing witness, to speak out for the people that nobody knew anything about, but for whom we have an obligation. I think once the conventions came into the statute books we believed that there would be a new world where we would be able to stop a lot of what happened from happening in the future. I think the reason I joined Amnesty was because I began to realise that that was not the case.

There is something else that has been achieved in my life, which is looking at ways to work with seriously traumatized and damaged people but bringing them into a life of meaning. There is spirituality in that as well as skill. There is something about a women emerging into a skill or into realising who she is and that we respect and honor her is so interesting. It is this creative side of our work that keeps me doing what I do. I've always been moved by people and their resilience and their ability to overcome terrible adversity. Very often, whatever the reason is, women make quicker recoveries than men.

Listening to people who have suffered is very important but recording and talking to the older generation is also significant because we have long memories and I think history is very easily forgotten. I'm only interested in my own history if it has a link to the present. I think that's very important. I don't want to dwell only on my husband's story and the effect it had on our relationship I want to relate it to present day men and women struggling with their relationship because of their suffering I think its important to listen to them. Someone asked me the other day whether I remembered horses in the street. I remember sitting in a tram in north London, alongside those huge carthorses, and seeing their breath in the cold air. The houses were so cold in those days, the whole family would huddle over one fire. I think it makes me appreciative of what we have and I don't want to lose that. I think it is very boring for children whose parents keep on and on about the past. The phrase 'when I was your age I had nothing' can be infuriating for young people today, but it is true.

I talk to a number of schools and I'm always astonished at the gravity of the children's questions and seriousness with which they tackle things and I learn from them as well. I would ask young people to keep an open mind and not to make quick decisions about other people, to walk in their shoes, just for a day and think about them. I think I did learn that quite early on. We all have our failures, our anger and our aggression, but it's about understanding ourselves, which is quite important and if we do hurt someone that we find a way of repairing it.

Nigel Cameron

2 May 1925
Uttarakhand, India

This is an extract from my diary, *A Fourteen Year Old School Boy's Wartime Diary*, which I wrote during the Battle of Britain in 1940 while living in Herne Bay in Kent.

24 August 1940. An air raid warning before we got up at one in the morning lasting 1½ hrs. Peter & I went to the woods. On the way another an air raid warning goes off and we saw the sky dotted with Ack Ack fire and could see the twisted course that the planes had taken. There was a dog-fight going on most of the time, so we took shelter behind a barn and watched. Then we went on and made our hut better (we had constructed a sapling hut in the woods). There were aircraft overhead nearly all the time. Then the all clear went. At ten to one, on the way home an air raid warning sounded again and once more we saw AA fire. Five planes, most likely our Fairy Battles.

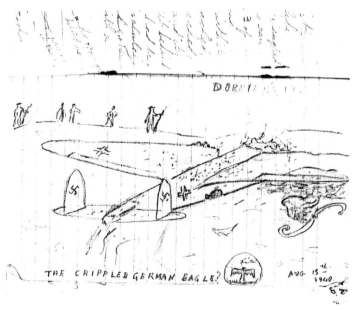

A sketch from Nigel Cameron's diary, 15 August 1940, a crippled German eagle

Nigel Cameron age 15, with his mum in front of a disguised pillbox in Herne Bay

After lunch there was a great deal of activity over us and, while Peter & I were looking for planes, we suddenly saw a parachute floating down towards the sea. It went quite quickly, so we immediately got on our bikes and raced to the front. Already quite a crowd had gathered. There was nothing to be seen of the parachute or pilot for he had landed about five miles out to sea. Then some fishermen rowed out and got into a motorboat. By this time Mum & Dodie had turned up. We watched the boat disappear over the horizon (almost) and saw it through binoculars. After a quarter of an hour or so, it turned round and started back. By this time the front was packed with people. Soon the motorboat was within a few hundred yards of the shore. The crowd increased (if that was possible) and the road was full of vehicles of every description, ambulances, trailers, even military lorries. Tin hats were to be seen in great abundance. All of this for one miserable pilot! The crowd surged towards the landing point. Police, Air Raid Precaution wardens, Home Guards and soldiers (all in tin hats) even a fireman, met him and made a gangway. Luckily I was very near and saw him well. He was a German. The whisper spread through the crowd "Jerry, German" etc. He had on a dingy blue-grey uniform, with wings sewn on and an iron cross (like every German airman appears to have). His hair was dishevelled and his face streaked with yellow grease. He appeared quite unhurt but extremely sullen for he wouldn't take his eyes off the ground. He didn't speak a word.

The crowd was silent except for a few remarks. The man next to me growled his disapproval and other remarks Mum, Dodie & Peter heard were "Now he'll taste some butter" and a policeman said "Treat him rough!"

He was bundled into an ambulance and that was the last we saw of him. The all-clear went just afterwards at 5.40! Four hours 40 minutes! My longest air raid warning so far!. Soon afterwards at 6.50 p.m. another air raid warning went off and lasted for about an hour.

25 August. It was very peaceful until about 7.40 p.m. when an air raid warning went off. Soon we could hear planes fighting all around. Once or twice we saw Hurricanes and Spitfires patrolling under a layer of cloud about 10,000 ft. up. Suddenly we saw falling from the sky, what appeared to be a great comet! It was the flaming wreckage of a plane crashing towards the ground. We were at Tankerton and saw it fall beyond Herne Bay.

At about 12.20 p.m. in the night I was woken up by a WHISTLING BOMB! Wheeoo-brump! I bounced out of bed. What a night! Searchlights were probing the sky, flashes from AA guns could be seen in the distance, while bren-guns and lewis guns crackled and lent a shimmering effect to the scene. Then the searchlights flickered out.

Nigel Cameron age 15 sitting in front of unexploded bombsite

Mary Ellen Watts

27 May 1925
London, England

The games I played when I was young were ball games, skipping and imaginary games. We had a swing, seesaw and trapeze in our garden. At school we played rounders, netball and later tennis and lacrosse. Indoors, we played pingpong, card games, darts and jigsaws. We had a toy theatre, which we put on the kitchen side of the hatchway, and our audience sat in the dining room, so they could only see the toys and not us.

In my teens I loved the fresh fruit from the garden and cucumber and tomatoes from the greenhouse. The food I remember the best is the food that I got fed up with, for example, root vegetables from Christmas to March, as no greens were available. I also disliked spinach intensely, which had to be picked and washed seven times to get rid of the sandy soil. Had it been available, my favourite food would have been ice cream. On 9 January 1946, I had lunch in Dickens and Jones restaurant in London and we had ice cream with chocolate sauce and crystallised violets. It had at last been made available, I think from the New Year. It was delicious.

My first job was to assist a lady who ran a 'dame's school' from 1943 to 1946. The school's pupils increased from 17 to 66 because there had been three schools evacuated from London to Mid Sussex and the local schools were already full. I was turned down from being 'called up' in order to stop my little school from closing down.

The medicines that I remember are Vinol, which was given to me for building up my strength. I thought it was lovely – like liquid toffee, but I think it was expensive so did not get it often. When my second set of teeth came through, they were soft through lack of calcium. I had half a teaspoon of white medicine from a thick blue glass bottle. It tasted of soapy water so I always called it that and I forget its proper name. When I was 10, I had whooping cough and had to take a tablespoon of brown mixture. It always made me sick and I hated it. When I was 11, I had the measles and mumps. I had cotton wool soaked in tea to wash the stickiness off my eyes each morning so that I could open them. I can remember wearing a flannel scarf around my throat when I had the mumps, which was quite mild. When I was 12, I had the chicken pox quite badly and I was given a pot of camomile on a saucer with some cotton wool to dab the spots when the itching was bad. My grandmother said I should have a bran bath and so my mother put a cupful of the rabbit's bran into the bath water. Unfortunately it stuck to me, and made the sore patches worse, so I had another bath to get rid of the bran. Granny explained that it should have been put in a muslin bag before adding to the bath water! When I was 17, I had pleurisy and stayed in bed for a month. Pneumonia threatened and my maiden aunts came to see me and dutifully shook their heads. But then the doctor appeared with a new wonder drug called M&B (which Winston Churchill had taken and was cured) and this did the trick. It sounds as though I was quite poorly but I think it was quite normal in those days.

In the 1950s the war was finally over;, rationing was coming to an end; the black-out was no longer necessary; men between 18 and 45 were seen out of uniform and best of all there were more men at dances. My first dance was with approximately 150 girls and nine men. I got to dance with Paul Jones so honour was satisfied. There was a great air of optimism, people seemed genuinely happy. I saw the Queen's coronation procession from Admiralty Arch, having got up at 3 a.m. and went home after the fireworks at midnight.

Given my time again, I most certainly would try not to be so shy. I would 'have a go' instead of standing back to let someone else do it. I would ask somebody to tell me that I was not ugly. Nobody ever said I was pretty so I assumed the worst. Possibly because of my lack of confidence I've never given any advice to anyone, except I did tell my granddaughter once to suck her sweets slowly and they will last longer.

Anne Kerr

3 June 1925
Bristol, England

The first thing that I remember is probably holding my mother's hand as we climbed up Christmas Steps. They were huge. It was a terrific effort for me to climb up just one of them. I was a forceps birth and in those days they used to say that this meant that you would have a dreadful memory, which has turned out to be true. I passed logic (which is now called geometry) but not arithmetic and algebra – and I think the latter need a good memory whereas logic is logic.

I lived in Bristol and was at school at St Brandons, a private school in Clevedon, but was evacuated to a school in Wells in Somerset where I became a border. I had lessons in the Bishops Palace and, when we all had measles, we were all kept in the Great Drawing Room and were nursed there together. There were rumours of a ghost, a lady in a green dress that roamed the house. One night, I thought I felt someone touch my bed, but there was no one there. I didn't tell anyone in case it was someone playing a trick on me and trying to frighten me. One girl was so terrified that she had to sleep next to the matron's room. Another time I remember rushing outside when we heard bombs to see if we could see them land but we were always taken back inside to safety. My memory is that is was always freezing there. We had to keep hot-water bottles in our desks. It was so cold we couldn't play the piano – our fingers wouldn't work properly. But I also remember paddling in the moat around the palace but it must have been summer when we did that. I was eighteen years old when I left.

I became a Land Girl after school, by accident really. It was the last thing that I wanted to do. I was on holiday at a farm near Crediton, in Mid Devon, and then became an unofficial land girl and was registered as a farm worker. I remember there were a few men on the farm who I suppose must have registered as conscientious objectors. Their fathers had fought in World War I and they didn't want their sons to go into this war. I enrolled as a chicken keeper at first but then spent most of my time on the farm, pulling parsnips and carrots. I damaged my back while doing that – it has never been the same.

I learnt to drive a tractor before a car when I was working on the farm and then I learnt how to plough. I remember the man who taught me kept saying, "Don't upset Cecil by getting as good as he is, he's our tractor driver. We don't want you taking over his job!" I must have been quite good, I entered a ploughing match but I wasn't as good as I thought because I didn't do very well – I ploughed too deep for sowing seeds. The same farmer gave a piece of his land for the village hall to be built on. He used to drink too much cider and would talk out of both sides of his mouth, like drunken men do. He would also wear this silly big hat. He would frequently upset the WI ladies by turning up in the hall, a little worse for wear, acting as though he owned the place. It is strange the little bits and pieces that you remember. I wonder why I've remembered these things.

I didn't particularly enjoy being part of the land girls, I don't think I was aware of what it meant. But also I didn't wish I was anywhere else. We didn't have choices. We just did what we were told to do.

We ate whatever was around during the war. I suppose being on a farm meant that we ate better than most people, at least we had fresh vegetables. One evening, I cycled to and from a dance in the next village with a friend of mine and when we arrived back to the farm, we found the left-overs of an apple pie on the table. It had been left over from dinner (that was what we called lunch in those days) and it was being kept for the next day, but we ate it all there and then. We were in a lot of trouble. I remember rabbit pie, too, mainly because I remember not being able to kill the rabbits. They would get flushed out of a field, as we were harvesting it. As we cleared the field there would be less and less crop for them to hide in and eventually there would be nothing. Someone would have to catch it and kill it. But not me. I wouldn't do it.

When the war ended there weren't any celebrations because so many of the men that we knew were still at war in the East. I don't remember any parties in Devon.

I met my husband, Jeff, in England. He had a civilian job in the RAF and we went to a party and met some people from Shell and he got a job in public relations – it was almost as easy as that in those days. This job took us to Brunei in about 1952 and we stayed there for about seven or eight years. In Brunei Jeff and a colleague started a press company and the English-speaking weekly community newspaper, Borneo Bulletin, for expatriates working in the area. He sold the company and newspaper to the Straits Times of Singapore in 1959. I taught English, history and poetry at a mission school while we were there. I didn't like the climate in Borneo but got used to it eventually. But I never got used to the sand flies and mosquitoes.

While we were there we had two sons. We had a Chinese nanny who looked after Andrew, my eldest, and she moaned all the time. Consequently Andrew ended up moaning all the time too. I looked after Peter, my youngest son. We came home from Borneo by ship because I was terrified of flying. I remember on the way to the port we had to cross two full rivers in a Land Rover and we had to manually shove cattle out of the road so that we could pass. It was dreadful on the ship, terribly stressful and there was no air-conditioning. Peter was crawling everywhere so he had to be contained in a cot, which made him very irritable and I was pregnant, which was probably making me irritable. We had to go to England via Hong Kong, as Jeff had to stop off there for work so he was only with me for a little of the journey. I was glad to be home when we eventually got there.

Gordon McCrea Fisher

5 October 1925
Minnesota, USA

I was born in St. Paul, Minnesota, in the northern Midwest of the USA. My mother and father remained together only until I was five years old. After her separation, my mother and I moved to her hometown, Little Falls, Minnesota, to live with my grandparents. Not long after we got there, my grandmother died unexpectedly of a heart attack. She and my mother were very close, and what with that death and her divorce, my mother had a hard time coping. When I was about 13, she was installed in a mental institution, diagnosed with what was called acute melancholia, which was considered to be a kind of insanity. Nowadays it might be called an extreme form of depression. When I was 14, my mother committed suicide while still a patient by drinking a bottle of Lysol, a disinfectant.

After my mother died, I went to Miami, Florida, to live with my mother's older sister, Thelma Leone Brown, and her husband Cuban-born Eduardo Marino Rebozo. I graduated from high school in the summer of 1942.

My first job after high school was as an apprentice electrician in a U.S. Navy shipyard in Charleston, South Carolina. After a few months, I became a radio technician and announcer at a radio station in Charleston. After a year or so, I was fired because I had learned to drink alcohol too well. I went to New York City, where I worked as a typesetter; a copy boy for a newspaper; a messenger boy delivering boxes of candy; and a busboy in a restaurant. I didn't keep any of these jobs for very long.

Finally, not long after I turned 18, I volunteered for military service. I went into the U. S. Navy in December 1943, and was sent to a naval base at Bainbridge, Maryland, for recruit training (boot camp). I contracted scarlet fever while in camp, and this progressed to mastoiditis (infection in the inner ear) and to the beginnings of a brain abscess. The antibiotic penicillin was quite new at the time, and I became one of the first people in the USA to be treated with it. It worked wonderfully. However, when I was released from hospital and sent to radio operator's school, I was put on KP (kitchen police) duty until there was an opening. My ear started to drain again while I was serving mashed potatoes. This led me to request to be transferred to hospital corps school where male nurses were trained. After I became a hospital corpsman, I was sent to a naval hospital in Portsmouth, New Hampshire for a while.

All this time, I had continued to become more and more addicted to alcohol. Already in Miami, I had been arrested a couple of times for public drunkenness, and spent some hours in jail, in what was called the drunk tank. I continued on this path in Charleston and New York, and into the Navy.

An incident involving drunkenness led to my being transferred from the hospital in Portsmouth to San Francisco, California, and then overseas to the island of Guam in the Pacific. The battle to retake Guam from the Japanese wasn't quite over when I arrived. Our group built a fleet hospital, where eventually we took casualties from such battles as those at Iwo Jima and Okinawa. I worked mainly as a corpsman in an internal medicine ward, and as a co-editor of a daily newsletter for the hospital, although I also spent a little time on loan to an intelligence group, which analyzed films taken by airplanes over Japanese installations and Japan itself. I note, incidentally, that I was at one point court-martialled for drinking on duty, and spent a week on bread and water in a jail cell.

After the war ended, I returned to the home of my aunt Thelma and uncle Ed, and became a student at the University of Miami in Coral Gables, Florida. I majored in mathematics and minored in philosophy, and got a bachelor's degree in 1951. I had the benefit of what was called the GI Bill for veterans of the war, and the U.S. government paid my university expenses.

In 1951, I started working toward an advanced degree in mathematics at the University of Miami, where I met my wife. In 1952, I joined Alcoholics Anonymous (AA). I continued going to AA meetings in three different cities for three years, and I have not drunk any alcohol at all since 1953. Three years later my wife and I got married.

After a year teaching at the University of Miami, Dawn and I were offered positions at Louisiana State University in Baton Rouge, where I got my Ph.D. in 1959, after which we spent three years in Princeton University, New Jersey. Thereafter, we spent time in New Zealand before returning to the USA in the early 1960s. I spent the rest of my working life as a professor of Mathematics and Computer Science at James Madison University in Harrisonburg, Virginia.

The purpose of this essay is to present something about what I have learned in 81 years of life, which I think, might be of value to young people today. One of the questions I have been asked to address is how I have managed to live so long. I attribute my longevity mainly to my wife and children. My wife has struggled valiantly to make me eat in a healthful way. In our old age, we still snuggle together at bedtime. We enjoyed being in the same profession, and we enjoyed sharing the experience of bringing up our two children. The moral of all this is a familiar one: happy family life is a good way to go, if you can manage it, and, as a certain song goes, have a little bit of blooming luck.

In any case, family life or not, my advice to a young person is to try your damnedest to find out what a good life for you might be, and to work persistently toward achieving it. However, don't be afraid to change your goal from one kind of good life to another kind of good life, as circumstances change during your time on earth.

David Davidson

5 December 1925
Aberdeenshire, Scotland

David Davidson age 13

I was born in Peterhead in Aberdeenshire and my first job was an office boy for a haulage contractor. I was 14 and worked from 0730 to 0930, I had an hour off and then worked from 1030 to 1730. My wages were 10 shillings per week with a deduction of 4 pence for unemployment stamp.

My first important decision was to leave the textile manufacturers employment in which I was a clerk to join the Civil Service at Aberdeen Airport in 1948 and my second was to apply and secure the post of Assistant Director of Glasgow Airport in 1965 in the employment of Glasgow Corporation.

In 1977 I was appointed General Manager of Glasgow Airport but my favourite decade was the 1980s. I achieved the highest position I was likely to attain. I was in airport senior management as deputy director personnel for British Airports Authority. My children were married and I had grandchildren. I had a retirement few could match. We had a round the world holiday and another in South Africa, which were both unforgettable. I have no regrets. If any circumstance or decision I had taken had, in any way, been different I would not have achieved the position where I am today.

The secret of my longevity, in the words of a recent centenarian, I keep breathing! I am still an active Scottish country-dancing participant. I have never smoked; I drink very little alcohol and I like walking. In my retirement, I have been involved in many voluntary organisations, often as Chairman or President. It helps one to keep active and not stagnate.

The world as a physical place has not changed (but could in the not too distant future by global warming) and people have not changed over the centuries; they still have the same aggression. However, the two greatest challenges, in addition to global warming, are the growing use of hard drugs and unlimited (possibly uncontrollable) criminal use of the Internet.

If there is one thing a teenager resents most it is being given unsolicited advice from any senior person. I would gladly give advice when it is sought, but there is an art in this. Always lead them (with your help) into working out the solution for themselves. It will stick and they will be forever grateful.

Oliver Bernard

6 December 1925
Buckinghamshire, England

I am a poet but I have worked as a book packer, an RAF pilot, I've been a postman, a repairer of London tramlines, an advertising copywriter, a nuclear disarmer, and a farm labourer. My first job was in 1942, at a wholesale communist bookshop and my salary was £4.10s per week. My last job was drama adviser for West Norfolk, from which I was wrongly dismissed for possession and cultivation of cannabis, but I was reinstated by an Industrial Appeals Tribunal.

My father was a stage designer and architect. He had worked as a set-designer in theatre and opera, in Britain and the USA, was a consultant artistic director to J Lyons and designed interiors for all the corner houses in London. He also designed the spectacular art deco entrance to the Strand Palace Hotel. He survived the sinking of RMS *Lusitania* during the First World War and made some drawings of the event, which were published in the Illustrated London News. He became a camouflage officer on the Western Front and was awarded the Military Cross in 1916. My father died suddenly when I was 13 and left my mother with many debts, so at 14 years old I had to leave school, as she was unable to pay the fees. She died in 1950, eight years after I left home. My mother's advice to me was 'you must never be late for the theatre' – she meant as a performer. She was an opera singer (her stage name was Fedora Roselli.) Whereas my advice to a teenager would be try to be true to yourself and if possible truthful to others as well.

The most significant thing that I have done in my life was to run away from home aged 16, having joined the RAF and the Communist Party. I thought the Communist Party were the only people who were going to do anything about the Nazis but what I didn't realise was that as soon as anyone got into politics, they started thinking about controlling people. Stalin was just power crazy, not a true communist. I ran away from home because I didn't get on with my mother. She was very unpleasant to my sister and said that she preferred her boys. It was complicated by the fact both my sister and my mother were actresses.

When the war was over I was free to go anywhere. I travelled and worked in France and Corsica, went to university, began to write poems, worked on farms, drank in Soho, talked to poets and painters, had love affairs and read a lot. On looking back over the years, I have three regrets: having too little Latin and no Greek, being too interested in sex, and not being able to sustain a long-term relationship.

Oliver Bernard age 17

I have been arrested perhaps a dozen times for "criminal damage" to fences of USAF air bases and to the Ministry of Defence during anti-nuclear demonstrations. I went to prison in Norwich in 1984 for refusing to pay fines.

Oliver Bernard wrote 'Getting Over It', an autobiography, published by Peter Owen Ltd, 1992; 'Verse Etc', published by Anvil Press poetry, 2001; his 'Apollinaire' translation and 'Rimbaud' translation are published by Penguin Classics.

Joan Down

28 December 1925
Devon, England

I was born in Torrington and my first job was helping on my father's farm in Bow near Crediton for no salary. I drove a tractor, an old Fordson, for the harvest, which was a work of art to change gear. I grew up in farming and then I married a farmer so I have done it all of my life. When I was young I played with dolls and friends; and imagination turned the roots of an old tree into many things – a shop, a hospital, a house. We were free in the fields and woods. How privileged we were.

I vividly remember the bombing of Exeter and Plymouth during the war. I remember standing in one of our fields adjoining Reeve Castle and feeling the thud of exploding bombs and seeing the fires at Plymouth. One night, from my bedroom window, I watched the glow in the sky, above Exeter and heard the distant planes. It was terrifying, especially because we had friends and family there. The next day, my dad drove up to fetch his sister and her family and managed to get through the chaos to their house but they weren't there. There was a huge crater in the ground nearby. He went to rest centres looking for them, with no success. On returning to their home, my father was told the hole contained an unexploded land mine and "Get out quick!" was the order. My father found my auntie wondering around carrying her canary in its cage, it was all she could grab before leaving the house. Once things were made safe, my family were able to return to collect any personal belongings they needed so they could come home with us where it was safe.

Exeter was so badly bombed that no one could go into the city. A month or two later I went to Exeter, to the St Sidwell area, there were no obvious streets any more. A pathway had been created in the rubble for people to continue their daily lives, I remember the debris and ruins, and most of all the smell of the dead buried there. I remember seeing a street in Exeter machine-gunned by a pilot in a German plane and there were holes in the cars and the garage doors. This made the war feel very close to us. Freak things happened too. I remember a story about a man who when walking his two greyhounds, one of them totally vanished, leaving him with one dog on a lead and another lead attached to only a collar. They say it was because when bombs landed, the ground waves would follow strange routes, perhaps along certain seams in the earth or soil and perhaps the dog got thrown into the air.

Before I got married I helped out at the congregational Sunday school, which had a children's choir, which we used to take around in a bus to sing in different villages. I've always been involved with church life and one day in 1960 the minister of the Rings Ash Circuit (a ring of Methodist churches around where I live) called and asked if I would like to take a service. Then Methodism made a rule that you had to study and be accredited to become a local preacher but I had two little boys and a farm at the time and I knew what took priority so I didn't do the studying until the boys were a little older. I carried on taking a few services but didn't take my exam until 1991.

I felt that my ability to preach was a gift and a calling. When I felt the calling, I had to follow it. I am a frustrated teacher I suppose, but being the only daughter I wasn't allowed to train when I was younger. I had to stay and help on the farm. I loved singing and used to take singing lessons but I had to stop when Exeter was being bombed as my lessons were with the Cathedral organ master and it was simply too dangerous to go there. I wish that I had continued. But now singing and playing the organ, which I absolutely love, are big parts of my church life. I only preach some weekends so that I can play the organ at other times. I go to congregational Methodists and Baptists churches – I go wherever I am asked to if I'm free. I regularly do the Ring's Ash Circuit.

Preaching isn't really in my family except my granddad was a preacher but not committed to Methodism. Several of my family have been Christians and, many years ago, my great grandparents gave some land for a church to be built on, about fifteen miles from where I live, and three generations of my family are buried in the graveyard. There is a plaque on the wall in the church for my uncle who, at 21 years old, was blown to pieces in the First World War, there was nothing left of him to bury so this is all we have. He was in the Seaforth Highlanders, so there is also a plaque for him in Edinburgh Castle. About five or six years ago the Baptist unions sold off the church because no one was going any more. We were never informed of this sale or what might come of the building and its land. A builder who wasn't interested in the church bought it and only uses it for storage – we would rather it had been converted into someone's home. We went up there recently to have a look inside and all the pews are still in place, and resting on the tops are canoes and crates of drink which the builder is storing. It is such a shame as the old pipe organ is still there, just gathering dust and falling into disrepair.

My advice to a teenager would be: no sex before marriage; girls should set a value on themselves, not be things to be used and cast aside. Live a clean life and treasure the things money cannot buy. Have fun. I would also like to pass on to those who don't already know it, Proverbs 3: verse 5-6. Trust in the Lord with all your heart; and lean not unto your own understanding; in all your ways acknowledge him; and he will direct your path.

Joan Down age 16 (front middle)

Elizabeth Baer

1926
London, England

Elizabeth Baer age 18

I grew up in a remote country house in Caernarvonshire, North Wales. My father was an impoverished gentleman farmer and estate owner, my mother came from a privileged London banking family. My uncle, architect Clough Williams-Ellis, married to Amabel Strachey, an intellectual writer, was a prominent figure in our lives, and his creation, Portmerion Hotel village, has always been an influence on our ideas of design and beauty. I was brought up to love the Welsh countryside and to hate the ugly things that people put up which spoiled the landscape and views. I was privately educated with a German governess until the beginning of the last war and I then personally signed myself in (aged 13) to an English school evacuated to Aberdovey from Switzerland, as I was very keen to learn languages and travel. Luckily my parents paid up! From there I went to Somerville College, Oxford, where I first met my husband, Derek, and I then took a secretarial job at Chatham House, St. James Square, London, hoping to get opportunities to travel.

When I married, at 21, rationing was at its worst so catering was quite simple as there was so little choice. My husband used to buy tins without labels and without coupons at the first and original Tesco store in The Cut, Waterloo, and the contents could be peas, pears or butter beans, all from South Africa, so our few guests often had a 'surprise' menu. It was difficult to entertain and all fabrics and clothes were on precious coupons so family passed-on curtains and covers were the only way to furnish. Oxfam was a good source for second-hand clothes but the 'new look' came in and the swirly long skirts had to be made from old curtains and cheap nylon velvet round tablecloths (very much the Scarlet O'Hara style).

We left London and with two small children, moved to Essex to a charming village house with a huge garden, and in order to pay for a part-time gardener we started selling plants at the garage door. Somehow this little enterprise grew over a few years and we soon found ourselves running a flower and garden shop in Harlow, the new town nearby. By the time we finished we had 16 employees and two shops and were almost ready to open a garden centre, which was a very new concept then. However, a growing family and my husband's busy City career made us decide to leave and sell the business, though we carried on in a large neglected Regency house near Colchester and kept a garden business going there. We opened the gardens which we had fully restored and had parties of 50 (a coach load) every day for two months; we gave home-made teas and sold plants and honey to our visitors, and our diary was filled every day each year; I spent nothing on advertising but put notices in the County Church and W.I Magazines and the Outings Secretaries were thankful to find a good venue with a good welcome and delicious cream tea, and signed up each year. There we no waste of tea and cakes as we knew the exact numbers who had booked to come.

I also sent huge quantities of fresh foliage from the overgrown garden to a leading London florist who needed long lengths of green and variegated leaves for important City Hall functions and society weddings. I found a lorry returning empty to Covent Garden, after delivering to local Essex greengrocers, who would deliver my stuff there. In addition, we let the fields for horses and cattle, and hosted caravan rallies. All these activities meant we could maintain the gardens properly and we opened them for three different charities, raising many thousands of pounds.

I converted all the derelict outbuildings into smart self-contained accommodation for single tenants, mostly for short-term tenants from Marconi, the Chelmsford company, and also restored some units for beginner workshops. By the time we left, on my husband's retirement, the whole small estate was in first class order and with the proceeds of the sale we were able to buy a good house near Bath.

I have always loved antiques and I improved my furnishings whenever I moved house. I was able to indulge this hobby when my four children had grown up and I enjoyed selling folk art items from Bath, and later from France. When I moved to the Bath area, I switched to dealing in decorative items and all kinds of soft furnishings. I still am wonderfully busy with this business, despite my age, and I have great fun finding things in France. I supply quite large quantities of old French linen for re-use for film costumes such as old hemp sheets for all the costumes of the Pirates of the Caribbean films besides selling finer examples of decorative stuff to top decorators who work on stately homes and Royal Palaces.

To me, waste is an abomination and to throw away anything useful and in good condition is an insult to the people who produced it. I also believe strongly that economy is a splendid and still under-valued way of inspiring invention and originality. Making the most of what you already have is common sense and would reduce the muddle and clutter that so many people have in their lives and their houses. Making the most of what you already have in the way of family, friends, marriage and career will give you satisfaction and make you a better person to know and follow. To the young, and to anyone seeking a change in their lives, I would say go for something that really interests so that you can give it your full effort. Make the most of any opportunities and do not be afraid to take a lowly position: so many people miss out and chances do not repeat themselves! Always be ready to move on!

My toughest job in old age has been to bring up my three grandchildren who came to live with me in the late eighties when my son became ill and their mother stayed abroad. I think I know a bit about teenagers now, but I would say, that like everyone else, they are all different individuals with different needs and responses so one way of life does not fit all! It's tough for them that many of the old restrictions and guidelines have been dropped and forgotten, they now have too many choices and so much freedom in society, and it is so difficult to steer some in the right direction. I just hope that a good home gives them the love and support they need, but also some limits and boundaries, so that they acquire gentle ways, with good behaviour and respect for their families, friends and workplace

Jane Brooker

1926
Birmingham, England

My grandfather, Benjamin Stone, was quite a well-known photographer in his day. He then became quite neglected soon after he died in 1914, but now he is becoming famous again. He took masses of photographs, I've been told, something like 25 000 – I think they are held at the Birmingham Central Library. I don't think anyone else documented Victorian daily life in the UK and abroad on such a massive scale. He was also a Conservative politician and industrialist, consequently he was very wealthy.

My father was the eldest son and disgraced himself when he left the family firm and set up his own business in Birmingham just before the recession. He went bankrupt just before I was born. We started off with two nannies but only one stayed with us until I was grown up. My father's family never accepted him back, even when he went to ask for help, mainly because he had left the family firm, especially as the eldest son, but also because of my mother. They didn't approve of her because she was very working class.

When my parents married, my father's family made my mother take elocution lessons and she was sent away to a finishing school to be turned into a lady. I think she prospered and rather enjoyed it. She fell in love with someone there, which she was always happy to tell us about. He became my godfather, though I don't remember meeting him. She was very good socially and had passed as a lady. She had lots of friends and got to know Lord Desborough and went to the Desboroughs' house in Maidenhead – they were very grand.

My father died when I was about nine. We were very fond of him. We were left in the care of my mother and she wasn't very well. She had a nervous breakdown and didn't have much to do with us; she was a proxy mother really and we weren't attached to her at all. Due to her mental illnesses she was taken away to recuperate many times and Nanny was the person that was constantly around and was much more like a mother. I have a sister, and a brother who died, I never met him. He had haemophilia so he was never at home; he never featured in our lives. We moved to a much smaller rented flat in Maidenhead after my father died where we lived until after my mother died, which was when I was 19.

Jane Brooker

One day I remember my mother was in the kitchen and frightening us because she was behaving very strangely so I threw some water over her, hoping to restore some normality. We rang the doctor and they took her away. She died soon after that but I'm not entirely sure what of. I can remember when they came and told us that she had died, I had a feeling of huge relief. She was a great worry. It was then that my sister, Betty, and I started to enjoy ourselves.

Even though Betty bullied me when I was little, she was also supportive in lots of ways. I depended on her a great deal so I was quite shocked when she went off and got married. I was bereft when she left, but a great friend of mine, who still is a great friend, moved in with me. She was quite a lot older than me so sort of looked after me.

I went to work in a very lowly place, screen-printing. Some of my grandfather's rich family from my father's side who had been keeping a look out for us, contacted us to tell us that there was some money for us that we could spend on doing something sensible so I went to art school, St Martins, which I'd always wanted to do. I hadn't been there for more than a year when I met my husband, who was also a student. We got married and I left college. Christopher turned out to be a very talented illustrator, and he worked mainly on children's books. He was such a kind and lovely person. He was wounded in the war, not fighting, but he was on Paddington station when they bombed it and he lost a leg but he never talked about it. He had only just been called up when he was hit. His brother also lost a leg before being called up. Neither of them had to go into the army after that, which I imagine pleased them somewhat.

We had three children – all boys. It was a very happy period of my life. Christopher was at home a lot and helped with the children, which was unusual for our generation. Nanny came and lived with us when Paul, my eldest son, was a baby. It was like my mother coming to live with us, but it didn't work out with Christopher, he didn't really like having a strange woman in the house. We had to ask her to go. We kept in touch with her for a long time, but she wasn't very happy and wanted to come back. It was a difficult time.

Gwendoline Hollingshead

1926
London, England

I left school at thirteen years old, in 1940, and a year later I started work in a shop where I took in laundry. I wanted to work in an office but I had no typing skills, so the Juvenile Work Bureau, who helped young people find work, placed me in an office, while I learnt typing and business skills at an evening class. Then

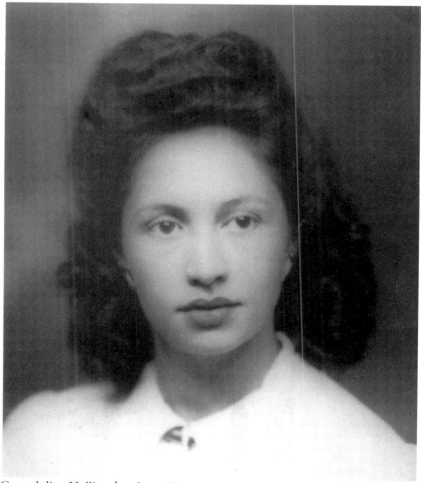

Gwendoline Hollingshead age 18

one day while travelling to work on the tube, I met a lady who worked for the American Red Cross. She asked me if I could dance; I had only taken ballroom dancing classes but she still asked if I would be interested in being a hostess at Rainbow Corner, the American Red Cross Club, in Shaftesbury Avenue, near Piccadilly Circus. I was. For twenty-four hours a day, every day, the club was open to American servicemen from 11 November 1942 to 9 January 1946. In addition to extensive recreation facilities and programs, the club offered an excellent food service.

I went for an interview with "Sally" (Mrs Helen Elting), and was offered a job. My hours would be in the evenings after I had finished my day job in the office. On my first evening on the dance floor, a G.I. asked me to dance and started jitterbugging, which I couldn't do. Fortunately, I could follow his instructions and picked it up very quickly. I had a good time dancing and talking with all the servicemen.

One evening, the crew from an LST (Landing Craft), which was in for an overhaul, said they would ask the Captain if he would allow the hostesses of the club to come on board. The Captain agreed, so we were taken on board to have a tour of the ship, and were given a splendid meal, which included ice cream (a special treat). Another happy day was our "picnic". We were able to get an open truck filled with straw for our "hayride". People had to look twice as we drove through wartime London to get to our destination. We had a great time.

Fred Astaire's sister Adele (Lady Charles Cavendish) was also at the club to help the boys, who had difficulty in reading and writing, write letters to their mothers, wives and sweethearts. She was a girl with a big heart. So, too, was "Ma" Whittaker, a volunteer who has sewn on over 10,000 stripes. She had a plane named "Lady Irene" after her. While she sewed on the stripes, she inserted a lucky farthing coin under the stripes for every boy who flew. I wonder if there are any airmen around who still carry their lucky piece? The boys really loved her.

Irving Berlin, George Raft, James Stewart, General Theodore Roosevelt and General Dwight Eisenhower were all seen at the club at some time or another and Glenn Miller made his "Eagle

Broadcasts" here. On one special occasion, Artie's Shaw's Navy Band played, with Sam Donoghue conducting and sometimes a young Petula Clark sang for us. The joint really rocked.

However, one day Mrs. Eleanore Roosevelt came to finally close the doors on a great building, which had helped so many servicemen and provided them with main meals, a barbershop, valet service, hot showers, and other amenities.

For a "Special Thank You" we were each given a letter and pin by Mrs. Roosevelt for our time and effort to help, especially as air raids had us rushing down to the basement for safety, as bombs were dropped close by.

Numbers grew from the opening day, 11 November 1942, when ten G.I.s were fished out of one of London's dense fogs and invited to see their new Red Cross Club, to VE Day when the club was so full that balconies might have collapsed with the weight of so many people. What a wonderful day it was for us all. There was so much joy – we were all singing, dancing and kissing each other.

Sixty years on, I am still very busy and recognise the importance of keeping active. I do all my shopping, cooking, cleaning and I walk a lot. I go to shows at the theatre.

To keep fit, I exercise my legs in bed before I get up. I do dumbbell exercises before breakfast and back exercises taught to me by my friend in the States. I take vitamins and fish oil tablets and practice self-healing

Diana Lloyd

1926
Leicester, England

I had always wanted to work on a farm so after school I went to Reading University to study agriculture and dairying. While I was at university in order to get work experience I worked on the Guinness farm in the holidays. Then I went to work on a farm in Bedford next to the aerodrome from where the Americans flew the bombers. When they flew out, we never knew if we would see any of them again. The only men around were Italian prisoners of war. We needed them for the heavy work. While I was there, I met Donald Woods, who was based at the aerodrome and went out with him a few times. His friends loved to ask me if I knew who he was. I didn't. When they told me that he was a film star, I didn't believe them, until I saw him in the movies after the war. He did ask me to go back to America with him but I didn't, unlike a few of the girls that I knew from there who ended up as GI brides.

I left university after only one year because I felt I wasn't doing enough for the war effort. All I could do at university was give blood and I really wanted to do something more useful so I joined the WRNS. I spent two of my three years at Bletchley Park. We knew we were doing something to do with decoding but that was all. We had to sign the official secrets act, of course, and we were never ever to tell anyone. It was thirty years before we could tell people but unfortunately my parents died never knowing what I did. Nobody told. I think it was a very well kept secret.

We worked eight-hour shifts, sometimes through the night. They were very good to us and gave us tickets to London shows. I saw Margot Fontaine dance at Covent Garden and we had tickets to the Queensbury Club, the Windmill and Rainbow Corner, which was the American Red Cross Club near Piccadilly. Although there was a black-out going on, London was still alive. Everyone was in uniform even when we went to clubs and dances. We weren't allowed civilian clothes at all unless we went home. We had two sets of uniform – we had a best one and a work one.

I was in London for VE Day, which was very exciting. We got a day off to stand outside Buckingham Palace and to see the Royal Family stand on the balcony. It was a great day, especially in London as everyone went wild with lots of street parties. After VE Day we were disbanded and I went to Chatham to the Royal Mail sorting office, which was very sad as many of the letters were from sailors who had gone down.

Around 1958, I did a television programme called 'Keep fit with Eileen Fowler'. Eileen Fowler was a keep fit specialist and started the Keep Fit Association. Throughout the war she broadcast keep fit on the radio but she was the first to do keep fit on the television, though it was quite rare to do it at all. The BBC had asked her to do a series of keep fit classes so she held auditions in the Birmingham area and I was lucky enough to be chosen along with four other girls. We were carefully trained and wore t-shirts with the initials 'EF' on our chests. We were on at 3.15 p.m., every Monday afternoon for three years. I still go to a keep fit class twice a week. I never stopped. I taught it for ten years after giving up the television programme, as well as keeping the family together. They were good times.

Diana Lloyd age 18

Michael Bond OBE

13 January 1926
Berkshire, England

Michael Bond age 17

I left school in 1940 aged fourteen and worked in a solicitor's office for ten shillings a week, and after a year I was given a rise to twelve and sixpence. After that I replied to an advertisement in the local paper for "someone interested in radio", which happened to be my hobby. The advertiser turned out to be the BBC and, being able to rattle off Ohms Law, I got the job, upping my pay to twenty-five shillings a week!

I joined the RAF at seventeen. I still vividly remember the images of refugees on the cinema newsreels; they showed people pushing prams with their belongings down country roads as they fled the German invaders. To me the sight of refugees remains the saddest sight in the world, no matter where they come from.

I worked as a cameraman at the BBC, which was the only channel at the time, and I filmed assorted programmes: a play a week, light entertainment, *The Sky at Night*, and the odd children's hour. On Christmas Eve 1956, it was snowing and I found myself in the children's toy department of Selfridges and I saw a bear left on the shelf. There is something about bears that I find beguiling; people throw out dolls, but not bears. I took him home for my wife Brenda, and he gained his name from Paddington Station near where we lived.

My first book *A Bear Called Paddington* (1958) started life as a doodle. I worked long hours at the BBC and I wrote in my spare time. Ten days later it was completed. It was well received by the public and placed on recommended reading lists.

I enjoyed my work in television; it was a good time of creating new boundaries. I worked with General Sir Brian Horrocks, a wonderful man; the sort of man I would have followed anywhere. By 1965 I'd had enough and left in order to write full-time. Television was expanding and changing, and I had done enough books to feel secure. The BBC was a good organization, it was well respected and they looked after their staff. I found it was a cold hard world outside, particularly when trying to get a mortgage as a writer.

For me the seventies was a great decade. I had found my feet as a writer, made lots of new friends and was in full flow in a new area of my life. Peggy Fortnum illustrated the Paddington books and her sketches were the result of hard work. She made him a living, breathing creature and had total belief in him. Bob Alley, an American, is also super, he also believed and things come to life in his black and white sketches.

When I'm working on Paddington, I'm thinking Paddington all the time. What would he do? What would he say? He's been around for over 50 years so Paddington is a big part of my life. I'm currently working on the latest Monsieur Pamplemousse. I write for my own satisfaction, to please myself without a particular audience in view. I have a love/hate relationship with writing. I sometimes may have wonderful ideas on the top of a bus, or in the middle of the night and I can't wait to get to a computer to put it all down; when I do, it's not quite what I pictured. I often have to get it wrong before I get it right. The more I write, the more I re-write. I work every day, even on Christmas day. My grandfather told me that I could do anything if I tried hard enough and I shouldn't give up. Perhaps that is the secret to success but so is sharing a bottle of red wine every day for the last 40 years or so, which could be the secret to a long life – my longevity certainly hasn't been down to good clean living!

I have a small flat in Paris where I go, which receives no post. Space is enormously precious to me as is thinking time. As the world speeds up, there seems to be less time and space around, which I think is a shame. Despite all the means we have at our disposal, communication on a human level is at a low ebb; one should always try to make time to keep in touch.

In 1997 I received an OBE for services to children's literature which I was in two minds about receiving, but my grandchildren said I must. Writing is what I do, I don't consider it special and I'd laugh at someone who seeks decoration; but for Paddington's sake I accepted the honour. The ceremony at Buckingham Palace was well organized, like clockwork, very impressive.

Odette Veazey

20 February 1926
London, England

Odette Veazey in her 20s

My first job was as a shorthand typist at the Daily Mail and then I worked for the News Chronicle, a well-known liberal newspaper. It stopped production in 1960 but my boss was head-hunted (not that that was what it was called in those days) and went to work at the Guardian when it started printing in London, as well as Manchester, so I went to work with him. After that I worked for a recruitment consultant in Tottenham Court Road but I eventually fell out with the owner, Winnie Johnson, because I felt that she wasn't very honest so I left and started my own recruitment consultancy in the 1970s, which I ran until I retired.

My grandmother, who was French, lived with us when I was growing up. She could understand English but refused to speak it, so consequently I grew up speaking French. She loved opera and there was this story told when I was younger that she took a radio back to the shop because it only played English opera not French. The only cure that I remember is being driven around the gas works on a Sunday afternoon when I had whooping cough. The smell from the gas works was supposed to be a cure.

My brother and I were evacuated in the phony war in 1939 to Hindhead in Surrey for a few months, until a suitable school was found for us to continue our education, which was in Midhurst. I stayed in Midhurst until 1942 when I returned to London and spent the rest of the war at home. I remember taking some material to a shop just off Oxford Circus for my father one day (he was a tailor) and it was arranged I should pick them up the next day. Only to my shock when I returned the shop had disappeared and when I phoned home, my father said he thought there had been a lot of bombs dropped in the West End that night so I had better come home without them. Another memory was having my tonsils out, I was in hospital (National Temperance Hospital) and the matron came in and told me and the other person sharing my room that if there was an air raid we were to get out of bed and get underneath it. Fortunately we did not have to. The hospital was fairly empty except for urgent cases as it was being kept as empty as possible for casualties.

We used to sleep in shelters and the one we used was virtually next-door, under what is now Christie's Auction Rooms in South Kensington. Being in that part of London, we heard a terrific amount of bombs. To this day, the exterior walls of the Victoria and Albert Museum which was a few streets away are scarred from shrapnel. Sometimes when the bombing had been quiet for a few nights, we slept at home on the floor between the windows so if they blew in we wouldn't be hurt.

South Kensington was considered a French area, probably because Charles de Gaulle lived at Baileys Hotel in Gloucester Road, which was quite close to the Lycee. From there he started, with our country's help, the Free French who were assimilated in to the British Army. My family and I met up with many of the Free French. One of them, Guy Chaumont, became a boy friend of mine, and he used to call and stay with us on his visits back to London when he reported to his bosses. I never knew who they were, although one in particular by the name of Rene was sent to clear us and make sure we were not fifth columnists. Guy was a parachutist and was dropped in France many times and on one occasion brought me a bottle of perfume, which he obtained (I know not how) as France was still occupied. These men were in the British Army and I think working for S.O.E. (Special Operations Executives were carefully selected and trained 'saboteurs' who were taught to create chaos in Occupied Europe and the Far East). When our part of the war was over Guy was sent to Vietnam. However when Guy was in the Far East after the war, I was invited to St Malo to stay with his parents where we met Guy's brother Henri who was now home having been with a different part of the Resistance run by a communist cell to fight the Nazis.

It was my 21st birthday in 1947. There was not much choice when it came to food but all our friends rallied round and managed to get hold of all kinds of food and drink. There was no birthday cake but we ordered an ice cream cake from Fortnum and Mason, which cost 25s0d (a fortune). We had no fridge so when I got it home I had to put it outside the window where it became covered in snow and we had to dig it out when the time came to cut it.

My favourite period of my life was between 1945 and 1951. This is because it was the end of the war and with it came the availability of many things like oranges and bananas. During this period, I remember learning to drive and taking the car to France and Spain.

I was arrested once, by mistake (in about 1980). The silly policeman transposed our car registration number and when he phoned the station to say he had arrested two people in a stolen car, he was told to unarrest us. He had such a red face.

The Rev & Rt. Hon Dr Ian Richard Kyle Paisley MP MLA

6 April 1926
Armagh, Northern Ireland

On 1 August 1946 I was ordained to the Gospel ministry. The first years of my ministry were marked with the conversion of many hardened sinners who were miraculously changed. At the end of that decade, I was married to Eileen, the love of my life. I was a Member of Parliament for North Antrim; a Member of Northern Ireland Assembly for North Antrim and I am a member of the Gospel of Jesus Christ our Lord. This was my favourite time of my life, although I wish I could have reserved more time for private prayer and greater preparation time for sermons and lectures. This still applies today as does the fact that I would also reserve more time for my visitation duties for the sick, aged, and the infirm.

My favourite saying is: "As for me that utterance might be given that I might open my mouth boldly and proclaim the gospel of Christ for which I am an ambassador in bonds." (Ephesians 6:19 & 20)

The Rev & Rt. Hon. Dr Ian Richard Kyle Paisley MP MLA (back left)

I believe that the love of money is the root of all evil. My heroes are C. H. Spurgeon, the greatest of all English preachers and Sir Edward Carson, Ulster's great Unionist leader and defender. I have been arrested for refusing to stop protesting against the ecumenical religious movements. The most important event that happened in my lifetime was the turning of the tide in the troubles of Ulster.

My parents instilled in me the importance of being honest and true by following the teachings of our Lord Jesus Christ and so I became a Christian and a follower of the Lord Jesus in obedience to his own precious words: "Him that commeth unto me I will in no wise cast out." (John's Gospel 6:37). I'm sure I have reached the age that I am by obeying the 10 Commandments. I would tell young people to day to receive Christ as your Saviour, read your Bible every day and use your talents to honour him. Stick to your convictions, and willingly help those you see are in need. Do justly, love mercy and walk humbly with God.

June Pringle

26 June 1926
Yorkshire, England

June Pringle

At 16 years I was called up and I chose to go into the WLA (Women's Land Army). My parents were happy to see me go away from the terrible air raids we were having in Middlesbrough in 1943. I had one month's training for which I was paid £1 per week. I was out in the fields until 8 at night then I had to go and do the milking. I saw my bed about 10 if I was lucky.

I had several postings. At one place of work near Darlington they had a large herd of milking cows, which I had to milk. I was always singing in those days and the farmer said I had to keep singing while milking as the yield was up. The funny thing was that two years later many of the farmers were putting music in the cow byres. There must have been some truth in it!

When winter came in I was on the move once again, to Great Ayton. I decided to hire a Land Army bike for one shilling a week to ride down to Stokesley for the dances. After the dance I had to push the bike all the way back to the farm where I would go into the dairy and get a scoop of milk and then get changed ready for milking once again. This was a mixed farm with plenty of interesting work. I was moved a few times on relief work to different farms. The farm at Robin Hoods Bay was the worst, there were cats all over the place, very large Persians, which the farmer's wife bred. It used to turn my stomach when I saw them on the table, which we had to eat off. Needless to say I ate nothing there and had my mother send me food. After 14 days I decided I must leave and I got my next place.

I was sent to Kilburn to a small mixed farm, which I loved. The farmers were like a real mum and dad to me. I made friends with a girl from the village who was also in the Land Army but she was on pest control. She asked if I was interested in joining pest control, as there was a vacancy. As I had looked after all types of animals, I thought it would make a change killing rats and moles! The farmer and his wife were very upset when I told them I was leaving and believe me I shed a few tears too when I left. By this time I was courting a local bus driver but away I went to digs in Thirsk.

Two years passed quickly and I got quite used to the killing but I missed the cows. The worst part of pest control was digging for worms on a cold frosty morning to cut up and mix with poison to go down the mole holes. I did not like gassing the poor rabbits either.

I worked with the big Clydesdale horses at one point. I had to stand on a box to put on the harness and tackle because of their height. My most vivid memories of my Land Army days are of being in the harvest field. It was lovely, especially at night, to see a field with its neat rows of corn stooks under a moonlit sky. We also had good food. I have a lot of happy memories of those days despite all the hard work. One of those memories is of severe winters and deep snow. We used to snuggle up to the cows when we milked them to keep warm. I remember how the pilots of Spitfires would fly low over the fields and wave to us.

While other services were given a uniform, the Land Army was issued with a topcoat, jumper and a pair of shoes and we received no money when we left the service. We always felt we were the hardest worked force but the least recognised. We were taking the place of the men who were fighting the war, so that the country still had food. By 1945 I was near the end of my Land Army days, and about to be married. After five years of stacking corn, turning hay, muck spreading, potato picking, hay making, milking, hedging and all the jobs that go to make up farming, I was at last going to marry the local bus driver, having been courting for four years. We were married on 6 March 1945. Three daughters and 37 happy years later there is still one thing I would like to do, have one year back on the land.

'Noah' Norbert Klieger

31 July 1926
Strasbourg, France

Noah Klieger
– this is the
only photo I
have of me
before I was
arrested.

My father sent my elder brother Jonathan Julius to England in 1935 on a students visa (my father had foreseen World War II) so he escaped the Shoah, but as we couldn't afford to go to an overseas country my father decided, in 1938, to move us to Belgium, hoping that Hitler would leave it as a neutral country. But this did not happen. My strongest memory of World War II was the German attack on France, Belgium, The Netherlands and Luxembourg on May 10, 1940. My parents and I (and hundreds of thousands of Belgians and French) tried to escape from the Germans to the south of France, but we didn't make it, as the Germans had bypassed, via Belgium, the Maginot Line and cut us off in the north and east of France. And on 1, 2, 3 June we watched the evacuation of Dunkirk, of the British expeditional troops ('the little boats' as it is called). I'll never forget the incredible behaviour and discipline of the British troops boarding these 'little ships' under the attack of the German planes and the navy gun-shelling. When I was 16, I was arrested and deported. My parents were caught later. We were the only family with all of its members, who were sent to Auschwitz, to come back. In 1944, my father arrived in Auschwitz 1, and my mother in Auschwitz 2 (Birkenau). I was in Auschwitz 3 (Monowitz) as a member of the boxing squad, which was put together by the commander of the camp (a boxing freak) for his and his crew's entertainment. In April 1945 I was liberated from the camp of Ravensbrück as the once proud German troops retreated in chaos and panic from the attacking Soviet troops.

Of course the Shoah first, and then the Exodus-Odyssey later changed my outlook on life. I presume I do not have to explain why the Shoah has had an influence on my life, let's only say that in the camps, especially in Auschwitz (altogether I was in the camps for 31 months) I did learn much about human cruelty and about human behaviour when in deep trouble and anger. In fact Auschwitz was for me a sort of school of life – the only university I've ever known.

As for the Exodus, this is for sure a different story. Destiny brought me, in the spring of 1947, to Marseilles, where I wanted to board one of the so-called blockade-runners, thus the boats purchased by the Haganah, the Jewish underground organization in Palestine, then under British rule, in order to bring in Jews without visas. When I say "destiny" I'm referring to the vessel, not my desire, as I wanted to go to Eretz-Israel, the Land of Israel, as we called this piece of land in the Middle East that had been, in history, the land of the Hebrews and where King David had made Jerusalem his capital. For two thousand years, since the Romans, after the destruction of the Temple had driven the then called Judeans, from the land and scattered them over all countries, they dreamt about going back one day.

In Auschwitz I had decided that should I survive (and I was sure I wouldn't) I'd become a militant Zionist, as I had realized that the only solution for the Jews is an independent state – a land of their own. And here I was in Marseilles where I registered for the next vessel to Palestine. Becoming a Zionist militant and going to Eretz-Israel, were the most important decisions of my life. This vessel was the American showboat President Warfield that under its name, given by the Haganah, *Exodus*, became the most famous ship in history. With over 7500 Jews aboard the ship, it took off from Sète, in France, on 10 July 1947, while being shadowed by British destroyers it sailed across the Mediterranean.

Eight days later there was a brief battle with the British Naval Commandos, on the high sea, some 25 miles off the coast of Palestine. The British ordered the ship to surrender. It didn't, so one of the destroyers rammed the bow and an armed party managed to board the ship, but it was met with a barrage of tinned foods. Two immigrants and a member of the crew were killed and about 30 wounded. The Exodus was then towed to Haifa, where the immigrants were forced into three prison ships that took them back to France where the ma'apilim (as we called the illegal immigrants) made the heroic decision not to accept

France's offer of hospitality but to stay on the ships, despite rapidly deteriorating conditions, until the British authorities would send us to Eretz-Israel or until we died on board. This convinced the world that the Jews needed a country immediately, and so, on 29 November 1947, the UN decided on the partition of Palestine, thus an Arab and a Jewish state. I'm proud to have been made a crewmember by Captain Ahronowitz and, commander of the Haganah, Yossi Hamburger. This heroic chapter has changed my outlook on life. All the (mostly) unknown Jews who fought the Germans in revolts in many ghettos and extermination camps. became my heroes as did Winston Churchill, the man who saved the world from the Germans. Also all the Israelis who, in less than half a century, have built from scratch one of the most advanced countries in the world, despite the continuous battles and wars against their Arab neighbours. No other people has, or could have, achieved such an incredible task. I spent the 1950s participating in the building and development of Israel.

My first job was as a journalist in the spring of 1946, for the Brussels daily "Le Cité Nouvelle". I covered the trial of 23 S.S. and the capo's of the Belgian concentration camp, Breendonck. I still work as a journalist for for Yedioth Ahronoth and have been doing so for over 50 years. I am a 'big shot' in the world federation of basketball (FIBA), I was chairman of Maccabi Tel Aviv, one of the Europe's outstanding teams and then, for over 30 years, I was chairman of the Maccabi Ramat Gan multi sports club. Since 1953, thus almost for 55 years, I have been the correspondent for the French sports daily, L'Equipe, and France Football, a twice a week magazine. Lastly, I am the Dean of Israel's Journalists – stories, grand reportage and many editorials. I'm still involved in radio and TV sport commentary and I quite often write editorials for our sports pages. I was inducted in the Hall of Fame, based in Los Angeles, and the Hebrew University in Jerusalem, in 1990.

No invention has in fact made a great difference in my life, not even when I had to start to deliver my articles on a computer as I just adjusted to this new technique. But the inventions that impressed me most were first the fax and later, of course, the cell-phone. I'm still amazed how one can call from a street in New York, for example, to a taxi driver in Tel-Aviv and ask him to come and get you from the airport when you arrive. By the way, I only use a cell-phone only for trips abroad and never in Israel. How far from a telephone can I be at any given hour of the day? 10 minutes, 20? So what's the rush? Those who have to communicate with me can wait for a few minutes in any case.

My advice to today's teenagers would be short. It's the advice of my parents when they educated my late brother Jonathan, who was a Rabbi, and me. Stay honest; respect people; try to know as much as possible as knowledge is the key to everything in life and finally give a 100 per cent in everything you do. But I would also like to add advice that comes out of modern times: don't rely only on technology to contact your friends – meet with people and speak to them. Human relations are even more important than S.M.S and email. You can learn more from people and books that you can learn from the Google and Wikipedia, which can give you information but not knowledge.

Noah Klieger wrote '12 Rolls For Breakfast'.

Warwick H Taylor MBE

7 August 1926
Middlesex, England

In July 1944 just prior to my 18th birthday, I was informed that, unfortunately, I had been selected, by ballot for services as a Bevin Boy in the coal mining industry. In October of the same year, I was instructed to report to Oakdale in Monmouthshire, a training centre colliery in South Wales. It was supposed to be a four-week training program, but the deployment of shovelling snow off the colliery railway tracks brought about an extension.

The young miners that would normally do the work had been called up or gone to work in munitions factories where there was better pay. The government had failed to make mining a reserved occupation and by 1943, the country was running out of coal to keep the factories operating. In December of that year, the minister for labour, Ernest Bevin, came up with the idea that men between 18 and 25 would be picked off for work in the mines as they registered for National Service. We were selected every fortnight, according to the last digit of our registration number. If we didn't show up the penalty was a heavy fine or even three months' imprisonment under the Emergency Powers Act.

While in my final week at Oakdale, I developed influenza and while waiting in the sick bay to be attended to, I collapsed, and fell unconscious. On the fifth day of lying in the sick bay, I started to haemorrhage from my lungs so they sent me to hospital. I made the journey by taxi, via a small mountain valley town, in order to pick up a pregnant woman in advanced stages of labour. Upon arrival at Newport Infirmary, I was unconscious. I was diagnosed with double pneumonia and was given one million units of penicillin every eight hours and, against the odds, I pulled through due to this new wonder drug. The other five patients in the ward were servicemen who had been seriously wounded in action in France and, spending time with these men, who were all about my age, made me realise that at least I was in one piece and that their plight was far more serious. This and my near fatal double pneumonia changed my outlook on life.

Having recovered, and after a short spell of sick leave, it was thought that a short period of temporary work in the fresh air would prove to be more beneficial than an immediate return to coal mining. I was sent to work on a heavy anti-aircraft gun site installation, which was being constructed just outside London. A few weeks later, after a medical examination, I was pronounced fit and was instructed to go back to the training centre colliery at Oakdale. When my training was over, I finally started working at the colliery. The majority of my time was spent on conveyor belts, keeping the walkways clear of coal spillage and loading the movement of drams.

When the war was over, I made an appeal to be released from the mines and be transferred to the RAF to complete my period of National Service.

My days in the service as a Bevin Boy will never be forgotten but, like so many, I looked upon the situation as a farce. We were forced into the industry, entirely against our will, while the regular miners were serving in the armed forces. However, I am aware that I could have gone straight into the RAF and been shot down or killed.

Warwick H Taylor age 18, in Wales (left of the instructor)

What made things worse was that Bevin Boys were not popular amongst the local people as they understandably felt at that time that we had come to Wales to take away the jobs from their own kith and kin who were serving in the forces. As we were of military age and not in uniform, we were suspected of being draft dodgers, deserters or conscientious objectors and were often verbally abused by the public and challenged by the local police.

I often wonder what has happened to my fellow Bevin Boys at Oakdale and the Welsh miners, who tolerated us, to all those men in that ward and what became of that woman expecting a child on that cold January day in 1945.

I think all teenagers should go through a form of National Service, where they would learn not only discipline, but also to respect parents, property and others, and to work as a team.

George James Alfred Houguez

22 August 1926
Alderney, Channel Islands

My first job was an as apprentice at an Army Technical school in January 1942. My starting salary was 11d per day (6s 5d per week in old money). Out of this we were allowed 2s per week to spend on soap, toothpaste, writing materials and stamps, blanco (a chalky material used for staining canvas equipment, belts etc in various shades of khaki) and metal polish, shoe or boot polish etc.

I remember medicines such as an iron tonic called 'Parish's Food', a linctus called Owbridge's lunch tonic and an opium based mixture called Paragonic for toothache. These were all were obtained from the parish dispenser. We had plenty of home remedies as well, these included a poultice made from carbolic soap and sugar, which not only drew the boil but also burned all the surrounding skin; a compress of spent tea leaves, which was applied to the eyes for conjunctivitis; and an infusion of chopped carrot and brown sugar in vinegar to 'keep the blood clean'.

When I was a child I mostly played buck and stick, which consisted of a fat piece of wood, sharpened to a point at both ends and a baton. The object was to strike the stick, with the baton, at one of the ends, causing the stick to jump into the air, when it was struck again with the baton (as in baseball or rounders). There were also marbles and, in season, conkers. I also played whip and top, and the hoop.

Undoubtedly the thing that has made the biggest impact on my life was the Second World War. From a personal view, it resulted in the death of my father by direct enemy action, the death of my favourite sister, as a result of illness, due to sub-standard wartime hostel conditions; and the premature death of my mother, as a result of poor living conditions, resulting from a totally inadequate widow's pension with three young children to feed.

George James Alfred Houguez, age 14, in Salamanca Barracks in Aldershot, in the Kings Royal Rifle Corps

One particular air raid in 1940 has stayed with me till this day. We lived in Strood in Kent, across the Medway from Chatham Dockyard. We were sitting at dinner when my father, with experience of the First World War, shouted, "Get away from the table". We jumped up and sheltered against the wall, away from the window, while bombs dropped outside in the street. It sent broken glass; lath and plaster from the ceiling; and bits of wood and dust all around the room. I recall running to the air-raid shelter, carrying my youngest sister, while the aircraft fired machine guns at each other. At the time, I thought they were firing at me.

Without doubt the most important deci-sion I ever made was to ask a young woman to marry me. I met my future wife while serving in Egypt and she worked for NAAFI (Navy, Army, Air Force Institute – the services shop). We became very close friends and then at a New Year's Eve dance I had a sudden thought that I might lose her. I don't know if it was the music or the Egyptian moon, but I proposed and she accepted. We were married for 46 years before she died. For most of the 1950s, we travelled around Europe, mostly in army quarters and in spite of the apprehension surrounding the Cold War, we enjoyed our life in Germany and Belgium.

My advice to a teenager would be perhaps Polonius's advice from Hamlet. "This above all, to thine own self be true and it must follow, as the night the day, thou can't not then be false to any man".

Major Iain Radford

27 November 1926
Switzerland

The evening had started quietly. Work was over for the day and our soldiers had gone for their meal. So we decided to leave our very competent Indian officer, Bal Ram Sahib, in charge so that we could explore the officers club in Rangoon, which was said to have a bar that was 50 yards long. As we were setting out, I remembered an order that no vehicle was to leave camp without one armed man on board, as there had been a bit of 'dacoity' on the roads. Our driver had forgotten to bring his rifle, so we returned to camp but the only spare weapon in the Guard Room, was a Verey Pistol, which was a fearsome-looking weapon, with a one inch bore, used for firing signal flares. Reckoning that that would satisfy any Military Policeman who asked whether we were armed, we set off again for the club.

We never did get our drink, for after a mile or two we found the road blocked with bamboo barriers and it was swarming with small brown-uniformed men with guns. This was clearly not casual banditry so we stopped. I was sitting in the front of the truck beside the driver and a man jumped up onto the running board, said nothing and shoved a .38 pistol into my face. So I quickly shoved my Verey Pistol in his ear, thinking that, at one inch range, a signal flare would do him no good at all. Time is not measured in minutes and seconds when you are looking down the muzzle of a gun but it seemed like a very long time while I wondered whether I would have time to fire my Verey Pistol if I saw his finger tighten on the trigger,

Thankfully he let us go, but we didn't get very far. We were intercepted by a military police patrol and told that all units were confined to camp until further notice. We learnt later that the Prime Minister, U Aung Sang, and half his cabinet had been murdered that afternoon. A Jeep, painted in Burma Army colours, had stopped outside Government House and four men in impeccably starched uniforms had got out. One shot the police sentry at the door, the others went in, straight up to the Cabinet room, and opened fire with their sten guns. Satisfied that U Aung Sang was dead, they climbed back into their Jeep and disappeared.

U Aung Sang must have been the only Commonwealth Prime Minister to have had a ten thousand strong private army. When the Japanese invaded Burma, he called this force the 'Burma Peoples Anti-British Army', but, when the Japanese proved to be a lost cause, he renamed them the 'Burma Peoples Anti-Japanese Army'. He then offered his services to Admiral Mountbatten, who, realising that Aung Sang was a Burmese patriot and the only person the Burmese would follow, appointed him the first Prime Minister, and allowed him to keep his 'praetorian guard'. These were the men who had stopped us on the road. As soon as they heard of the murder they had thrown a cordon around the city, and the coup failed.

There was no fighting, and after two or three days we were allowed out of camp. We heard on the BBC that U Aung Sang was to lie in state and that sorrowing crowds were assembling. Neither my friend, Gerard, nor I had seen a murdered prime minister lying in state, so we left Jemadar Bal Ram in charge, and went off to have a look. The queue outside the Victoria Hall, an imposing colonial gothic structure, stretched from the front door to breakfast-time. However, we took our places, hoping to be inconspicuous, and waited. Unfortunately everyone else in the queue was about five foot six tall and dressed in clean white shirts and coloured 'lungies', while Gerard was over six foot, and we were both in green uniforms with pistols in our holsters.

We had been waiting for no time when two young men approached us and politely but firmly indicated that we should accompany them. This we did with considerable trepidation. They led us to a side door and through a maze of corridors to emerge in the main hall where the body was lying in its coffin, covered in flowers, with only the face visible. We were somewhat taken aback, but, when we had had a good look, I instructed Gerard, under my breath, to salute. We then thanked our escort and marched out through the front door, mightily glad to be safe outside.

Next day the sky fell in. We were summoned to General Headquarters where a very senior officer asked us whether we were the two young idiots who had gatecrashed the lying in state. Apparently, while Governors and Generals, like angels fearing to tread, had been wiring London for instructions, Second Lieutenants Noel and Radford, of Queen Victoria's Own Madras Sappers and Miners, had been the first representatives of the British 'Raj' to pay their respects. We were not popular!

Major Iain Radford age 17

Geoffrey R. Mason

12 December 1926
Derbyshire, England

I was born at a very early age and my earliest recollections were being wheeled round in a wheelbarrow on a building site by an older boy when granddad was having his new house built. Granddad was a farmer so in the summer time I used to go and play in the hay and ride on the hay drays, which in those days were pulled by horses. As I grew older I used to go and watch the grass being cut with a mowing machine pulled by two horses. Granddad said when he was young they used to mow by hand, up to ten men with scythes would start at dawn and mow a field before going to work in the quarries or boot factories.

As a boy I suffered with boils and carbuncles, which in those days were lanced and dressed by the doctor. One day a lady, a retired nurse, asked me if I drank cocoa and when I said that I did, she advised to stop. So I did and the boils cleared up. I haven't touched cocoa since and have had no more trouble.

We always got plenty of advice when we were young – 'speak when you're spoken to'; 'mind your manners'; 'don't put your elbows on the table'; 'don't speak with your mouth full'; 'if you want to leave the table, say please may I leave the table'; 'don't eat with your mouth open'; how to use a knife and fork and set a table; 'show respect to your elders; on a bus or train give your seat up to a old person or a lady if they are standing and there are no seats'; 'take care of the pennies and the pounds will take care of themselves'. When I started going out with girls, Mom said "show them respect, we don't want any trouble". One other thing, in those days when the national anthem was played we were told to stop and stand to attention – every one did until it was finished, it was a mark of respect. Now I suppose I have plenty of advice. It would be not to smoke or take drugs and if you have a drink know your limit and stick to it. If you go abroad behave sensibly – remember you become a representative of your country, don't let it down.

I left school at 14 in 1940 and started work as an apprentice joiner and wheelwright. My first wage was 8 shillings a week of which my mother took 7 shillings and gave me 1 shilling and I thought I was well off. The pictures cost 4 pence in the Mechanics Institute and 6 pence if you went to the matinee at Bakewell Picture House. Apart from going to the pictures we also made bows and arrows to play Robin Hood; scoured local tips looking for old prams for the wheels and axles to make trolleys, and old bicycles also for their wheels. We cut the spokes out and used the rim to make a hoop. You put a stick in the rim and just pushed it along – they were really manoeuvrable.

Between 1940 and 1945 I was in the Navy, which I thoroughly enjoyed. The comradeship and meeting people from different walks of life was a real experience for a country boy. When my demob came through, my commanding officer asked me if I would like to stay on. I was very tempted, but Dad had died, so I came home to help Mum out and went back to work as a chippy. I went to work at Stoney Middleton for Lincoln, an uncle, in his joiners shop. When he retired my brother and I bought the business from him. Times were changing fast; making and repairing farm carts with wooden wheels hooped with iron tyres then altering them, fitting new axles with rubber tyres, cutting off the shafts and fitting a drawbar so they could be pulled by an old car or a Fordson tractor.

I think the first 50 years of my life were the best. In the last century, we were just getting over the First World War and the general strike. I know people were out of work and there wasn't much money, but things began to pick up during the thirties. Even when Mr Hitler turned up things as a whole in this country seemed the same. We still had the village bobby on his beat and we could catch a bus day or night into town without fear of getting mugged. Come 1939 war broke out. We had the black-out and rationing queues, but the whole country seemed to pull together. Every one was friendly and had a tale to tell. We had the black market, which some people think was a bad thing, but I don't know what would we have done without it. We stuck together as a nation and we won the war. Things began to improve: wages were better, young people could afford to buy a house and could get jobs – there was an air of euphoria everywhere. We had the welfare state or maybe today it should be called the farewell state. Things were good. We had never heard of the *Elf and Safety* brigade – if you fell in a hole or slipped on a banana skin, you just thought *'silly fool, you'*, now it's *'who can I sue?'* The country has gone stark raving mad.

John Edward Dimond

25 December 1926
London, England

John Edward Dimond age 16

In 1964, I was 38 years old with a wife and three small daughters, all under six years old. I was a qualified civil engineer in a good job, which I enjoyed, but I was frustrated because of a lack of challenge and poor prospects for promotion. I had always hankered after the idea of living and working somewhere abroad but had never been able to do so.

One day I saw an advertisement for Perth, Western Australia. Australia was about the only place in the world at that time not beset by some trouble or another and we heard that Perth had a wonderful climate.

After applying for a position, having been interviewed twice, and being offered a post, we decided to go. My wife and I both realised what a big step we were taking to move with our three little girls away from all relatives and friends to start a new life and career on the opposite side of the world. Regular air flights to Australia had barely started and the thought of four weeks at sea made it seem much further away than it does today. But we had made up our minds and excitement at the prospect took over from our doubts. I was very fortunate that I could opt to have my pension frozen and resumed again if I choose to return to my old job.

On the morning of 6 April 1965, we were up at 7 a.m. and a taxi took us to Liverpool Street Station where we boarded our train for Tilbury. We passed through the formalities and joined the SS *Orcades* in a state of high excitement.

This was the time of the £10 "assisted passages" when hundreds of British families were being encouraged to emigrate to Australia often without any real idea where or to what part of Australia they would be going. We knew that most of the passengers on the *Orcades* would be emigrants but as I was going as a professional engineer to work for the State Government we were given superior accommodation on the ship in the form of two adjoining cabins on A deck.

General shipboard life was most enjoyable. Our little girls hated the noisy playroom but were much happier on the outdoor play deck. We shall never forget the excitement of seeing a man overboard in the middle of the Indian Ocean and my daughters never forgot the sight of the Captain out on the bridge in his pyjamas as he oversaw the rescue.

It was a wonderful day when we arrived in Fremantle. We were met on the ship by a young English engineer, his wife and two small daughters. However, while we were waiting in the Customs shed the engineer told me that I would find my position considerably inferior to that which I might reasonably expect given my experience, due to higher levels of engineering in Australia. This rather dampened my excitement but he was right and this fact coloured the whole of my Australian experience.

Apart from my work, life was very pleasant in Perth; neither my wife nor I had fully realised what a tremendous difference climate could make on our lives especially when we had young children. For most of the time the weather was wonderful, my wife was able to take the girls to the beach almost every day in the summer and the winter days were frequently as good as most English Summer days.

Towards the end of 1966 we rather reluctantly came to the conclusion that we should return to England at the end of the bonded two years. There seemed no hope that I would be able to gain much job satisfaction if I remained in Australia. Once we had made the decision to return to England I wrote back home and was duly re-appointed. My next step was to find a passage back home, which this time would be at my own expense. I booked on the MV *Flavia*, to take us to Southampton via the Suez Canal.

Our journey home was quite eventful as after crossing the Indian Ocean and entering the Gulf of Aden we heard that war had broken out between Israel and Egypt and the Suez Canal was closed. We spent 36 hours in the heat and dirt of Djibouti Harbour along with 30 or 40 other ships before it was decided we would have to proceed around the Cape. So we set off down the east coast of Africa but after two days we were told the war was over and we were heading back to Suez. However the next day we heard that the Canal was blocked so again we turned round and finally headed for the Cape. When we eventually reached Southampton we had spent 44 days at sea and the only times we had set foot on shore were for half an hour at Djibouti (and that was half an hour too long) a Saturday evening in Durban after dark and a Sunday morning in Las Palmas when everything was shut. We were glad to be home.

I was then, during two separate periods, involved with the planning and construction of the Channel Tunnel, which has been voted the top civil engineering project of the 20th century. I ended my career as Director of Transport in charge of the southwest region of the Department of Transport responsible for all the motorways and major roads in the seven counties of the southwest.

Ruzena Deutschova

1927
Dombo, Czechoslovakia

My grandma lived with us when I was growing up and I remember her gravestone was bought many years before she died and was kept in the garden. She loved to garden and collected rose petals and made syrup from them. She collected many kinds of herbs, if a cure was needed, she found one for almost every malady.

In Dombo, we went to a river to swim. It was large enough for them to float rafts of cut trees down it to the sawmill. Dombo was in a mountainous area, full of forests. We drove the geese up to the top of the mountain to mind them, and we played a lot then. The ground was clay, I remember, we made all kinds of biscuits out of it, which we decorated with little flowers.

My favourite subject was history. I love it to this day. But my favourite teacher was Zoltan Reisner. He came back here after the war and wanted to marry me. I would have married him for sure, if I hadn't become the woman of Herman Deutsch in the meantime.

In 1938, when the Hungarians came in, the very next week, they expelled us from the village, saying that Father was a 'Bolshevik'. We didn't even know what it meant at the time. In December, it was already freezing, my parents were railroaded out into the cold, under the open sky with six children. The Jews from a nearby town immediately intervened as well as they could and sent a car for us. That was the first time I ever rode in an automobile. Straight away we got a furnished room with beds, which was also arranged by the Jewish community. They even went so far as to get us a residence permit, but my father still had to report to the border police every day.

I had eight siblings. Between my oldest brother Beno and the littlest, Miksa, there was a difference of fifteen years. I only vaguely remember my youngest siblings, since I was with them a relatively short time. My youngest brother, Miksa was just four years old when he and Mother, Sari, Manci, Eszter and Sandor were gassed.

I was together with Hana, my little sister, in the Allendorf labour camp (a sub-camp of Buchenwald). When we were liberated, we went home together, but in 1946 she left for Palestine from where she and her husband caught a boat to Israel where my sister was conscripted as a soldier.

The so-called 'Jewish Codex' put out in 1941 fundamentally changed our lives. It was a series of laws and regulations that stripped Jews of our civil rights and means of economic survival. We all felt like we had been robbed of everything. They robbed me of my entire childhood. In Galanta, where I was living, in 1944 they locked up the Jews in the ghetto, from here, we went out to work in the fields. We were moved from place to place, living in horrible conditions, where we couldn't cook or wash and there was no toilet. We hoed corn and radishes, spinach, and picked poppies; whatever there was. The whole family was still together then, except for Father. He was assigned to forced labour in Mateszalka.

Eventually we were dragged off to the new town brick factory, where we stayed for two weeks. We slept where the bricks were stored. We didn't work, just waited to see where they would take us next. One day, Hungarian constables hustled about 40 or 50 of us into one boxcar, but I don't know how many of us there were in total. They stopped the train periodically on route to take off the people that had died. We finally found out that they were taking us to Auschwitz, but didn't know what fate awaited us there. We constantly threw little notes out of the cattle cars along the way where they were taking us, hoping that they would be found and we would be rescued. We had no food or water and there was no toilet, just one bucket for all those people, it stank horribly. After two days travelling, we saw Auschwitz. My mother said, "There's no way out, any more". She felt that we'd arrived in a bad place. She knew what was happening.

When we arrived, the train stopped. A man, who they later said was Mengele, just waved and shouted: right, left. My mother and siblings went one way, me and my sister were sent the other. My sister got lost among all the people in the meantime. I ran after Mother to help her with all the kids. Mother sent me away to *'find Hana, because you've got more brains than her, the family should be together'*. I don't know about my older brother either, he also got mixed up in the crowds. As I ran around looking for my sister, Mengele gave me a slap, and shoved me over to the other side, which saved my life. I broke down in tears because I couldn't help my mother.

They housed hundreds of us in a barrack. Every night someone went insane. They would count us at dawn. They poured coffee into a *'csajka'* (a tin or aluminium plate with high sides) for breakfast, towards evening we got a little piece of bread with a bit of meat. We were continuously hungry. The only water came from the cistern, which you had to stand in line for. The SS soldiers hit the women with the metal on their belts, as they scuffled for the water. If someone was hit in the head, it could kill them. There were always a couple that died.

New prisoners arrived daily. One night we heard from the gypsy camp people yelling, *"Help, help! They're taking us to the crematorium"*. In the morning, everything was quiet, there was no one left. We smelled it, it stank, the smell of burnt meat lingering constantly.

I was in Auschwitz from June until mid August and I found out about the death of Mother and my sisters in the July. I met my mother's younger brother, Uncle Alter, in Auschwitz. He unpacked the trains. He told me to work if they would take me. He told me that my mother had already gone to a good place. He worked in the crematorium, where they would sort the clothes and personal belongings from the people who were to be burnt. We reported for work a couple of days later when there was a *'selection'*. They took a thousand of us for work.

In August 1944, when we ended up in Allendorf, we lay down on the ground and kissed it. There were little flowers growing in the camp. Everybody got one bunk and we got a little blanket and a sack of hay each. Life, here, was more humane. My knowledge of German helped me get work in the kitchen where I stayed until the end of our time in the lager.

We stayed in Allendorf until March of the following year when we were evacuated. We marched day and night, for I don't know how many days. The Germans were going to Berlin, but we didn't know where we were going. They locked us in a pen where there were sheep grazing where we heard they wanted to burn us. The female supervisors were really horrible, but there was a guard, Adolf Hupka, who couldn't help us enough. He told us that the next day we would be free but he didn't know what would happen to us. The next day the guards took off the death-head insignia from their caps and coats, and we fled into the forest. I think it was the Black Forest. We just kept fleeing until a Pole took us into his manor, and told us to be quiet. The manor was full of tanks and German soldiers so we thought we'd fallen into a trap. All at once a black tank stopped in front of us. They were blacks. Americans. Soldiers. Officers. They even spoke Hungarian. They said, 'Stay here. We'll come back for you tonight'. And they came back for us, took us into a village, and housed us in a school there where we ate tinned American food. It took a week for the Mayor to come and see us, when an American officer threatened to hang him if he didn't find us places to stay. After this the Mayor personally came and wrote down everything that we needed.

I was together with my girlfriends and my sister, Hana, all the way. We went to Kassel, to the American military headquarters, so that we could get home. My girlfriends wanted to go to America since they had nothing to go back to, but Hana and I still hoped that mother or our siblings would come back. We wanted to go home. We travelled by truck all the way to Pilsen, where we were handed over to the Russians. It was a horrific experience. Whatever we had left, the Russians took from us. Some of us were raped. We finally got home to Galanta. It was then that I found out that our father was living in Pest. So I went to find him. By chance I saw him come out of a building where returning prisoners were being housed. We both started crying. Everyday he had been going to the train station to see who came home. He didn't know anything about any of us.

I married Hermann Deutsch in 1947 in Prague. My husband borrowed my wedding dress from an acquaintance of his. I met him in the Jewish kitchen, where I was working as an assistant cook. There was a 24 year age difference between us. My husband was Jewish, and that was very important to me.

Almost all of our friends emigrated to Palestine by 1948 – they went home. My husband and I also got ready to leave; we even packed for it and labelled the crates. But I was pregnant so we felt we couldn't go. That was really painful for me. I would have gone.

We were very glad about the formation of the Israeli state in 1948. Even today, if we sing the Israeli anthem, my tears start gushing. We were really sorry then that we didn't leave for Israel, but we were really scared that they would put us in prison. It was enough to just say somebody was a Zionist, and they were locked up. My husband's business partner was locked up for five or six years because he wanted to go to Israel on an airplane.

During the latest census, I considered myself of Slovakian Nationality. I live here, in Galanta, so I consider myself Slovakian. At the same time, I haven't given up my Jewish religion. That's 100 percent.

Printed with kind permission of Centropa (www.centropa.org). Interview by Martin Korcok

Marigold Mcneely

1927
Somerset, England

I was a 13-year-old student at La Retraite Sacred Heart Convent when war broke out in 1939. Living in the country in Burnham on Sea, Somerset, was supposed to be somewhat safe from the bombs and the blitz. However, although our town was not a military target, we did have our share of bombs dropped on our small seaside resort. This was sometimes caused by the crippled German planes trying to jettison their bombs to get across the Channel lighter and quicker. We also heard many dogfights between the English Spitfires and the German fighter planes over our houses. Sometimes the shells from the bullets would rain down on our roofs. We had many air raid alerts while at school and during the night too. We were bundled up and sent down to the underground shelters or cellars, carrying our gas masks that everyone (even babies) were issued with. Every day in school we would have to wear our gas marks for the duration of at least one class. The funniest sight was the nuns in their black habits wearing a gas mask and trying to hold class.

I was 17 when I graduated from the convent and joined the W.R.N.S. (Women's Royal Naval Service). I was trained to decode and worked on the first type of computer, which broke the Nazi enigma code. I spent most of my training at Bletchley Park, which was a top-secret post about an hour north of London. Everyone who worked at Bletchley signed the official secrets act, which I think lasted for about 30 years and consequently I think we repressed our memories. There is so much of what happened there that I don't remember. Nobody knew exactly what we working on at the time. All we knew was that we were working on the bomb. We were told that if the machine stopped, we had achieved our goal, so when it stopped, we all cheered. I didn't find out exactly what we had done for years afterwards until I met a historian who was looking into what was achieved at Bletchley and he gave me some information, which I was able to piece together and guess what we did. We worked eight-hour shifts around the clock for a week or ten days and then we had a three-day leave. That is when we hopped on the train and dashed up to London, regardless of the threat of bombs. London although taking a terrible licking was very exciting. The only people you saw there were service people – many from other countries such as our allies, Canadians, Aussies, Poles, Free French and later the Yanks.

I can remember when we got off the train in London, in our navy uniform, tin hat and gas mask that the first thing we would notice was the smell of the smoke from the hundreds of smouldering buildings. I remember the sidewalks glistening in the sunlight from the shattered glass that had been ground into the cement from the force of the bombs and the huge craters that they left. The wail of sirens would go off day and night, and we had to take cover usually in the underground. We could not come up until the long wail of the "All Clear" went off. Then, we would come up from the shelters only to find more smoke and fires, and many buildings destroyed. The night time was really eerie because there was a complete blackout all over Britain. All of the windows had to be boarded up or have blackout curtains. There were no streetlights. People used torches and the car lights were shielded. The only thing lighting up the skies over London were the huge search lights which criss-crossed overhead looking for enemy planes and sometimes bright sparks like huge firecrackers when the ack-ack would shoot at the enemy planes overhead.

It was strange. Somehow, we were not afraid to be in London. We went to the service dances and the Stage Door Canteen and had some fun among the ruins. Being young, we did not think about dying, and yet, there was evidence of death everywhere we looked, with the ambulances screaming by, police and the bomb squads everywhere. Sometimes, after a raid, we saw people, their bodies all bloody and broken, lying in the ruins or sometimes part of a body – an arm or something – hanging up in a tree next to a broken chair or clothing flapping in the wind. The incendiary bombs that rained down day and night had London all lit up in a ghostly orange glare with the skeletal ruins of old buildings and spires of churches all blackened in the background

Thinking back on all this chaos now seems like a hazy movie from so long ago – a bad dream. However, the thing that I remember the most was how everyone pulled together and tried to help one another through all of the good times and the bad times. It did not matter if you were a total stranger. We would sit down in a shelter or a bunker with a cup of tea and become friends, not knowing what the next hour or day would bring. We were all bonded in a common cause – VICTORY.

After the war I was going to go into occupational therapy but before I started I went to stay with a friend in Houston, Texas. My mother fell ill while I was there and I had to come home to look after her so I went home to England on a freighter ship. As I was boarding, with another lady, the First Officer pointed to me and told his cousin that I was his. I had never met him before. By the time we arrived back in England, I was engaged to him, and we were married back in New Orleans some months later and I have been here ever since. My husband is a retired Mississippi River pilot.

Marigold Mcneely age 17

Peter Oakley

1927
Norwich, England

My young life was spent during the war in Norwich, which was heavily bombed. We had to cycle to school through all the air raids and the bombed streets, which I found quite stressful. I wasn't officially evacuated but my father sent me to my aunt's for a short while.

I was drafted in to the forces when I turned 17, towards the end of the war. It's not something I want to drag up from my memory. I didn't like the training, it was a very brutal initiation. It was basically a boot camp system where your brain was scrambled and you were taught to pull the trigger without question, on demand. We grew up very quickly and were changed from boys to men in six weeks.

Peter Oakley

The most exciting things that have happened to me in my life have happened since I retired, which should be encouraging to people. I have a presence on the website called You Tube where I am sort of a celebrity, or very popular person, you could say, with loads of subscribers. It started in mid 2006 by accident really. I was fascinated in what youngsters could do with the technology. At the time all the social networking sites were only for young people. I began with a short series of about five minute autobiographical videos and it seemed to pick up an audience immediately. I got a lot of attention and things started to grow and in turn, I got addicted to it. I just wanted to bitch and grumble about life in general from the perspective of an old person who's been there and done that. I talk a lot about growing up during the war and what that was like.

It takes up a lot of my time as I get invited to all sorts of events. I attended the World Economic Forum in Switzerland a few years back where the topic was 'The Power of Collaborative Innovation'. It's a very exciting time and a lot has come from making these silly little videos for You Tube.

Another thing that has come out of my experience on You Tube was when I made my first television appearance in early 2007 on The Money Programme, which talked about how the video websites were going to affect the future. I met this man who had worked on a series for the BBC and the last programme was about raising awareness of the elderly. He told me about this idea of getting together some of the old people he had met during the making of the programme to make a record. The group is called 'The Zimmers'. I was invited to be one and we made a record, which raised money for the charity Age Concern. I have been to many places with the Zimmers, including Washington DC towards the end of 2007 as a guest of the American Association of Retired Persons.

Margaret Hallett

7 February 1927
London, England

On 26 January 2002 Laura and I attended a party with our siblings, children and grandchildren in the Plaza Hotel, New York.

It was Laura's 75th birthday and, her children had planned it as a surprise. Laura was lured to the Plaza on the pretext of a cosy dinner with her daughter.

During the course of the evening it occurred to me that if my parents had not taken her into our family all those years ago, none of her children and grandchildren would have existed and I would never have known her as my sister. My mind returned to those turbulent days just before World War II, which have had such a tremendous effect on both our lives.

It began in January 1939 and I was not quite 12 years. My mother told me that we were going to have a refugee, a little girl, to live with us. I didn't know what 'refugee' meant but I was very excited about having another girl in the family, my only sister being not much more than a baby and my two brothers being somewhat chauvinistic.

The night that Lore (as she was then called) arrived we had very little sleep. We giggled a lot and managed to understand each other regardless of the different languages.

The next day we went to the cinema to see Deanna Durbin in "That Certain Age". I enjoyed it but was quite unprepared for the effect it had on Lore. She appeared to be transported and spent the next few days reliving every moment of the film. I realised many years later that she had been unable to enjoy a visit to the cinema in freedom for many months.

Lore soon settled into the family and into school. It seemed no time at all before her command of English was better than that of some of the English children, and at home she would captivate my little brother and sister with her own fairy stories. We discovered that we were born just nine days apart and celebrated our twelfth birthdays together.

We went roller-skating together at weekends and became great film fans. When summer came my father would drive us all to the seaside for the day. During those first few months the bond was created which has lasted all through the years.

Then as summer drew to a close Lore's parents, who had been able to get out of Germany in the nick of time, arrived. I learned later that this was largely due to help from my father, but to me it meant that I had another aunt and uncle to join my large family. Only a few days after the arrival of these lovely people it was September 3 and we were at war with Germany. All the lights went out, gas masks became part of our school uniform, boys at school dug trenches on our playing fields, food and clothing were rationed, a scenario many will recognise.

Life continued normally for us for the first few months of the war. Then in September the Blitzkrieg began and London was the target of German bombers night after night, week after week. At first we congregated under a table in the morning room of our house, outside which my father had erected a blast wall, but it soon became apparent that this did not offer enough protection and we moved to an underground shelter a few yards from the house.

Laura (née Lore Eichengrün) and I (left), in our school uniform. It was taken in the garden of our house in Finchley in the summer of 1940 when we were 13 years old, a year after Laura's arrival in Britain.

When the warning sirens sounded in early evening we would take our clothes, pillows and blankets down to the shelter, where we would sleep spasmodically to the dull sound of exploding bombs, the sharp rat-a-tat of the anti-aircraft guns and the broom-broom droning of the enemy planes as they made their way back to base after setting London on fire.

In November 1940, when the Blitz was at its height, Lore left us to go with her parents to America. Neither of us understood why this had to be, but I remember the morning she left, the tears we shed at parting and our promises never to forget each other.

It seemed a long time till we got news that the family had arrived safely in New York after their convoy had been attacked by U-boats in the Atlantic Ocean. Lore Eichengruen became Laura Oakes and we spent the next few years exchanging letters and photos.

In 1944 my brother, who was in the RAF and training in Canada, spent a few days leave with Laura and her family in New York. He was completely bowled over by the lovely 17-year-old and nicknamed her 'personality kid'.

After the end of the war we continued our correspondence. In 1948 I married, and a year later Laura married. In 1954 we both had our first child. Laura had two more children, I had just one more.

In 1968, shortly after my first marriage collapsed, my parents celebrated their Golden Wedding and Laura was able to fly in to join us. It was as though we had never been separated. We giggled all night like a couple of teenagers.

Over the next ten years we saw each other a couple of times and from then on, visits were frequently exchanged on both sides of the Atlantic Ocean.

She is an active member of the Kindertransport Association in New York, and I am privileged to attend some of their meetings during my visits there. We contrive to spend a few days every year together in London too.

Now we are both widows. We have suffered pain and bereavement together as well as the joys of parenthood and becoming grandparents. Who would have thought all those years ago that in 2002 we would be celebrating our 75th birthdays together in New York with our children and grandchildren?

It was certainly a night to remember, and I forever bless my parents for bringing Laura into my life on that day in January 1939.

Patricia Jack

21 April 1927
Illinois, USA

I was born in Waukegan. Growing up, the only thing I ever wanted to be was a journalist – I read constantly, anything I could lay my hands on. After a philosophy degree at the University of Texas I got my first job on the *New York Times*, as a runner, where I was paid almost nothing. I went to university with Howard Hughes' brother's daughter and I spent holidays with the family during the summer. I was also friends with Jawaharlal Nehru's daughter (Nehru was India's first Prime Minister).

I was close to my father, who was a civil engineer, but he was always working. My parents weren't the sort that gave out advice, although I remember one thing my father said about me when I was young. 'She's not frightened of the dark or anything in the dark'. Not being fearful has helped a lot in my life.

My father and I were in Japan when Pearl Harbor was attacked. He managed to get out right away but it took him some months to rescue me. I spent about six months in a POW camp in Japan. I saw much brutality there. I still don't like the Japanese. As soon as war was declared young men chose to join up and get killed. My older brother enlisted immediately after the attack on Pearl Harbor. So many navy people were killed and my family had strong connections with the navy.

In 1951 I was deported from Libya for writing an article criticising Colonel Gadaffi – which at the time I thought no one would see. I was the assistant to the American Ambassador. He had army officers reading everything that came in to the country. I retreated to Malta and stayed with friends. This is when I started to write. I am still not able to go back to Libya.

I've been a journalist all my life and I am still working. I worked my way up and became a reporter, eventually becoming a war correspondent. Vietnam was the first war that the *New York Times* sent me to cover and that experience changed my whole life. I saw some horrific things, but the image that really sticks in my mind is of a US flame-thrower attacking 100 Vietnamese men in a cave. They were burnt alive. I lost my sense of smell and my faith in God. I visited Cambodia during Pol Pot's regime when I was sent to report on Errol Flynn's son who was killed out there. Again, there were death camps where people were buried alive. Today, I admire the Cambodians, and have been back to visit the country. They are kind, nurturing people with a strong work ethic, well educated and a strong sense of community.

I got married and divorced in the 1960s. My husband divorced me because I wouldn't quit work and start a family. I didn't want it at the time. I got married again (twice) but the marriages fell apart for the same reason. I am a complete workaholic – work has always come first, nothing interrupted it. The most disappointing thing in my life has been my three husbands!

I put my longevity down to a strong work ethic, quantities of alcohol including vodka, red wine and scotch. Lifting a glass was exercise enough. I also surround myself with like-minded people – intelligent, bright and fun. I don't have any regrets about my life and I would do the same all over again.

I'm not really interested in food – I don't enjoy cooking at all or eating out. I don't even like handling food. Part of this is down to an incident in the 1950s. I was living in Florida and my husband was away in Canada on business. I woke up to find a man at the end of my bed intent on injuring and possibly raping me. He had broken in using a baseball bat and used it to hit me over the head. Somehow I managed to run out and scream. A Swiss kid heard me, lifted me over a hedge for safety and called the paramedics and police. I was on a drip for a long time and it changed my attitude to food for ever. In fact the psychiatrist assigned to me said that this is a common reaction to anyone who has been on a drip for sometime. I asked him how long it would last, he said for ever. He was right!

Extensive travel probably has had the greatest impact on my life – it has made me more aware and observant, probably because I always travel with local people. Recently I've been to Cambodia, Ethiopia and China. I've also lived in France,

Bahrain and India where I worked for the *Times of India* and I hope to go to Burma soon.

I do believe the world has changed for the worse in that the value system has deteriorated with youth, and education has also gone downhill. I recently heard an interview on the radio when the interviewer asked a young man whether he thought he had the life he deserved. This probably sums up what I think is so wrong today – everyone needs to earn their own life. The Government does too much for young people and the work ethic is very poor. We do our young no favours at all if we do not equip them for times of hardship and crisis. You learn and grow so much when faced with difficulties and decisions. I'd say to any young person to work hard and get the best education you are capable of.

'Avi' Arthur Livney

26 April 1927
New York City, USA

I was raised in Brooklyn and I remember when I had whooping cough I was taken down to the East River to breathe in the night air. At age 13, I worked Saturdays at the American Museum of Natural History, where I prepared boxes for mounting insects in the Department of Entomology. From the age of 15, I belonged to the Hashomer Hatzair Zionist youth movement, but of course this wasn't a job.

I am a retired member of a kibbutz in Israel and I worked in poultry and the kitchen. Prior to moving to Israel, 30 years ago, I worked at the Statehouse in Trenton, New Jersey. I was responsible for the insurance matters of the State government. I was also involved in environmental affairs as administrator of the New Jersey Spill Compensation Act. Prior to that, I commuted daily to Manhattan where I served as an assistant vice-president and assistant secretary of a company of builder-owners of office buildings and hotels.

I was in New York City during most of the war but, at the end of it, I served in the Hospital Corps of the U.S. Navy. While on dispensary duty at a naval ammunition depot in New Jersey, I learned of the participation of American volunteers in the illegal transport of European Jews to Palestine. After repeated enquiries, I was finally able to join the crew of what became the *Exodus* and was given the role of purser-pharmacist. The *Exodus* was a converted 200-berth Chesapeake Bay steamer, which was originally sold for scrap and bought by the Agency for Illegal Immigration. During World War II, the vessel had been converted into a troop ship for the British navy but after taking part in the Allied landing at Normandy, the ship was taken out of service and anchored in the ships' graveyard in Baltimore. It was an embarrassment not a ship.

In January 1947 I met the rest of the crew in Baltimore after the ship had been restored and we set 'sail' for Europe. The

European Jews would be moved from camps in Germany to transit camps in the south of France and with the help of several French socialist cabinet ministers, we were able to pick them up. About 20 miles out to sea, the *Exodus* was intercepted by British destroyers and after an extended struggle, the *Exodus* was towed into the port of Haifa, I was sent back to Europe on a British prison ship, *Ocean Vigour*. After disembarking in France, I made my way to Venice, where the *Pan Crescent* (Atzmaout), another immigrant ship, was being repaired before its voyage from Romania to Palestine. I sailed on the ship from Venice to Constanza, where it was soon joined by a second ship, the *Pan York*. When Romanian authorities refused to allow the would-be immigrants to board the ship, they sailed to Burgas, Bulgaria, where over 15,000 Romanian and Bulgarian Jews boarded the two ships. Both ships were soon intercepted by British warships and forced to sail to Cyprus. Disembarking from the ship in Famagusta, in January 1948, I was arrested, put into a military lockup of the Duke of Cornwall Light Infantry, interrogated several times and put into a detention camp for Jewish refugees. Two weeks later, I escaped to Palestine in a fishing boat. I will never forget the bestial behaviour of the Nazis towards Jews; the concentration camps and crematoria; Auschwitz and Hiroshima; the total killing and destruction; the inability, and sometimes refusal, to save innocent lives; and the waste.

However, the 1940s were an extraordinary decade because of the events that took place and their effect on the lives of everyone. They include the rise and fall of Nazism, Fascism, and the Japanese empire; the atom bomb; the creation of the United Nations; the admittance of a black man for the first time into the ranks of American professional baseball; the creation of the State of Israel; independence of India and Pakistan; the creation of American aid programs for people elsewhere; the G.I. Bill which gave millions of Americans an opportunity for a university education; the creation of sulfa drugs and penicillin;, the death of President Roosevelt; and the Iron Curtain. However, the most important of all of them for me is the establishment of the State of Israel.

I've been most fortunate in my life in that I was born in the United States of America. If I had been born in Eastern Europe, in all likelihood I would not have survived the war. I grew up in the richest and most free country on earth. In my travels I have seen poverty, prejudice and worse in such diverse places as the former Soviet Union, Uzbekistan, Kenya and China. However how could I not have been most influenced by my first meeting with Jewish refugees from the Holocaust and trying to help transport them to Palestine on a ship called the *Exodus*?

'Avi' Arthur Livney (middle)

John Lumsdon

May 1927
Newcastle, England

The small community Felling Shore, on the south bank of the River Tyne, in which I was born, was murdered in the 1930s with 72% unemployment.

The main source of employment was a paint-manufacturing firm, International Paints Ltd. As a child, I remember standing with others outside the factory gates begging for food that the workers had left at the end of the day. Monday was always a good day. I suspect this was because some had too much ale to drink at the weekend.

Our recreation areas were often derelict coal yards which were potentially hazardous. A few hundred yards from our house were some old wooden coal staithes built on the banks of the River Tyne. I was attempting to jump across a hopper one day, once used to discharge the coal from wagons down a chute into the ship's hold, when my foot slipped and I fell into the chute. It was only my plimsolls that saved me as I spread my legs with a foot on either side of the chute, the rubber soles acting as a break. Shaking slightly, I looked down to what may have been my watery grave before being extracted by some older boys.

Living near the river, inevitably people drowned, some accidentally, others by suicide. One man, Pinter Wilson, had been drinking and made a wager that he could swim across the river and back, but, as he got half way across, he disappeared. His body was recovered three days later by a boatman, Bunker Russell. Another incident occurred when children were playing on some steps used by merchant seamen who came ashore from their ships. One boy pushed a girl into the river, another boy dived in to rescue her, but, as she struggled with fear, the boy who attempted to save her was drowned. Another boy got her back to the steps.

I didn't like school very much so sometimes I didn't go. Instead I went fishing for sticklebacks and newts in the clay hole pond and once I was arrested for stealing turnips. I also liked to watch the merchant ships moving up and down the river, wondering what parts of the world they had been to, or were going to, and thinking, one day, I would join the merchant navy and see the world. The Tyne was a very busy river with ships of all shapes and sizes.

I was pleased to leave school at the age of 14 and start work in the paints factory. The firm supplied me with overalls, clogs and gloves but the overalls were far too big for me, so my mother had to alter them to make them fit me. My job, in the Varnish Making Department, was to take away the rubbish when the materials had been used. I took the empty barrels to an old man, who was a copper by trade, and he repaired them before they were sent back to the material manufacturers. On one occasion three of us were instructed to take a load of empty canisters on a four wheeled bogie to a department at the top of an inclined road. After completing this task we decided to ride back down the hill instead of walking, and I elected to steer this vehicle by means of a metal bar at the front, which was attached to a swivel that turned the front wheels. There were no brakes on the wheels because it was supposed to be pushed or pulled at walking pace. We started on our way and soon began to pick up speed, and before long it was travelling too fast to jump off. My heart was in my mouth as we approached the junction in the road. I decided to turn right but the speed was too fast to negotiate the turn, and the bogie overturned and threw us head over heels to the ground. Fortunately none of us were seriously hurt, just a few bumps and bruises. As we began to pick ourselves up, we realised the foreman was standing over us. He promptly suspended us for one week.

On another occasion while filling a container with White Spirit, a highly inflammable liquid, it slipped and I was soaked in it. I went into the building beneath the Varnish Making Department and stood in front of a heating element to dry out my overalls. A few of my mates were in there and as I was drying, one of them said that if someone threw a lit match at me I would go up in a blue light. Another laughed saying this was untrue. Soon enough, a lit match was thrown in my direction and of course, I burst into flames. Luckily a man was passing by at that time and he smothered me in an overcoat, putting the flames out. Luckily I only suffered singed hair and eyebrows.

My wages were 19/6 per week (97½p) and I received 2/6 (12½p) pocket money. My first thought with all this newfound wealth was that I would buy a Gramophone on weekly terms. Jack Jackson was the radio disc jockey and the top song was *"Here in my Heart"* sung by Al Martino, so naturally this was my first record. But as I could not afford to buy any more, as my pocket money would not stretch to buying records as well as paying weekly for the Gramophone, I played this constantly to the annoyance of every one.

John Lumsdon age 12

The working hours were 8 a.m. until 5 p.m. with one hour for dinner. One could take raw potatoes and an egg, and the canteen staff would make you egg and chips. Alternatively you could buy a canteen dinner. If any employee clocked in one minute after 8 a.m., fifteen minutes pay was deducted from the wages, so the late comers, not wanting to lose any time, ran to get in before eight and the noise of their clogs was deafening as they stampeded to the factory gates.

When I retired I was a coal miner and had worked for 34 years on the coal face. I was nearly buried alive in the pit, but this wasn't the only time I was close to death – the other occasion was while serving in the army in Egypt 1946-1948.

'Kit' Catherine Russell

25 May 1927
London, England

'Kit' Catherine Russell age 16

I can still hear Neville Chamberlain's announcement that war had broken out. It was expected but as a twelve–year-old I was still very frightened and didn't really know what was going to happen. When I was evacuated with my little brother and niece I was told that I was in charge of them and that I had to take care of them. I was very anxious about the responsibility that this gave me and I wasn't happy about leaving my friends and family. West Norwood, where I lived, was bombed quite severely and I remember many fires raging and bomb holes left in place of buildings, but people just gritted their teeth and worked hard together to put things in some sort of order. One day later in the war, while going to work with some friends, machine gun fire was sprayed everywhere from a plane overhead. A passing man threw me to the ground to protect me. We still went to work and our feeling was that we had to because it was a war, which we had to win. I also remember the excitement I felt when one of my big brothers was repatriated from a prisoner of war camp, minus a leg, but still my big brother. And lastly, I will never forget the end of the war in Germany. There were wonderful street parties, everybody was so happy and the feeling of real bliss when the lights went on again. Lovely. I think it is a very sad state of affairs that World War II was supposed to end all wars, and yet ever since there has been a war somewhere in the world. One thing that I have learnt in my eighty (plus) years is that war is futile.

I think I have lived life to the full and have treated others how I wanted to be treated i.e. with respect. This is what I would like all following generations to do. It seems that today there is less of this around, certainly people are more off-hand and less neighbourly than when I was a girl. Despite there being a war when I was growing up, there seems more anger in the world now. However, I am pleased that women get a better chance in business these days, but it could still be better.

Herta Scherk

7 October 1927
Cernauti, Romania

I currently teach rehabilitation awareness through movement and perception, the method is called Feldenkrais.

In 1940, the Red Army occupied my hometown of Cernauti, which then became part of the Soviet Union and between 1942 and 1944 it was occupied by the Germans. In 1944 they were driven out and my hometown then became part of the Ukraine. I arrived in Israel at the end of April 1944 and it was here that I got my first job. It was any job that I could get with any salary. My job up until then had been being a survivor.

In about 1945, I left Tel Aviv for Haifa, where my parents, grandmother and young brother lived in a one and a half room apartment, which the Jewish agency found for them. I worked as a children's nurse, giving my salary to my parents, as my father, who was a dentist, had to wait for his licence before he could work. After a year and a half I got a job in a bank where I met my first husband. We got married in 1947, I adopted my husband's daughter, and we had two more children.

My friends and comrades, of this time, were involved with the bombing of the King David Hotel, in Jerusalem. They were part of Irgun (or Etzel), an armed militant Zionist group. My first boyfriend, a member of the Stern Group, another militant Zionist group whose aim was to forcibly evict the British authorities from Palestine, had home arrest. He had to report to the police station twice a day. I often sheltered him, as a couple was less suspicious. I think it was after the killing of Lord Moyne (the British politician, who in 1942 had attacked the Zionist proposal to bring three million Jews to Palestine after the war) that he was deported. He, nor I, had anything to with the murder.

When he came back, the state of Israel was already a reality and he became involved with social work and youth bands. He married and lived with his family in Tel Aviv. His nervous system must have been very damaged as he committed suicide a couple of years later. I saw him only once after he came home, as by then we both had our own families to consider.

One young girl that I knew was a leading activist in a bomb attack on the airport, causing much damage and harm. I hadn't been active for a long time, when one day she arrived at my front door and broke down with exhaustion. I spent some time looking

Herta Scherk as a teenager in Israel

after her before she went to live in Brazil. I had no connection whatsoever with the former illegal organizations or have any information about militant groups, but they were all founded with the aim of creating the Jewish state.

The things that have changed my outlook on life are the inability to change one's fate and the disappearance (apparently) of loved ones. It made me agree with Yves Montand's saying, that in order to grow old positively, don't forget 'l'humour, la lucidite, la tendresse'. It sounds better in French, but roughly translated, it means you should maintain your sense of humour, your lucidity and your tenderness. I'm still trying to survive accordingly.

My advice for a teenager would be to choose a profession, which he or she is interested in. If possible, the heart and the brain should be involved or at least one of them.

Anita Greenwood

26 December 1927
Lancashire, England

I was born at a time when most of the town's population worked in the cotton weaving mills. We didn't have any money at one point during a period of mass unemployment in the early 1930s. I remember when my grandmother bought some fish, which we had to share with an aunt's family.

We had a regular life style, when I was growing up, not luxurious, but treats were great. I remember receiving a brand new bike for my eighth birthday, which my father carried home from the shop on his shoulder. My summer holidays were spent with my aunt in Blackpool as my parents were working. My uncle looked after a deck chair stand on the 'prom'. He looked very important with his peaked cap, leather money bag and ticket machine! I would sometimes take a lengthy bus ride just so that I could bring him his lunch –. then I would walk to Olympia to ride on the electrically operated boats. Being a frequent visitor, I did get the occasional free ride! Sometimes for a change I would go to Stanley Park's open-air boating lake where they had wonderful red-hot pokers in the gardens.

The days of having goose grease rubbed on chest and back and swallowing a daily dose of cod liver oil and malt, on what seemed a large spoon, are long gone. My standards were set, not by parental advice, but by their comments and example. It was also an era when acting outside the considered norm was severely frowned upon (or hidden).

In 1939 while in Blackpool I heard the declaration of war via the open window of a stationary police car as I was pulling my bike on to the pavement nearby. I sped back to tell my aunt. Nelson, my hometown, was not in a danger area but sirens got us up and into the indoor coal place where we had provisions, as directed, until we got tired of the pointless exercise. I was at Nelson Grammar School where we received an influx of Manchester evacuees, doubling the school's numbers. They were billeted in nearby homes, one at my aunt's, who now owned a fish and chip shop. My father, wanting to do his bit as in World War I, worked in a munitions factory in Coventry, a much-bombed city. We feared for his safety. He returned eventually to work in Nelson where he joined the Home Guard (formerly Local Defence Volunteers).

I spent much of my time at my grandmother's, where there was a strict timetable for housework. Washing was done on Monday. It was hung out on the line stretched across the unmade road to the hens' pen on the other side (this was my grandfather's responsibility). Ironing was done on Tuesday and baking was done on Thursday. There was a cleaning day too. Newspaper had to be cut up into suitable pieces and threaded on string to put in the outside toilet in the yard. Ashes from the fire were put in a bin, which could be accessed and emptied from the roadside by the Nelson Corporation lorry. All work in the house took place in the morning. After lunch my grandmother washed herself, changed her clothes and carefully brushed her long hair, tidying it up into a 'bun'. The afternoon was for relaxation or maybe Chapel. Shopping took place briefly as required at the local butcher, Co-Op, baker and small general store next door. Sometimes it did rain on Monday, which upset the system. Sometimes the coalman would deliver on Monday! Messages were hastily passed along the road and washing salvaged if the owner had gone out!

The fire supplied the heat for the oven and for the kettle to boil water as well as rising heat to dry washing on the overhead rack. Cockroaches were a pest. Sticky paper was left overnight on the floor near the range and removed in the morning! As a child there was always plenty to do, be it work or play. I used to play plenty of card games and board games with my grandmother. I also rode many miles on the arm of the sofa, using the dangling ropes of the overhead rack as reins.

I was in the hockey team when I was a teenager with the daughter of Lord Learie Constantine, one of the world's most distinguished cricketers. A dark face was an unusual sight to see in Lancashire in those days (see photo). It's shocking to think that before 1944 it was common for black people to be refused accommodation in West End hotels as he was. He sued and won a case for this. It was said that he had a first-class status as a cricketer but he had a third-class status as a man.

Ballroom dancing was another activity a group of us enjoyed on Saturday evenings. Sometimes we went to a local dance school, a small clubroom, at Nelson's Imperial Ballroom (alas no longer there). As we had to use public transport to get there, we would have to walk home from Nelson town centre, as it was too late for buses, singing and whistling all the way. Another leisure pastime was cycling. I sometimes cycled to Blackpool for the day at the weekends, which was about 45 miles away. A couple of times, for a short break, I cycled on my own to my cousin's in Derby, which was about 90 miles away. The roads were calm and peaceful; there were no motorways.

Things are so different now but I suppose my personal world has gradually got better, particularly with the invention of television, which gives me much pleasure, information and relaxation. Despite that, globalisation has caused tension in many forms and children have lost their childhood, and with it anticipation, wonder and trust. I find it hard to think that the world is a better place. I find it difficult, impossible even, to offer any advice to today's teenagers. I don't want what they have and they can never have the peace and freedom that I experienced.

Anita Greenwood (bottom row, 2nd in from the left)

Lorrene Lemaster

1928
Oklahoma, USA

I was born in a farmhouse near Stillwater in Oklahoma I had five brothers and two sisters. I married at age 17 to a service man who had just returned from a tour of duty during World War II and had been discharged from the US Air Force. We moved to Yakima, Washington where we had three children and where I remained for the rest of my life, however, sadly I was widowed in 1990. My children and grandchildren live in the same state and I have six granddaughters and three great grandsons. Our only grandson was killed in an accident when he was twelve years of age. These days I read a lot and enjoy my television and computer.

I still have one friend left from my ancient past. We have been friends now since we were at school together in the 1940s. Her only son, brothers and husband have passed on and she is unable to walk so she lives in a nursing home in Oklahoma. Her only remaining family is a daughter-in-law and two adult grandchildren who live in another state. We still exchange snail mail, but she doesn't seem to have much to write about. In her last letter she said she had not heard from any of her family in over a year. I'm sure they don't realize how lonely she is, but she has a tiny room, which she shares with another lady and rarely sees anyone else. On Sundays the carers sometimes fail to make her bed because they only have limited staff on duty at weekends. An aide is supposed to walk with her each day to strengthen her legs so she might be able to walk again but sometimes the aide just doesn't have the time. She looks forward to the walks so is thoroughly disappointed when they don't help her. Meals are something else. Once she told me in a letter that the menu said a grilled burger on a bun, what she actually received was a boiled wiener on a bun. Little disappointments are huge when your world has got so small.

When we come into this world everybody loves us and they can't give us enough attention and then when we get old the tables get turned around. When people advance into their senior age they do not become less deserving, but sometimes it sure seems that way. Some have health issues that affect their ability to care for themselves as they once did and they usually end up stored away in a Nursing Facility and forgotten about. Yes, I mean forgotten about. What a sad thing to leave the world feeling that nobody cares.

Marinus Boon

9 July 1928
Leiden, Netherlands

I was the sixth of twelve children in my family and I started kindergarten at the age of three under the care of the Franciscan Sisters. I still remember a chap who boarded at the house next to our school. He had a mop of black, curly hair and used to watch us playing. Years later I found out it was Albert Einstein who spent some time at the University of Leiden.

Being Roman Catholic we spent a lot of time praying, enough to find our voice and to last us for the rest of our natural life. As soon as I turned six years old I had to take Holy Communion daily. It was taken very seriously. In those days it meant abstaining from eating and drinking after midnight. Easily forgotten by a child of 6 years of age, this is where my father showed me to walk the line by pushing my head in a bucket of water and saying it was better to drown than commit another sin. As a result none of my siblings nor I are churchgoers.

On the day that war broke out in the Netherlands, 10 May 1940, at 5 a.m., I saw German paratroopers jumping from hundreds of planes. They were heading for Valkenburg and its airport. The town was flattened in one hour. The last time I saw my father he told me to take care of the family and very soon after that I became the oldest male in the family. I started filling sandbags, got the bedding downstairs and took care of getting food into the house. Looking back I was quite fearless about it, and have been like that for the rest of my life. In August 1940 I lost my sister, she was 15 years old. We were riding our bikes when a car hit her and she died twenty minutes later. This is something that stays with you for the rest of your life.

In the winter of 1942 I contracted diphtheria because food and hygiene had started to deteriorate, and I was hospitalized. The hospitals were full, with beds in the hallways, lined up and down both sides. My bed was placed in the bathroom next to the bath, which was never used due to water restrictions.

Marinus Boon age 13 in a wood workshop

During the war, the Germans used to go around from house to house to look for men, aged 16 to 40. They were caught by the thousands and then transported off to work in Germany. I built myself a good hiding place in a ceiling cavity of the room that I was living in, with only enough room for a mattress and I stayed there from 7pm until 9am. In 1944 the whole country only had running water for one hour a day and there was no electricity, or any form of heating. All the shops were closed, as there was nothing to sell. We used to get food from a central kitchen where every citizen was entitled to one litre of soup and two slices of bread. The constant hunger was the worst thing about the war. The glass in the windows of our apartment was blown out during a number of bombardments aimed at a railway bridge nearby. The bridge survived the bombing but half a street was flattened and many died. When I was 15 years old I used to smuggle food to innocent people who were held in jail at the fortified police station. One of the prisoners, a 62-year-old farmer, told me that as soon as he was out of jail that I had to go and see him. They released him in February 1945 and despite the fact that no one was allowed outside after dark, I travelled to his home in Noordwyk. It took me two hours to walk along the back roads. I was instructed to go to the house of a young lady who would take me to the farmer's place in the dunes. I had to walk through a minefield in order to reach his house where they had plenty to eat, but I had to work for it. My job was to make syrup out of sugarbeet. All through the dunes the Germans had put up posts connected by wires with bombs attached in order to stop paratroopers from landing. The farmer's sons showed me how to dislodge the bombs by cutting the wires with pliers and throwing them in a hole. These poles were cut up and used for firewood to make syrup out of sugarbeet for the black market.

In 1952, I applied to emigrate to New Zealand, probably more for an adventure rather than from common sense. The Immigration Authorities decided I had sufficient funds to pay for my fare so I landed in New Zealand, after a five-week sea journey, with ten pounds in my pocket and a small amount of clothing.

My girlfriend's parents wanted me to find out a bit more about the country before she, too, emigrated. I managed to save her travel costs in three months and my wife-to-be, Joanna, arrived in August 1953 and I married her in New Zealand in November of that year. We had three daughters and one son, who now have children and grandchildren of their own, but sadly my wife passed away at 70 years old of heart failure.

At 74 years of age I married a lovely woman, Pat, who encouraged me to take up indoor rowing. At the age of 75, while watching Master Games indoor rowing, I mentioned to her that I could beat 'that lot'. She dared me to try and that is how it all started. I bought myself a Concept 2 rowing machine, trained and studied the art of indoor rowing. Sport hadn't played a big part of my life up until this point. I stopped smoking and drinking alcohol at the age of 52 and started weight training, which I did three to four times per week and I jogged a bit, but that was all.

In October 2009, age 81, I will try to better all my previous records, which means training four to six times a week, one hour per day. Over the last three years I have beaten world records in Masters Games in New Zealand for the age group 75+ and I am still looking for improvements.

Wolf Blomfield

31 January 1929
Berlin Charlottenburg, Germany

I came to Britain when I had just turned ten. I was a Kindertransport boy and came over on a train full of German Jewish children, on 15 March 1939. All we were allowed to bring was a small suitcase that we could carry, so for a ten-year-old it wasn't very much. My father put me on the train in Berlin and had tried to explain what was happening. I think I was too bewildered to completely grasp it. Just before the war my family and I were going to go to America via England but when war broke out the U-boats were sinking the boats coming from Europe to the States so I stayed in England. My mother had already left Germany and gone to Shanghai. She had remarried and her husband was in a concentration camp and the only way she could get him out was by emigrating and Shanghai was an open city. They took people when they weren't accepted anywhere else.

We arrived in England with little placards round our necks saying who we were. None of us spoke English and, when we arrived, there were kind ladies behind trestle tables offering us a drink, which I'd never seen before. I was very suspicious of it, but it was only tea with milk. We were all sent to children's homes and I was allocated to one in Croydon. It was staffed by German Jews so the food I got was familiar, which was helpful. It really would have added to the trauma if we were given food that we didn't recognize.

My father worked for a Jewish refugee organisation and he was able to put my name down on the Kindertransport list, which was very hard for him. We were very close and we loved each other very much. He thought I would be safer in England. He stayed in Berlin for a while, but then he was sent to a concentration camp in Poland where he died. We were able to correspond with each other for a short while, via the Red Cross, but then the letters ceased. Then at the end of the war I checked with the Red Cross lists of names of who had died where it was confirmed that he died in 1942. My mother stayed in Shanghai and then got a work permit to come to England and worked as a domestic, to her horror, and then got a better job and worked in an old people's home. She stayed in this country for about 20 years but eventually she went back to Germany, where she died aged 93 years old.

Wolf Blomfield age 15

There were many differences between England and Germany, but at the time the biggest one for me was there were no Gestapo or SS here and it felt safer. My memories of Germany before I left are of the lakes around Berlin, but the Kristallnacht is indelibly marked in my mind. Coming home from school, I would pass the synagogue that I attended and I would always watch for it as I passed by on the train. One day I looked for it and it was on fire. It was terrible. My father tried to explain what was happening, about the Gestapo, the SS and told me to be careful. I think, in a way, my father protected me from some of the terrible side of what happened because I do have good memories as well.

It took me a long time to go back to Germany. Then one day I just felt that I had to go back, I suppose to lay some ghosts to rest. I finally went when the Berlin wall came down. I travelled with Robert, my best friend, who I had met on the train coming from Germany back in 1939. He had returned long before me. Berlin wasn't that different to how I remembered it as they had rebuilt much of it exactly the same. The Palace where I used to play in Charlottenburg is still the same.

Dr Katz, a Rabbi who taught me history and Hebrew gave me *Psychopathology of Everyday Life* by Sigmund Freud when I was about 16 years old. It was a very good introduction to psychoanalysis. It was then that I decided to do social work. One way of getting into social work was to do residential work so it was arranged for me to go to Lingfield House to work at a home for children who had been in concentration camps. Alice Goldberger ran the home. Alice was one of the most important people in my life. I knew her in Berlin as a young child because she ran the 'Hort' I attended every day after school. She moved to England before the war and trained with Anna Freud as a child psychoanalyst. Alice was crucial in my development, both in Germany and in England. I don't think she is recognised enough for her achievements. In 1949 when I went along to Lingfield House, I didn't know that Alice worked there, It was fantastic to see her again. I was maybe four or five years older than the oldest children in the home. The gap between us was quite narrow. It's strange because I never felt lucky next to these children, even though if my father hadn't put me on that train, I may have ended up as one of these children instead. I know now I was lucky. I am forever grateful to my father for his foresight.

I am still in touch with some of the Lingfield House children. When I go to Israel I always see one of the girls that I looked after, who is now a grandmother. It feels important to me to still know people that I knew back then.

I qualified in 1975 as a psychotherapist and I still work as one today, but I don't give advice as such. I try and help people to understand themselves and find their own solutions. As a teacher and psychotherapist I am often reminded of a quote from Hillel who wrote 2000 years ago "from my teachers I have learned much, from my peers I have learned more, but from my students I have learned most of all". However, there are some basics to pass on such as being sensitive and empathetic towards others, and to remember that it is important to love as well as to be loved.

Dr Jean Pain

7 June 1929
London, England

When I was a child I enjoyed roaming on my own for hours in the unspoilt countryside until my father, who worked in Customs and Excise, was evacuated to Blackpool during the war, and we had to go with him. I hated the place, mostly because I had to leave Rayleigh where I had been very happy. I was so different from both of my parents and from seven years old my mother began to ask me for advice so I learned to plan for the future and make my own decisions at an early age. Any advice given to me by my parents was scanty and of no practical use.

I have been ambitious since the age of five. In my teens my ambition was to get a scholarship to university. I succeeded. This was the first step to get away from the kind of people around me in childhood and to find some intelligent people I could talk to about the matters I was exploring.

Since 1992 I have been a practising psychotherapist and completed an MA and PhD based on my own work. I dish out many SAYINGS ad nauseam to my clients. Three of the best are "You are the only one that can help yourself. Trust your own judgement", "Why do you hate me? I haven't helped you." and "He (or she) that expecteth nothing shall not be disappointed." However I am disappointed that so many women have not made the best use of the opportunities that are now open to them, compared to when I was growing up. In my lifetime women's opportunities have opened up tremendously, it is such a shame that so many women ignore them.

In my life I have experienced both failure and success. I learned more from failure than from success. Failures taught me something new about myself, successes merely reinforced my belief in myself. All my experiences have been useful one way or another. I have learnt that people who are devoted to their work can never be lonely. It took me many decades to learn to choose my friends wisely and learn to enjoy my own company. I think that is very important, as is aiming to please yourself. You are the best expert about yourself. You are your own best friend and your worst enemy. Therefore learn as much as you can about yourself.

Throughout my life, I have taken risks, never asked for advice, trusted my intuition and followed my star. I never wanted to be married nor to have children, however my hormones decided otherwise. I married after graduating and had three children. I am now a grandmother. I unwittingly created for myself what I needed and never had in my natal family, people I like and have much in common with. I expected to be successful in my work, but I never expected to be successful in the family that my husband and I created.

Dr Jean Pain age 19